PREGNANCY
AND
FAMILY HEALTH

VOLUME ONE IN

THE CHILDBEARING FAMILY

PREGNANCY
AND
FAMILY HEALTH

A Programmed Text

BETTY ANN ANDERSON, R.N., M.A.

Instructor, Maternal and Child Health
Roosevelt Hospital School of Nursing, New York

MERCEDES E. CAMACHO, R.N., B.S.

Instructor, Psychiatric Nursing and Nursing Fundamentals
Roosevelt Hospital School of Nursing, New York

JEANNE STARK, R.N., M.A.

Assistant Professor, Maternity Nursing
Miami Dade Community College, Miami

VOLUME ONE IN

THE CHILDBEARING FAMILY

A Blakiston Publication

New York   St. Louis   San Francisco   Düsseldorf   Johannesburg
Kuala Lumpur   London   Mexico   Montreal   New Delhi   Panama
Paris   São Paulo   Singapore   Sydney   Tokyo   Toronto

Pregnancy and Family Health, Volume One in the Childbearing Family

1234567890 DODO 7987654

Library of Congress Cataloging in Publication Data

Anderson, Betty Ann.
     Pregnancy and family health.

     (Her The childbearing family, v. 1)
     "A Blakiston publication."
          1.   Obstetrical nursing—Programmed instruction.
2.   Family medicine—Programmed instruction.
I.   Camacho, Mercedes E., joint author.   II.   Stark,
Jeanne, joint author.   III.   Title.   IV.   Series.
[DNLM: 1.   Maternal welfare—Programmed instruction.
2.   Pregnancy—Programmed instruction.   3.   Pregnancy
complications—Programmed instructon.   WQ200 A545c]
[RG951.A66   vol. 1]   618.2′007′7s   [618.2′007′7]
ISBN 0-07-001681-X   73-15786

This book was set in Press Roman by Creative Book Services division
of McGregor & Werner, Inc. The editor was Cathy Dilworth; the
designer was Creative Book Services; the production supervisor was
Judi Frey.
R. R. Donnelley & Sons Company was printer and binder.

CONTENTS

PREFACE

The authors' involvement in research germane to parent and child health revealed the absence of any sophisticated and comprehensive textbook approach to content and methods of instruction in this subject. This book and the second volume attempt to fill the void by employing an up-to-date teaching approach which leads the student toward a better understanding of the problems affecting families during the childbearing cycle. In addition, they develop new methods of family nursing during this crucial life experience, utilizing family health, stress, and roles as themes through the program. The first volume defines health and establishes this concept as a basis for actions throughout the childbearing cycle; the second volume explores interruptions of the health status. The level of the text is applicable to any and all nursing students.

Through the use of a programmed text, the authors endeavor to engage the learner actively in the discovery of new subject matter. The uniqueness of the authors' system lies in the use of two methods of programming—linear and branching (scatter)—to provide reinforcement of learning throughout the text and enable students to learn at their own pace. The linear method enhances the acquisition of specific information and theory. The branching, or scatter, method provides for applications of learned theory to realistic situations.

The comprehensive body of knowledge concerning the family during the childbearing process has been delineated by specific objectives that guide students' learning. Tests following chapters and units enable the students to recognize their difficulties as they encounter them; the program then directs them back to review specific material.

The text also assists the student in developing a personal philosophy with positive attitudes toward membership within a family.

ACKNOWLEDGMENTS

In the process of writing this book, we became indebted to the many colleagues and friends who, through their words of encouragement, supported our efforts in developing a new approach to the teaching of maternal-child health.

Principally, we gratefully acknowledge the contributions made to our project by Jeanne Chernay for assisting us throughout by lending her time and nursing expertise during the many months that it took to write these two volumes; by Jane Skolinsky for her illustrations; by Dorothea Wagner for acting as consultant on the material regarding the newborn; and by the School of Nursing at Roosevelt Hospital and our many students for their enthusiastic participation and encouraging reception as we tested out programmed materials.

Finally, the many months of continued work would not have been made possible without the constant support provided us by our families.

Betty Ann Anderson
Mercedes Camacho
Jeanne Stark

TO THE STUDENT

This volume has been developed to assist you in the study of the family during the childbearing cycle. Major emphasis will be on health, family members and their roles, families' adaptation to stress, and the role of the nurse in meeting identifiable needs.

Some chapters are preceded by pretests. The objective of the pretests is to acquaint you with the content covered in the chapters and to allow you to identify areas to be learned.

The core chapters are not preceded by pretests because we consider this material fundamental to your complete understanding of the program. We suggest that you study these chapters thoroughly.

Throughout this program, two different types of programming are used:

1. *Linear*, in which the answers are on the same page on which the material is presented. These answers are to be concealed as you study the material and uncovered to check your learning. The mask enclosed in your book should be used to conceal the answers while you read. An arrow appears in the upper right-hand area on pages where the mask should be used. As you study, you may write your answers in the spaces provided in the text.

2. *Branching*, or *scatter*, in which you are directed to turn to other pages to reinforce your learning.

Achievement tests follow each chapter and each unit so that you can check your comprehension of the completed material. Remember that when you answer the evaluation questions, you are not competing with anyone else for a grade. Rather, you are evaluating your own understanding to see if there are any sections of the material that you did not comprehend. Directions following the questions will help you decide how much of the material you will need to review.

TO THE INSTRUCTOR

The purpose of this volume is to provide nursing students with a comprehensive body of knowledge concerning health and the family during the reproduction cycle. The programmed approach of this book will enable the student to learn at his or her own pace with immediate reinforcement. Units in the book discuss major content areas, and each unit is built upon the knowledge and understanding acquired in the preceding ones.

To assist the student in exploring topics in greater depth, pertinent reading lists are provided at the ends of most chapters. Pretests precede most chapters to enable the student to review knowledge already acquired and identify areas for further study. Achievement tests follow each chapter and each unit. This double testing is intended to further reinforce the knowledge assimilated in the program and to direct the learner to portions of the chapter or the unit which may need reviewing.

This program can be used by the instructor as a basis for seminars, role-playing exercises, and teaching in the classroom or clinical laboratory. Family models introduced in the text can be used to engage the students in realistic situations requiring them to apply their understanding of the concepts learned in the various units.

UNIT I
THE DEFINITION
OF FAMILY HEALTH

CHAPTER ONE
HEALTH

OBJECTIVES *Identify the four components of the definition of health.*

Apply this concept of health to specific situations.

GLOSSARY *Health:* A state of being in which homeodynamic systems are in harmony. Health is never static, is dependent upon the individual's potential, and exists on a continuum.

Homeodynamic: Related to the continuous interaction of biological systems or of human beings and their milieu

System: An organization of parts that are related or functioning as a whole or unit. In man, the total organism is a system and any of its integral parts are subsystems; e.g., the urinary system is a subsystem of the total human system.

Interaction: A mutual exchange between two or more systems

Homeodynamic system: The continuous interactions of related parts functioning as a unit

Dynamic: Characterized by constant change; actively engaged

Potential: The optimum level of a person's resources

Variable: Any factor that is subject to change or is able to produce change

Ecological: Related to the interactions between man and the environment

Continuum: An infinite scale of measurement in time and space

Health status: The degree of homeodynamic harmony

"Health for all" is the ideal motivating nations, regardless of political persuasion, to participate in the World Health Organization. To professionals in the health field, the rapidity of changes taking place in the modern world has automatically voided the standards for health as it is defined in the World Health Organization (WHO)'s constitutional preamble: "a state of complete physical, mental, and social well-being." In spite of the agency's frequently quoted definition, the formulation of what constitutes an "ideal" state of health remains elusive, relative, and controversial.

To unquestioningly accept WHO's definition would imply that we adhere to an absolute standard of health for all people. Recent national and world events, however, point to the fact that we cannot use our own frame of reference to establish pragmatic scales for measuring the health of every individual in the world. Complex variables such as culture, nationality, geography, politics, economics, religious beliefs, population density, technology, and education, which interact to make up the individual's "lifestyle," understandably influence all interpretations of health. Thus, it becomes apparent that health is not a constant, static state defined in terms of absolutes; rather, health can be viewed only as the result of a dynamic interaction between individuals and all of those variables in their environment.

In this light, health can be defined only in terms of its essential components: *First,* health is dependent upon *each individual's potential* to achieve and maintain a state of well-being. *Second,* health is not static; rather it is based on each person's ability to achieve a *homeodynamic* relationship[1] between the psychosocial, ecological, and physiological forces acting upon him. *Third,* health is relative; it *exists on a continuum* upon which individuals are placed according to their potentials.

It follows that health is represented by harmony in the *homeodynamic systems* that exist between the individual and his environment.

Based on the preceding information, let us see if you can identify which of the following statements includes the essential criteria for defining health:

A. Health can be measured only by comparing the health status of individuals with the health status of other individuals in the same national, ethnic, and cultural group and geographic area.   Go to page 6.

B. Health is a relative term that may mean different things to different individuals and is dependent upon each individual's potential to achieve a homeodynamic relationship with his environment.   Go to page 5.

C. Definitions of health can be developed only through comparison with nonhealth states (disease). That is to say, one is healthy only when one is not ill or being affected by some disease process.   Go to page 7.

Excellent! You have chosen properly. By selecting statement *B* you have indicated your ability to identify the major criteria that we will be using to define health. Furthermore, you were able to understand that health can neither be defined as an absolute nor be measured on a comparative scale. Indeed, it is doubtful that anyone could identify clearly what a complete state of health is at any given instant or in relationship to a constant standard. To illustrate this: you may consider yourself the healthiest individual in this school, but at this very moment there may be several forces operating which will affect your future health status. However, does the presence of these forces make you a sick individual as we define "sickness"?

By accepting our definition of health, you then are free to identify more easily nonhealth states for any given individual or group of individuals, regardless of their national, geographical, cultural, or ethnic membership. As well, you are better equipped to predict the actions that you may initiate as means of overcoming the forces producing the nonhealth states.

Advance to page 8 and take the post-test.

You have not understood our statements regarding the essential components that determine the criteria for health. In selecting statement *A*, you have failed to recognize the individuality inherent in our definition of health. We defined health in terms of each person's ability to be healthy relative to his own potential to achieve health. In choosing statement *A*, you have developed a standard for health which might be a difficult criterion to meet. Can you say that a person who has had an amputation is less healthy than you because he cannot compare with your physical wholeness? No, because an individual's health status is measured relative to his own potential for health. By defining health in terms of absolutes you create standards that are impossible to meet for most individuals.

Return to page 4. Review the material and choose another response.

Incorrect. By selecting statement *C* you have defined health in terms of negative absolutes. Look at it this way: Can one say that something is black just because it is not white? What about all the other colors in the spectrum? In selecting this statement you have committed yourself to saying that there is *only one* state of health and that this state exists only when disease is not present. This, in effect, places health in almost unachievable terms, since it is doubtful whether anyone at a given point can be considered totally free of forces leading to nonhealth states. In fact, at this very instant, there may be several forces operating on you which ultimately will affect your health status. But we will talk about this later.

Return to page 4. Review the material and choose another response.

POST-TEST   Indicate whether each statement is true or false by circling the appropriate letter. Then turn to page 9 and check how well you have done.

1. Health can be considered a goal that is the same for all individuals regardless of their socioeconomic status.   T   F

2. A positive state of health refers only to physical well-being.   T   F

3. Health cannot be measured in absolutes.   T   F

4. The health status of the individual is dependent solely on his environment.   T   F

5. When evaluating the health status of an individual, it is important to recognize and remember that this status is in a constant process of change.   T   F

6. Health is represented by harmony in the homeodynamic systems.   T   F

In the specific areas with which you had difficulty, return to the material and review.

REFERENCES
1. Martha Rogers: *An Introduction to the Theoretical Basis of Nursing,* F. A. Davis Co., Philadelphia, 1970, p. 102.

BIBLIOGRAPHY
Abrams, Herbert K., "Neighborhood Health Center," *American Journal of Public Health,* Vol. 61, p. 2236 ff., Nov. 1971.

Bernstein, Betty, "What Happened to Ghetto Medicine in New York State?" *American Journal of Public Health,* Vol. 61, p. 1287 ff., July 1971.

Dolfman, Michael L., "Health Planning—A Method for Generating Program Objectives," *American Journal of Public Health,* Vol. 63, p. 238 ff., March 1973.

Freeman, Ruth: *Community Health Nursing Practice,* W. B. Saunders, Philadelphia, 1970.

French, Ruth: *The Dynamics of Health Care,* McGraw-Hill Book Co., New York, 1968.

Holder, Lee, "Education for Health in a Changing Society," *American Journal of Public Health*, Vol. 60, pp. 2307-2313, Dec. 1970.

Jamann, Joann S., "Health is a Function of Ecology," *American Journal of Nursing,* Vol. 71, pp. 970-973, May 1971.

Matheney, Ruth, et al.: *Fundamentals of Patient Centered Nursing,* C. V. Mosby Co., St. Louis, 1971.

McGrath, Eileen, "Guidelines for New Community Nurses," *Nursing Outlook,* Vol. 19, pp. 478-480, July 1971.

National Commission on Community Health Services: *Health Is a Community Affair,* Harvard University Press, Cambridge, Mass., 1966.

Rogers, Martha: *An Introduction to the Theoretical Basis of Nursing,* F. A. Davis Co., Philadelphia, 1970.

POST-TEST ANSWERS   1. F   2. F   3. T   4. F   5. T   6. T

CHAPTER TWO

STRESS ADAPTATION

OBJECTIVES   *Identify the three components of stress adaptation.*

Apply this concept of stress adaptation to specific situations.

GLOSSARY   *Stressor:* A force within or without any given system (e.g., the human system) which is capable of inducing or producing change

Stress: A state in which a system is affected by a stressor and harmony or balance is disrupted or is not achieved

Equilibrium: Harmony or balance between systems or within a system

Dissonant: Characterized by a negative or nonharmonious force

Adaptation: A dynamic process of adjustment or change following the introduction of a stressor

Resources: Positive strengths and abilities present within a system

Central to our concept of health is the idea that various forces act upon and are reciprocated by the organism as it attempts to establish a homeodynamic balance. These forces may be interpreted by the organism as being positive or negative, favorable or unfavorable. In either case, a temporary imbalance occurs, causing the organism to attempt to reestablish an equilibrium. When the force is interpreted by the organism as being dissonant or negative, a process takes place which is called *stress adaptation. Stress* is the state that exists when a force is interpreted as dissonant, and *adaptation* is the responsive process of the organism as it attempts to remove, conform to, or alter the dissonant force.[1]

A dissonant force is any agent that produces a state of stress. The strength of this force (which will be referred to hereafter as *stressor*) is influenced by other variables. For example: When the stressor is of a psychological nature (such as concern over studying for an examination), it may be accompanied by a physiological manifestation such as a headache, and the ensuing result will be an intensified stress situation.

You will remember that health was defined in terms of an important characteristic, the organism's own potential to achieve a new homeodynamic balance. Therefore, during the process of adaptation a new equilibrium will ensue which represents a new state of health for that individual. Should the adaptive mechanisms fail and should the stressor be prolonged, the individual will be unable to overcome the stressor's strength; a serious nonhealth state, and at times death, results.

When you chose the correct response to the section on health, you went on to find that possibly, at this moment, there may be some stressors that are causing you to mobilize your resources socially, emotionally, or physiologically as a means of adjusting to these stressors. Not only that but, in the process of adapting, you will, in all probability, produce changes in these internal and/or external forces or variables (such as the environment). As this process occurs, your health status has changed. How can this be?

Let us see if we can clarify this. Look at the following situation, which, although somewhat simplistic, will give you an idea of what we mean. After reading it, see if you can adequately match the terms with the parts of the situation they describe. Before doing this, you may want to go back and reread the section on stress adaptation.

This is Mary Smith's first day at college, and she has been given quite a number of reading assignments by her instructors, who expect her to get them all done by the following day.

Mary is employed on a part-time basis as an assistant librarian. Although she had hoped to get some of her readings done during work hours, everyone in the campus appeared to be using the library and required her attention. As she returns to her room after work, she suddenly begins to feel tense and nauseated and is perspiring. In addition, although she has been away from home for only a few days, she is beginning to feel "homesick."

She leaves her room, meets another student, and begins to talk about her pressures. After some conversation, she returns to her room and decides to develop a working plan to handle her study time. She makes a schedule for evenings in which she assigns study hours to different subjects while at the same time allowing two hours free time so that she may socialize. She also makes sure that she will go to bed at a reasonable hour.

Having done this, she then decides to call home and find out how everyone is. She talks to her mother and to her boyfriend, who happens to be visiting her family. They all make plans for a party on the following weekend. She returns to her studies with new determination, realizing that school makes certain demands that must be met.

Now, then, let us see how well you can identify what might have occurred.

Match the terms in the left column with the parts of the situation they describe.

1. Stress   _____   A. Making up study schedule
                                    Talking to classmate
                                    Calling home
                                    Planning for party   C

2. Adaptation   _____   B. Job
                                    Reading assignments
                                    Separation from home   A

3. Stressor   _____   C. Tenseness
                                    Perspiration
                                    Nausea
                                    Homesickness   B

If you got any of these wrong, return to page 11 and review the material.

POST-TEST Indicate whether each statement is true or false by circling the appropriate letter. Then turn to page 14 and check how well you have done.

1. Stressors are present only in nonhealth states.   T   F

2. A stressor can originate within the individual.   T   F

3. Adaptation occurs as the stressor is modified by the interaction of the individual with the stressor.   T   F

4. The individual achieving a homeodynamic balance after being in a state of health will return to a former state of health.   T   F

5. The strength of a stressor may be increased by additional stressors.   T   F

6. Stress is primarily the result of psychological conditions.   T   F

In the specific areas with which you had difficulty, return to the material and review.

REFERENCES   1. Hans Selye, "The Stress Syndrome," *American Journal of Nursing*, Vol. 65, p. 98, March 1965.

BIBLIOGRAPHY   Aguilera, Donna, Janice Messick, and Marlene Farrell: *Crisis Intervention, Theory and Methodology,* C. V. Mosby Co., St. Louis, 1970.
Caplan, Gerard: *Principles of Preventive Psychiatry*, Basic Books, New York, 1964.
Parad, Howard S.: *Crisis Intervention*, Family Service Society, New York, 1967.
Selye, Hans: *The Stress of Life,* McGraw-Hill Book Co., New York, 1956.
———, "The Stress Syndrome," *American Journal of Nursing,* Vol. 65, p. 98, March 1965.

POST-TEST   1. F   2. T   3. T   4. F   5. T   6. F
ANSWERS

CHAPTER THREE

LEVELS OF HEALTH CARE AND NURSES' ROLES

OBJECTIVES *Identify the three levels of health care.*

Identify the nurse's role in the areas of promotion and prevention.

GLOSSARY *Maximization:* The achievement of the highest possible level
Promotion: Activities that serve to maximize potentials
Prevention: Activities that lead to the elimination or reduction of a stressor
Restoration: Activities that reestablish harmony of the homeodynamic system

It has become apparent that health cannot be defined in terms of absolutes and that, if an "ideal" state of health is truly related to the individual's capacity to achieve a homeodynamic balance with those external forces interacting with him, then the goal of health care services should be to provide conditions under which an individual's maximization of his potential to live, work, and be a happy, contributing member of society is ensured. The three levels of health care are prevention, promotion, and restoration.

According to Dubos,[1] aspirations for the attainment of high health standards require a continuous dynamic approach to the methods employed in ensuring such maximization of individuals' potentials. Thus existing and future health care programs should aim at instituting actions, the goals of which are the *promotion* and provision for maintenance of the individual's ability to react effectively to stressors so as to achieve a positive homeodynamic balance and the *prevention* of nonhealth states.

Primarily, preventive activities are measures that thwart the emergence of stressors that could become threats to health. Promotion measures, on the other hand, maximize individuals' ability to achieve their potential within the health continuum. Activities such as depolluting the environment, for example, are preventive measures since, among other things, they avert the emergence of respiratory difficulties. In the process of forestalling these difficulties, however, these preventive measures become promotion activities since, by blocking the entrance of injurious agents, they ensure the respiratory system's ability to function at its optimum level.

The concept of prevention applies to all phases of health care.[2] Whether health workers are engaged in curative activities, that is, activities that lead to the elimination or reduction of a stressor, or in *restoration*, that is, activities that assist the individual in achieving a homeodynamic balance after a stressor has been introduced, prevention of further imbalances within the homeodynamic system is instituted.

In addition, prevention requires that projections be made regarding the effectiveness of the actions that are taken to preserve the integrity and homeodynamic balance of the organism.

From the preceding discussion, it is seen that prevention is a dynamic, constantly evolving aspect of health care; it is all-encompassing, since it may involve more than one area, and future-oriented, since it requires that actions instituted now be examined in terms of their possible effects tomorrow.

All too often, health care services and activities have been equated primarily with actions that would lead to cure and restoration. Obviously, cure is not a goal that may be achieved equally by all, particularly when physiological, biological, and environmental stresses may have so debilitated the individual that his adaptive resources are in jeopardy. Therefore, focusing solely on curative and restorative measures circumvents the issues, since these measures by themselves do not deal with the stressors that were the original causes of the nonhealth state. However, if effective prevention and promotion measures are instituted so that the emergence of the stressors is anticipated and blocked, the homeodynamic balance of the organism can be ensured and maintained.

In establishing meaningful criteria for judging the maximization of the individual's potential to achieve a positive state of health, the methods employed should be able to differentiate between those goals that clearly are achievable and those that may be desirable. It is desirable, for example, that all people live under highly hygienic conditions; that they be guaranteed a stable, adequate source of income; that social conditions be such that social harmony and stability is ensured; that housing conditions be the best available; that all possible harmful biological, chemical, and psychological stressors be totally eradicated. All of these goals are indeed desirable; yet, are they attainable? What seems possible are programs and services the objectives of which are the prevention of nonhealth states and the promotion of the individual's optimum level of functioning.

The objective of *health care systems* is to serve the needs of the people. Since the function of health care systems is to improve the human condition and environment, and since health services are people-directed, it is only through the interaction of people in their various roles as patients, consumers, family members, friends, legislators, and health team workers that health care programs can be funded, designed, developed, and implemented.

Nurses as part of the health care system have the unequalled opportunity of effecting good preventive and promotion methods. Through their understanding of health concepts, their awareness of the many stressors that are bound to emerge and threaten individuals' homeodynamic balance, and their ability to intervene when such measures are indicated, nurses can and do become essential components and translators of the prevention and promotion objectives of health care services.

POST-TEST   Indicate whether each statement is true or false by circling the appropriate letter. Then turn to page 19 and check how well you have done.

1. Future health care programs should function to ensure maximization of the individual's homeodynamic balance.   T   F

2. Prevention and promotion measures are geared only to curing the individual when he is in a nonhealth state.   T   F

3. Prevention is the averting of the emergence of stressors that could produce a nonhealth state.   T   F

4. Health care systems should exist to meet the needs of those able to afford them.   T   F

5. Nurses' participation within the health care structure, through assessment and intervention measures, can provide for the prevention of nonhealth states and the promotion of positive homeodynamic balance.   T   F

In the specific areas with which you had difficulty, return to the material and review.

REFERENCES   1. Rene Dubos: *The Mirage of Health*, Harper and Row, New York, 1959, p. 13.

2. Irene L. Beland: *Clinical Nursing—Pathophysiological and Psychological Approaches,* The Macmillan Co., New York, 1970, pp. 57-62

BIBLIOGRAPHY   Dubos, Rene: *The Mirage of Health*, Harper and Row, New York, 1959.

Kintzel, Kay Corman: *Advanced Concepts in Clinical Nursing*, J. B. Lippincott Co., Philadelphia, 1971.

POST-TEST   1. T   2. F   3. T   4. F   5. T
ANSWERS

CHAPTER FOUR

THE FAMILY AND ROLES OF ITS MEMBERS

OBJECTIVES *Define the concept of family.*

Apply the given definition of family to various situations.

Identify the four functional roles that may be occupied by family members.

GLOSSARY *Family:* "The relationship recognized by a man and a woman and between one or both of them and their children"[1]

Role: A position occupied by an individual or group of individuals in response to other persons or situations

Functional role: A position occupied as a result of behavioral responses

Assigned role: A position occupied as a result of sex, e.g., brother

Positional role: A position occupied as a result of ranking, e.g., according to age or position within the family

Norms: Behaviors that are set as standards by a group

Mores: Values established by a group

Supportive role: A position occupied by a family member when dealing with human relations within the family

Companionship role: A position occupied by a family member when sharing the interests of other members

Power role: A position occupied by a family member who assumes the authority within the family unit

Status role: A position occupied by a family member who provides a source of income or position within the community

Since the beginning of history, the most widely shared characteristic of the human race has been its ability to organize into family groups. Indeed, it is through the family that society endures and constantly regenerates itself culturally and biologically; it is the family that helps mold and adapt its members to established social norms and mores; it is the family that provides the individual with a sense of protection, security, and love. It is the family that creates the pattern of life for men and women to emulate and provides the means for self-perpetuation after death.

What *is* a family? When and how does it begin? In this era of changing life-styles, when traditional mores are questioned and sometimes discarded, the concept of the family has not escaped attempts at revision. Although one may prefer other definitions, for our purposes we will focus on a definition that is centered on "the relationships recognized by the participants, between a man and a woman and between one or both of them and their children."[1] Keeping the given definition in mind, which of the following statements *best* describes a family?

Married couple and their two children — Go to page 24 top.

Unwed mother and her child — Go to page 29 top.

Widower and his two children — Go to page 27 middle.

All of these — Go to page 25 bottom.

Since you recognize that there are interactions within families, you must now focus on the roles of the participants and how these serve to identify the nature of the relationship.

It has been stated that a role is a "goal directed pattern or sequence of acts, tailored by the cultural process, for the transactions a person may carry out in a social group or situation."[2] It is important that we clarify the fact that no role exists in isolation; rather, any role is a reciprocal response to the role occupied by another individual or group of individuals.[3] It also must be recognized that individuals occupy different roles at different times and that often they assume more than one role at the same time. Let us examine the following situation as an example:

It is six o'clock and Mother is sitting in the living room breast-feeding her newborn baby. Father arrives from work and sits opposite her and begins to share with her some of his difficulties at the office during the day. At this point, Mother is occupying two roles: she is taking care of the physiological needs of her child and thus is engaged in a supportive role, and at the same time she is occupying a companionship role as a wife.

Now, can you think of any situation in which you did not meet the criteria for occupying a role? *Stop for a minute and reflect on this.*

Did you recognize the fact that there is not a single situation in which you are not occupying a role by being involved either in an activity or in a relationship with other people? Even right now, as you study this unit, you are occupying a role, that of being a student! Therefore, you are never without a role.

Literature dealing with the subject of roles points to the many criteria that may be utilized to categorize them.[4] For example, roles within a family may be occupied by *assignation* according to sex, such as roles of "brother" and "sister"; or they may be assigned according to *position*, that is, relating to age ranking, such as being the "first-born" or the "youngest" child. Finally, roles may be categorized according to *function*, that is, in terms of the behaviors exhibited by individuals as they interact with one another.

In defining the types of roles occupied by family members, we will assign roles according to *functional* category. The four major roles that may be occupied according to function are:[5]

> *Power role:* The role occupied by the member who assumes the authority within the family.
>
> *Status role:* The role assumed by the family member who provides the source of income and position within the community.
>
> *Supportive role:* The role occupied by a family member in dealing with human relations within the family. Its basic elements are understanding, impartiality, caring, and concern.
>
> *Companionship role:* A role occupied by a family member when sharing the interests of other members.

The selection of these four functional roles is based on the fact that family member activities may be categorized easily under these four major headings. Thus, identification of role alterations that occur as a result of stresses created by family changes in strengths, economics, emotional aspects, and interpersonal relationships can be understood more clearly.

It is important that we clarify the fact that these roles may be interchangeable as well as being shared by several family members at any given time.

Now that you have acquired some of the basic concepts related to a definition of role, can you identify the role that Mother is occupying in the following situation?

Father comes home from work early, as promised, in order to take his wife and son to the basketball game, an event that he has eagerly anticipated and planned for. As he arrives, he finds Mother overwrought because she had a flat tire while shopping, was late for her dental appointment, and does not have dinner ready. She expounds on the family's lack of concern for her plight until finally her husband agrees to cancel the game and take her out to dinner.

Of the following statements, which one *best* illustrates the role being occupied by Mother?

Power role

Status role

Supportive role

Companionship role

Go to page 29 middle.

Go to page 27 bottom.

Go to page 26 middle.

Go to page 24 middle.

Now, can you point to the *role* occupied by *Mother* in the following situation?

Mother comes home from her shopping outing to find her eldest daughter, Jane, in tears. She asks her daughter what has occurred and is told that the younger sister has borrowed Jane's tennis racket and broken it.

Mother pours some lemonade. As she sits with her daughter, she reflects on the fact that Jane must be very upset; after listening for a while, she calls in the younger daughter, explains Jane's feelings, and asks her sister if she has any plans for either fixing or replacing the tennis racket.

Power role	Go to page 30 top.
Status role	Go to page 28 top.
Supportive role	Go to page 24 bottom.
Companionship role	Go to page 26 top.

Now, then, look at the following situation. Can you pick out the role Father is occupying?

Mr. Forum, a prosperous banker, comes home early because he has to attend a meeting at the Moravian church of which he is a member of the Board of Directors. He makes dinner from leftovers in the refrigerator while Mother is preparing for her bridge club and their young son is doing his homework.

Power role	Go to page 29 bottom.
Status role	Go to page 28 middle.
Companionship role	Go to page 26 bottom.
Supportive role	Go to page 25 top.

So far you have done well and have done lots of work. Let us find out if you can identify what role Mrs. Moore is occupying in the following situation.

Mrs. Moore, a widow, is a retired schoolteacher living with her only daughter, Mary, who works as a secretary. Since she knows that Mary has become an accomplished painter, Mrs. Moore has planned a surprise outing to the Museum of Modern Art for both Mary and herself.

Power role	Go to page 25 middle.
Status role	Go to page 27 top.
Companionship role	Go to page 30 bottom.
Supportive role	Go to page 28 bottom.

Your choice, "... married couple and their two children," is not the best answer. It is true that this is *one* type of family. However, if you notice, the given definition identifies relationships within the family as existing not in a legal sense but rather in terms of *how each participant recognizes them.*

Return to page 21. Review the material and choose another response.

———————————————

Wrong. In choosing the companionship role you are saying that the mother was sharing her family's interests and planned activities. If she had been in the companionship role, she would have ensured that the father and son attended the basketball game as anticipated.

Return to page 22. Review the material and choose another response.

———————————————

You have answered that Mother is in a supportive role, and this demonstrates an excellent understanding of the dynamics underlying the behavior of a person occupying this role.

Indeed Mother is being supportive by helping the members of her family work out their interpersonal problems without showing partiality. She has done this by listening to all parties involved, understanding their feelings, and allowing them to express themselves.

Turn to page 23 middle and continue with the program.

We caught you napping! Your answer was "supportive role" for this situation. However, none of the activities identified indicate that Father is offering any type of support to any of the family members at this particular time. Remember the essential elements differentiating a supportive role from others? Reread your definitions!

Return to page 22. Review the material and choose another response from page 23 middle.

You have said that Mrs. Moore is occupying a power role? How did you arrive at that conclusion? Look at the situation again: Is mother exercising any form of authority over her daughter's decisions and actions?

What is it that she is really doing?

Return to page 22. Review the material and choose another response from page 23 bottom.

Excellent! In choosing all of the examples as being descriptions of families, you have grasped the real meaning of the definition. Indeed, the relationships that define a family do not have to be delineated by any given set of social expectations, such as legality of union, or by predefined membership. It is the reciprocity of the interaction and the recognition of its existence that make a family.

Turn to page 21 middle and continue with the program.

You said that Mother was occupying the companionship role. No. You are confused about the various role definitions.

Mother is not sharing Jane's interest in tennis. What is she really doing?

Return to page 22. Review the material and choose another response from page 23 top.

Your choice of "supportive role" is wrong. Can you identify any activity or behavior on the part of Mother which may be classified as being supportive to any of the family members? Did she show understanding of her family's previous plans? If she had been occupying the supportive role, would she not have participated in the activities decided upon earlier?

Return to page 22. Review the material on roles and choose another response.

You said, "companionship role"? Not this time! Father is not sharing any particular interest expressed by any other family member.

Return to page 22. Review the material and choose another response from page 23 middle.

Oops! "Status," you say? How so? In the last given situation you were able to identify the correct criteria applying to a definition of a status role.

Is Mrs. Moore engaged in a situation in which she is providing income and position within the social structure for the family? Sorry, but you have to recheck the definition.

Return to page 22. Review the material and choose another response from page 23 bottom.

In your choice of "widower and his two children" you were partially correct. This example falls within our definition of family although one of its members (the mother) is absent. However, this is not the best response. Note that the definition makes reference to the recognition of relationships by the participants, whether or not any of them are married.

Return to page 21. Review the material and choose another response.

You are confused. How do you see Mother occupying a status role in this situation? You have not understood the meaning of this role; she is *not* providing for financial support or actively engaged in any community activity that which provide for family recognition.

Return to page 22. Review the material and choose another response.

Your choice of "status role" is a wrong one. How is Mother providing for income or family position for the family unit through her interaction with Jane? You are really confused. Better go back to the beginning of the chapter and get the various roles clearly defined!

Return to page 22. Review the material and choose another response from page 23 top.

Return to page 22. Review the material and choose another response from page 23 top.

———————————————————

You have picked the status role for this situation, and you are quite correct. Father is occupying a status position by assuming a role within the community as a member of the church. As well, in his position as a banker he occupies a role that is a source of financial security to his family.

Turn to page 23 bottom and continue with the program.

Turn to page 23 bottom and continue with the program.

———————————————————

No. Mrs. Moore is not in a supportive role. If you recall the situation, there is nothing in it to identify the basic components of a supportive role, that is, understanding, impartiality, etc. You had better return to the original definition, check your terminology, and try again.

Return to page 22. Review the material and choose another response from page 23 bottom.

Return to page 22. Review the material and choose another response from page 23 bottom.

Your selection of "unwed mother and her child" is a good one, since it points to your ability to identify the concept of "mutually accepted relationships" as the core idea that defines a family as we see it. However, in this context it is not the best possible response.

Return to page 21. Review the material and choose another response.

––––––––––––––––––––––

Great! You were able to discern that this is a matriarchal unit, in which the mother in the power role has the authority to regulate the activities of the family. Furthermore, it is to your credit that you have been able to identify the fact that "power" does not only mean use of physical force but also may be utilized in subtle ways such as through social or psychological pressures.

Turn to page 23 top and continue with the program.

––––––––––––––––––––––

Wrong! Although power may be vested in Mr. Forum because of his positions as a banker and a church board member, you have not grasped the definition of the power role as it applies within the family unit. Where in the situation can you identify Mr. Forum utilizing authority as a family member?

Return to page 22. Review the material and choose another response from page 23 middle.

You've missed on this one! Mother is not occupying the power role. Look at the situation: Is she telling anyone what to do? In fact, she is not acting as an authority figure, who would be forcing the young daughter to do something specific. Rather, she is fostering a situation in which both sisters can work out their problems and make their own decisions.

Return to page 22. Review the material and choose another response from page 23 top.

Congratulations! You have identified the fact that Mother is occupying the companionship role in this situation by becoming interested in her daughter's hobby and participating in this activity.

Advance to page 31 and take the post-test.

POST-TEST Indicate whether each statement is true or false by circling the appropriate letter. Then turn to page 32 and check how well you have done.

1. It is necessary that a relationship between a man and a woman be legal in order for them to begin a family.   **T**   **F**

2. The most important factor in a definition of the concept "family" is the mutual acceptance of the relationships between the members.   **T**   **F**

3. The power role within the family may be identified when one member exercises some form of authority over another member or members.   **T**   **F**

4. The power role within the family emerges *only* when the physical use of authority is applied.   **T**   **F**

5. The status role when held by the mother means that she wields the authority with the family unit.   **T**   **F**

6. Status roles may be occupied simultaneously and shared by Mother and Father within the family unit.   **T**   **F**

7. When in a supportive role, a family member helps to mediate when difficult interpersonal conflicts arise between other family members.   **T**   **F**

8. A mother occupying a supportive role will try to impose her own ideas and feelings on other family members.   **T**   **F**

9. When Mrs. S begins to take golf lessons because this is her husband's favorite sport, she is occupying the companionship role.   **T**   **F**

10. While occupying the companionship role, the mother would be sharing the interests of other family members.   **T**   **F**

In the specific areas with which you had difficulty, return to the material and review.

REFERENCES

1. Norman Bell and Ezra Vogel: *A Modern Introduction to the Family,* The Free Press, New York, 1968, p. 1.

2. *Ibid.,* p. 393.

3. Lelia Calhoun Deasy: *Persons and Positions,* The Catholic University Press, Washington, D.C., 1969, p. 13.

4. *Ibid.,* pp. 3-102.

5. Ernest R. Mowrer, "The Differentiation of Husband and Wife Roles," *Journal of Marriage and the Family,* Vol. 31, No. 3, pp. 534-540, Aug. 1969.

BIBLIOGRAPHY

Bell, Norman and Ezra Vogel: *A Modern Introduction to the Family,* The Free Press, New York, 1968.

Deasy, Lelia Calhoun: *Persons and Positions,* The Catholic University Press, Washington, D.C., 1969.

Goode, William: *The Family,* Prentice-Hall, Englewood Cliffs, N.J., 1964.

Horton, Paul B: *Sociology and the Health Sciences,* McGraw-Hill Book Co., New York, 1965.

Krech, David, Richard S. Crutchfield, and Egerton L. Ballachey: *Individual in Society,* McGraw-Hill Book Co., New York, 1962.

Mowrer, Ernest R., "The Differentiation of Husband and Wife Roles," *Journal of Marriage and the Family,* Vol. 31, No. 3, pp. 534-540, Aug. 1969.

POST-TEST ANSWERS

1. F   2. T   3. T   4. F   5. F   6. T   7. T   8. F
9. T   10. T

CHAPTER FIVE
FAMILY HEALTH

GLOSSARY   *Family system:* An organizational structure and mode of functioning within the family which exists as a result of the members' relationships

We have previously stated that the existence of the family is dependent upon its members' recognition or acceptance of relationships such as mother-father, parent-offspring. The sum total of these relationships therefore constitutes a family system.

A family system may be thought of as being the broad, all-encompassing view of the family's organizational structure and modes of functioning. Thus, the family unit will emerge as a *unique organism* with identity, characteristics, interactions, and adaptive resources of its own dependent upon how relationships and roles are assumed.

We have stated that the intricate interaction of variables such as culture and economy has a direct influence on the degree of health enjoyed by a given individual. Likewise, these same variables come into play as we address ourselves to what we mean by family health.

The dynamic interaction of variables may affect families either in a general way, i.e., by exerting stressing forces on the total *family system*, or merely by affecting a single member. In either case, the presence of a dissonant force will evoke a systemic adaptive response to it. Therefore it can be said that, regardless of the direction of the stressor—either to a single member or to the family as a whole—the family system will react to it as a total organism in order to maintain the homeodynamic balance needed for health.

Let us look at a situation in which a family achieves a homeodynamic balance as it responds to a stressor that is generally directed (that is, affecting the whole system), such as the loss of economic resources. If the father loses his job, family members may react as a system by seeking employment, decreasing expenses, etc. In so mobilizing its adaptive resources, the family has exhibited its ability to function as a unit and has been able to decrease the strength of the stressor and therefore achieve a homeodynamic balance.

In another situation, the force of a stressor may be directed toward a single member. Father may come home quite upset over a trying day at work due to arguments with his superior. To the family, the father's mood becomes a dissonant force to which it may react as a unit.

Family members may become supportive by decreasing distressing stimuli by listening to him and, when appropriate, by assuring him of the validity of his feelings. Through this process, the family has assisted the father in dealing with his problem. The family's ability to react as a unit, utilizing roles and interactions adequately in dealing with a dissonant force affecting a single member, has served to establish a homeodynamic balance for Father. It is important to clarify the fact that, if this force had not been dealt with, it would have continued to disrupt the family's system of interactions.

It should be understood that there are certain situations in which simultaneous adaptation to a stressor by all members of a family system may not be possible. The resources available to a six-month-old child, for example, are limited in comparison with those of other older members of the family. Successful adaptation in such cases lies in the rest of the family's abilities to dispense with or assume necessary roles for the member who is at that time unable to mobilize sufficient resources to overcome the stressor.

Let us see how well you have understood our concept of health as it applies to the family system. In the following situation, can you identify the response that best illustrates a family system adapting most successfully to a stressor?

Mother awakens at 6:00 a.m. experiencing symptoms of the flu. Her two children have to be at school by 9:00 a.m. and Father leaves for work at around 8:30 a.m. Usually Mother is responsible for preparing breakfast for the family and packing the children's lunch while Father gets the children dressed and ready for school. Today, Father insists that she stay in bed while the rest of the family go about their usual routine.

A. Father fixes breakfast for the children and himself and prepares their lunchboxes while the children get themselves ready and dressed for school.

Go to page 37.

B. Father prepares a light breakfast for his wife and himself, and the children's lunches, while the children get themselves ready for school and prepare their own breakfast.

Go to page 38.

C. Father dresses the children, fixes their breakfast and school lunches, and then prepares breakfast for himself.

Go to page 36.

In choosing response *C*, you indicate your lack of understanding of the material presented in this particular section. Are you not placing an undue burden on the father? Are you considering the *whole* family system? Is this truly the most successful mode of adaptation which may be exhibited by this family system?

You had better return to the beginning of the section (page 34), review the material, and then choose another response from page 35.

Your selection of *A* indicates that you have not clearly understood the meaning of successful adaptation by the whole family system. It could be argued that in carrying out the described actions, the family has exhibited a certain degree of adaptation. In fact, the same thing could be said of all of the choices provided. Yet, haven't you overlooked an important aspect?

Return to page 34. Review the material and choose another response from page 35.

Your choice was *B*. Great! This situation clearly exemplifies a most successful way in which this family has been able to adapt to the stressor introduced by the mother's incapacitation. All other members of the family have been able to mobilize resources available to them in carrying out the routine, while at the same time providing for the mother's immediate needs.

Advance to page 39 and take the post-test.

POST-TEST   Indicate whether each statement is true or false by circling the appropriate letter. Then turn to page 40 and check how well you have done.

1. The health of the family is dependent upon its ability to mobilize adaptive resources as a unit.   T   F

2. All family systems tend to assume the same characteristics, relationships, and roles.   T   F

3. All family members should always simultaneously adapt in the same way to any given stressor.   T   F

4. A general stressor is one that tends to affect a single family member.   T   F

5. The sum total of all mutually recognized and accepted relationships constitutes a family system.   T   F

6. A family system tends to develop a structure of its own.   T   F

In the specific areas with which you had difficulty, return to the material and review.

BIBLIOGRAPHY   Craven, Ruth Falk and Benita Hall Sharp, "The Effects of Illness on Family Functions,"
                    Nursing Forum, Vol. 11, No. 2, pp. 186-193, 1972.
                Finch, Joyce, "Systems Analysis: A Logical Approach to Professional Nursing Care,"
                    Nursing Forum, Vol. 8, No. 2, pp. 176-190, 1969.
                Sobol, Evelyn and Paulette Robischon: *Family Nursing—A Study Guide,* C. V. Mosby
                    Co., St. Louis, 1970.
                Tinkham, Catherine W. and Eleanor F. Voorhies: *Community Health Nursing Evolution
                    and Process*, Appleton-Century-Crofts, New York, 1972.

POST-TEST   1. T   2. F   3. F   4. F   5. T   6. T
ANSWERS

CHAPTER SIX

THE NURSING PROCESS

SUGGESTED BACKGROUND REFERENCES

The following list of suggested references includes those techniques and methods of interviewing and communications which you should have mastered before advancing with this program.

Kron, Thora: *Communication in Nursing*, 2d ed., W. B. Saunders Co., Philadelphia, 1972.

Lewis, Garland K.: *Nurse-Patient Communication*, 4th ed., William C. Brown Co., Dubuque, Iowa, 1971.

Mercer, Lianne S. and Patricia O'Connor: *Fundamental Skills in the Nurse-Patient Relationship—A Programmed Text*, W. B. Saunders Co., Philadelphia, 1969.

OBJECTIVES

Identify the four steps of the nursing process.

Identify the nine steps in carrying out nursing assessment of the family.

GLOSSARY

Nursing process: The actions carried out by the nurse to meet the needs or problems of the individual and family. These actions are assessing, diagnosing, intervening, and evaluating.

Nursing diagnosis: A statement of an identified patient problem based on data gathered through assessment, observation, interview, and history.

Nursing intervention: An act that serves to prevent, alleviate, or solve any given patient problem

Hypothesis: A provisional idea of a causal relationship

Theory: A set of related definitions, assumptions, concepts, and hypotheses designed to predict and explain relations between observable phenomena

Nuclear family: A social organization based on the relationships of a mother, a father, and offspring

Extended family: The extension of a nuclear family to include others such as aunts, uncles, and grandparents

Preventive medicine: That branch of medicine which concentrates on averting the emergence of health problems

Nursing assessment: The gathering of data that will serve to identify the specific patient problem or need

Problem solving: A systematic, analytical, and scientific method of objective thinking requiring the application of five distinct steps:

1. Identification of the existence of a problem
2. Definition of the problem
3. Formulation of hypotheses leading to the determination of solutions
4. Testing of the solution through practice
5. Evaluation and interpretation of the outcome

The introduction of a new member to the family unit produces stressors that, because of their complexity, must be taken into consideration if the family system is to function at its optimum degree of health. The stressors of pregnancy, which affect both the mother and the father, can readily become disruptive forces that will effect changes in the family unit and alter its homeodynamic state. The childbearing period introduces change in role; threatens economic security; alters social status; and involves physiological, biological, and psychological changes. All of these stressors require the family system to mobilize its adaptive resources.

Awareness of the stressors that may be impinging on the health of the family becomes of primary importance to nurses if they are to assist individuals toward achieving their optimum homeodynamic state.

As they interact with families, nurses will be called upon to exercise objectivity in evaluating needs presented by the family system as a whole or by any of its individual members. This is not to mean, however, that the nurse's feelings and reactions are to be overlooked. They can and often do become another set of variables that influence the nurse's responses and modes of interaction.

The accurate identification of these variables and stressors is a necessary part of the nurse's role. Through the *nursing process*, the nurse is able to assess, diagnose, and intervene in meeting the family's or individual's needs or problems. This process can be better understood if it is compared to the problem-solving method of investigation; it requires the application of the following steps:

1. *Assessment:* The essential variables are distinguished. Pertinent data related to the family and its members is collected and analyzed.

2. *Development of a nursing diagnosis:* On the basis of the data collected, the nurse is able to formulate a hypothesis of the nursing problems and needs presented by the family system or unit. This will guide intervening nursing actions.

3. *Establishing and initiating nursing intervention:* This step requires the definition, formulation, and application of those actions falling within the nurse's responsibility. Measures are instituted as means of assisting families toward successful adaptation and thus toward maintenance of their homeodynamic balance.

4. *Evaluation:* Finally, no action can be assumed to be effective without its being evaluated. The whole nursing process as it was applied to the particular family unit is assessed and appraised as a means of determining the success of the intervention measures put into practice. Also, the evaluation helps in identifying whether there is a need or problem that has not been solved by

the original assessment and intervention activities. This is significant since it will point to the need for the nursing process to be repeated until adequate solutions are found.

The following description of the nursing assessment of the family will require you to apply the steps of the nursing process.

We have said that the success of the nursing process and, thus, of the intervention measures being instituted as means of assisting families or individuals toward the attainment of their optimum homeodynamic balance, is highly dependent upon the identification and assessment of the variables influencing their health status.

In this light, it is essential for nurses involved in the assessment process to take into consideration the fact that the families with which they come in contact, as well as their individual members, are quite different from each other. Also, family members often exchange the roles they occupy, affecting their interactions and their perceptions of the various situations surrounding them. Therefore, attempts to identify the psychosocial variables affecting families' and individuals' role occupations, interactions, and perceptions should become an integral part of the assessment interview and should include:

1. Identification of type of family.
   a. Nuclear (is the family an entity in and of itself?)
   b. Extended (does the family include as immediate members of the group others such as grandparents, aunts, or uncles?)

2. Identification of cultural heritage.

3. Identification of socioeconomic levels. Who provides the principal source of income?

4. Identification of patterns of communication employed by family members.

5. Identification of how each family member perceives and interprets the same situation.

6. Identification and recognition of needs present in the family.

7. Identification of family goals with respect to:
   a. Economics
   b. Education
   c. Social status

8. Medical history.

9. Identification of feelings about preventive medicine and medical care.

This initial assessment will give nurses a beginning knowledge of the family and will guide them in setting priorities for further investigation and intervention and, at times, will lead them to make referrals to appropriate members of the health team and professional agencies.

Let us see how well you can apply the objectives given you in assessing a family situation.

You have met Bill and Jean Garry during your experience at the Outpatient Center and have been assigned to carry out a nursing assessment interview. At this time you find out that they have made an appointment for their annual physical checkup.

During the interview you find out that both Bill and Jean work, are American-born, and have a college education, and that they live in a comfortable apartment while at the same time saving money so that Jean will be able to stop working in another year to start a family. As you talk to the couple, you notice that they share in information-giving and frequently exchange glances to get reinforcement that what they are saying is correct.

As you discuss the various tests that are a part of the complete physical examination, Jean seems to be somewhat nervous and her husband reaches out to take her hand. He explains that she has a tendency to faint during blood tests and is concerned about it. He asks you if he could be with her during that part of the examination.

Based on the preceding information, which of the following statements includes the correct assessment?

A. This is an extended family, American, middle-class, utilizing verbal communications, and one in which the power, status, and supportive roles are equally shared. The family members are educationally oriented and have positive values toward health.

Go to page 46.

B. This is a nuclear family, American middle-class, utilizing verbal and nonverbal communications. While the status role is shared, during the interview the husband occupies the supportive role. The family members are both educationally oriented, and they have a positive set of values toward health.

Go to page 47.

By choosing response *A*, you evidence the fact that you do not clearly understand all of the following:

    1. Differences between an extended and nuclear family.

    Return to page 44 and review the material.

    2. Classification of roles. Although the status role was shared, the supportive role was not. As well, the situation did not include any information that would identify who was in the power role.

    Return to page 22 and review material on roles.

    3. Communication methods. Your assessment of the communication methods being utilized did not include nonverbal components which were indicated by the description of the couple's glances and the holding of hands by the husband.

    From bibliography, select any of the reading dealing with patterns and methods of communication. After this, return to the program and select another response from page 45.

Excellent! In choosing *B*, you were able to identify the fact that this was a nuclear family; culturally: American-born; economically: middle-class. Furthermore, you utilized your observational skills quite well when you identified their nonverbal communications as well as listening to their verbalizations. The fact that they are both working validates their sharing the status role, and Bill's response to Jean's fear did indeed place him in the supportive role.

Finally, you recognized that their educational orientation and the fact they chose to have an annual checkup indicate their positive attitude toward preventive medicine.

Advance to page 48 and take the post-test.

POST-TEST   The first part of this post-test is made up of completion problems. In the spaces provided, fill in the word or words that best complete(s) the statements. Then turn to page 49 and check how well you have done.

1. The four steps of the nursing process are:

   a. _____

   b. _____

   c. _____

   _____

   d. _____

2. As they interact with families, nurses should be able to exercise _____

3. The nursing process is akin to a method of investigation known as the _____

   _____ method.

The second part of this post-test is made up of true-false items. Circle the letter of the correct choice. Then turn to page 49 and check your answers.

4. In assessing a family the nurse defines what type of actions are needed.   T   F

5. Among the variables that nurses must identify during the assessment interview, the most important one is that of age of family members.   T   F

6. An extended family includes grandparents, aunts, uncles, etc.   T   F

7. The objectives of the nursing assessment process serve to identify priorities for intervention.   T   F

In the specific areas with which you had difficulty, return to the material and review.

BIBLIOGRAPHY

Byers, Virginia B.: *Nursing Observation*, William C. Brown Co., Dubuque, Iowa, 1971.

Carriere, V. K., et al., "Components of the Nursing Process," *Nursing Clinics of North America,* Vol. 6, pp. 115-124, March 1971.

Johnson, Mae M., Mary Lou C. Davis, and Mary Jo Bilitch: *Problem Solving in Nursing Practice*, William C. Brown Co., Dubuque, Iowa, 1970.

Little, Dolores and Doris L. Carnevali: *Nursing Care Planning*, J. B. Lippincott Co., Philadelphia, 1969.

McCain, F. R., "Nursing by Assessment—Not Intuition," *American Journal of Nursing*, Vol. 65, p. 82 ff., April 1965.

Pardee, G., et al., "Patient Care Evaluation is Every Nurse's Job," *American Journal of Nursing*, Vol. 71, pp. 1958-1960, Oct. 1971.

Peterson, Grace G.: *Working with Others for Patient Care,* William C. Brown Co., Dubuque, Iowa, 1971.

Tapia, Jayne Anttila, "The Nursing Process in Family Health," *Nursing Outlook,* Vol. 20, pp. 267-270, April 1972.

Tayrien, Dorothy and Amelia Lipchak, "The Single Problem Approach," *American Journal of Nursing,* Vol. 67, pp. 2523-2527, Dec. 1967.

Tinkham, Catherine W. and Eleanor F. Voorhies: *Community Health Nursing Evolution and Process*, Appleton-Century-Crofts, New York, 1972.

Zimmerman, Gohrke: "The Goal Directed Nursing Approach: It Does Work," *American Journal of Nursing,* Vol. 70, pp. 306-310, Feb. 1970.

POST-TEST ANSWERS

1. a. Assessment b. Developing a nursing diagnosis c. Establishing and initiating a nursing intervention d. Evaluation 2. Objectivity 3. Problem-solving 4. F 5. F 6. T 7. T

CHAPTER SEVEN
FAMILY PLANNING

OBJECTIVES   *Identify the three criteria for ensuring the effectiveness of conception control.*

Identify the effectiveness of ten methods of conception control.

GLOSSARY   *Conception:* The process of becoming pregnant, involving fertilization and implantation

Contraceptive: An agent or method used to prevent pregnancy

Coitus: Sexual intercourse

Lactation: The process of milk production in the mother

Condom: A rubber sheath that is used over the penis as a method of contraception, also termed "rubber"

Prophylactic: Relating to prevention or protection; the term is often applied to the condom

Diaphragm: A round, rubber dome, which is placed in the vagina to occlude the cervical os as a contraceptive device

Spermicide: Any agent that will kill sperm; usually a chemical in combination with a jelly, cream, or foam

Rhythm: A method of birth control using abstinence from sexual intercourse during the woman's fertile period. It requires careful calculation of this period from her menstrual cycle.

Intrauterine contraceptive device (IUCD): A plastic or metal mechanical device that is placed inside the uterine cavity to prevent pregnancy

Subcutaneous: Refers to the layer of tissue underneath the epidermis

Enzymatic: Relating to the activity of enzymes

Vasectomy: The cutting of the vas deferens

Sterility: Characterized by the inability to procreate

Tubal ligation: The process of cutting and tying the fallopian tubes

External os: The lower opening of the cervical canal into the vagina

Implantation: The process that occurs when the ovum penetrates the decidua and becomes enclosed by this uterine lining

Tumescence: Referring to the erection of the penis

Douche: An irrigation of the vagina

Endometrium: The inner lining of the uterus

Pituitary gonadotrophins: Hormones secreted by the pituitary gland; they control the growth and function of the ovary and testes

Nulliparous: Referring to a woman who has never given birth to a baby of viable age

Morning-after injection: An intravenously administered contraceptive drug, given after sexual intercourse

Silastic implant: A drug in a capsulelike form which is placed under the skin and releases a specific drug level over a long period of time

Prostaglandins: A group of chemicals that are produced by the body; in therapeutic dosages used to produce uterine contractions

Phaser: A tube that is put into each vas deferens with a valve to open or close the lumen

Nidation: Implantation

PRETEST   In the spaces provided, fill in the word or words that best complete(s) the statements. Then turn to page 71 and check your answers.

   1.   The function of a contraceptive method is to _____

      _____.

   2.   Three of the ways conception control methods function in order to prevent pregnancy are:

      a. _____

         _____

      b. _____

      c. _____

Indicate whether each statement is true or false by circling the appropriate letter. Then turn to page 71 and check your answers.

   3.   Postcoital douche is an effective method of birth control because it washes out all of the sperm.   T   F

   4.   Coitus interruptus is not considered an effective method of contraception because it is difficult to control.   T   F

   5.   Prolonged lactation functions as a method of birth control by preventing ovulation.   T   F

   6.   The condom is applied immediately before ejaculation.   T   F

   7.   The vaginal diaphragm can be used successfully either alone or with spermicidal cream or gel.   T   F

   8.   Vaginal spermicides should be removed by douching immediately after intercourse.   T   F

   9.   If a woman has a consistently regular menstrual cycle, rhythm can be utilized effectively to prevent pregnancy.   T   F

 10.   Oral contraceptives prevent ovulation.   T   F

 11.   The IUCD prevents implantation from occurring.   T   F

 12.   The contraceptive subcutaneous implant is being widely used.   T   F

 13.   The "day-after" injection is best because it means safety only when needed and has no side effects.   T   F

It is generally accepted throughout the world that overpopulation presents a major problem to the ecological systems. Overpopulation has come under increasing research and debate by scientists and religious and governmental bodies. And so, developments continue to improve the varieties of safe, effective, inexpensive, and acceptable methods of birth control to enable couples to choose whether or when to have children. Furthermore, studies have proven that the health and well-being of the mother and infant are positively affected when a minimum period of one to two years elapses between pregnancies.

The nurse has the responsibility of being cognizant of the actions of current contraceptive practices and any contraindications to their use if she is to participate in effectively meeting the health needs of the community.

Since the discovery of the relationship of coitus to pregnancy there have been attempts to prevent the latter from occurring, and many methods of conception control have been utilized. However, contemporary methods have proven to be the most effective in producing contraception. It must be kept in mind that all methods of *contraception* are temporary and can be reversed at will, thus differentiating them from sterilization and termination of pregnancy.

In order for any form of conception control to be effective—that is, to prevent pregnancy until a couple decides that a child is desired—it must meet one of the following criteria:

1. *Prevent the union of sperm and ova:* An agent forms a barrier that may be mechanical or chemical and prevents the sperm from entering the cervix.

2. *Prevent ovulation:* A chemical agent interacts within the hormonal system of the female and stops or represses the maturation and the release of the ovum.

3. *Prevent permanent implantation:* An agent creates a noxious environment for the fertilized ovum, usually by enzymatic reaction caused by the presence of a foreign body.

Let us check whether you can remember the given definitions. Fill in the blanks within the following statements with the terms identifying the criteria.

An agent forming a barrier that prevents the sperm from entering the cervix following ejaculation is effective because it _____

_____.

prevents the union of sperm and ova

An agent that either prevents the fertilized ovum from implanting or rejects an implanted fertilized ovum functions by _____

_____ .

preventing permanent implantation

An agent that causes cessation in the ripening and releasing of ova functions by_____ .

⟱

preventing ovulation

We have said that there are varied methods of preventing conception from taking place. We have classified these as folk, traditional, and modern,[1] and the following pages will provide you with information regarding their degree of safety and effectiveness.

Some of the folk methods of birth control that are still being used are: coitus interruptus, postcoital douche, and prolonged lactation. Let us look at these:

> *Coitus interruptus:* The withdrawal of the penis from the external female genitalia and vagina prior to ejaculation has proven to be of very limited value since there are seminal secretions around the meatus prior to actual ejaculation and there is much difficulty in controlling the actual time of ejaculation.
>
> *Postcoital douche:* The administration of a vaginal irrigation immediately following coitus. This, too, has proven ineffective since it may propel the sperm closer to the *external os.*
>
> *Prolonged lactation:* Was thought to prevent ovulation since menses often are delayed in the breast-feeding mother. Studies have proven that ovulation does occur and pregnancy may take place during this period.

Now, then, according to the criteria for effectiveness in a contraceptive, which of the following can be considered to be good contraceptive measures?

A. Coitus interruptus

B. Postcoital douche

C. Prolonged lactation

D. None of these

Go to page 66 bottom.

Go to page 68 middle.

Go to page 63 top.

Go to page 65 bottom.

Let us examine some of the more traditional forms of contraception. These are: the condom, the vaginal diaphragm, spermicidal agents, and rhythm.

> *The condom:* A thin latex or collagenous sheet sometimes lubricated. This device is to be fitted over the penis after tumescence and prior to vaginal insertion. It acts as a barrier to the union of sperm and ova. Its efficacy is doubtful since it may leak, break, or come off during coitus. It is, however, effective in preventing the spread of venereal diseases during vaginal intercourse. It is considered to be more effective as a contraceptive device when used in conjunction with a spermicidal agent.

The vaginal diaphragm: To be used with a spermicidal cream or gel, it is a rubber dome with a firm rim formed by an enclosed metal or spring ring. This device must be fitted to the individual initially and refitted after pregnancy or after a light weight loss or gain. It is fitted by vaginal examination. The inserted diaphragm acts as a barrier preventing the union of ova and sperm since it occludes the opening into the cervix. A spermicidal cream or gel must be put on both sides of the diaphragm prior to insertion in order for it to be effective.

In addition, an applicator full of the cream or gel must be inserted into the vagina before additional acts of intercourse. A diaphragm can be inserted any time before intercourse and is not to be removed or a vaginal douche taken for six to eight hours after the last act of coitus. When used as directed, this device is considered to be extremely efficient in preventing pregnancy.

Vaginal spermicides: May be a foam, cream, or gel that is inserted into the vagina by applicator immediately prior to intercourse and must be reinserted for subsequent acts of coitus. It acts to prevent the union of sperm and ova by causing the destruction of the sperm. Douching to remove these agents is unnecessary; however, if this is desired for aesthetic purposes it is not to be done for six to eight hours after the last act of intercourse.

Rhythm: Is based on the determination of the individual's ovulatory or fertile period. During this time, abstinence must be practiced in order to prevent the union of sperm and ova. The fertile period may be calculated by the calendar temperature method. This is often difficult to do in women with irregular, very short, or very long menstrual cycles. It also must be remembered that a menstrual cycle can be affected or altered by any kind of stressor.

Which of the criteria for an effective contraceptive do all of these traditional methods (condom, vaginal diaphragm, vaginal spermicide, rhythm) of conception control meet?

A. Prevent union of sperm and ova

Go to page 63 middle.

B. Prevent ovulation

Go to page 67 top.

C. Prevent permanent implantation

Go to page 66 top.

Now let us look at some of the newer advances in conception control:

Oral contraceptives: Chemical preparations that inhibit ovulation by acting on pituitary gonadotrophins; by putting the endometrium out of phase, preventing implantation; and by causing the normally thin cervical mucus to become more viscid, inhibiting the passage of sperm. These preparations are taken daily, starting on the fifth day of the menstrual cycle, for 20 or 21 days. Within 72 hours after the preparation is stopped, withdrawal bleeding will start. This is considered the first day of the new menstrual cycle, and the preparation will be resumed on the fifth day of bleeding. If bleeding does not occur, the pills should be restarted on the seventh day after they had been stopped. This method of birth control is contraindicated when there is a history of circulatory disturbances, liver dysfunction, malignancy, or undiagnosed vaginal bleeding, and in breast-feeding mothers. These preparations are prescribed in two forms, the combination pills and the sequential pills. Both types provide estrogens and progesterones but in different proportions.

Intrauterine contraceptives: (IUCDs): These are mechanical devices constructed of plastic or metal in varying shapes, which are introduced through the cervix into the upper portion of the uterine cavity. These devices are left in place until conception is desired. They usually are inserted during the menstrual period. If excessive bleeding, pain, or infection occurs, the device is removed. The IUCD is thought to be effective in preventing pregnancy by causing the endometrium to secrete an enzyme preventing nidation. These devices can be inserted in nulliparous women.

Which of the criteria of conception control is met by both the oral contraceptive and IUCD?

A. Prevent union of sperm and ova

B. Prevent ovulation

C. Prevent permanent implantation

Go to page 64 bottom.

Go to page 65 top.

Go to page 63 bottom.

The morning-after injection: This method is currently being used only in instances where the usual method employed has failed (as in the case where a condom has broken or come off in the vagina, or where the participants in the coital act have been unable to utilize their usual method of contraception). The drugs being given most often are Premarin intravenously, or Stilbestrol orally in extremely high dosages. The latter drug has side effects such as severe vomiting; this is one reason why this drug is not widely used. In addition, it is considered dangerous to administer high dosages of hormones frequently.

Let us go on and examine new methods of contraception presently being tested and predicted for use in the near future. Research is currently being carried out in order to develop safer, easier-to-use methods of contraception. Among the many methods under consideration are:

Subcutaneous silastic implants of megestrol acetate: The chemical is absorbed by the system over a period of nine to 12 months, preventing ovulation.

Prostaglandin vaginal suppositories: To be used after intercourse. These produce uterine contractions, thereby preventing pregnancy; may be a common method in the future.

Male contraceptives: The once-a-month injection, once-in-three-months injection, and pills or injections for the man are only a few of the other methods that may be available in the near future. One of the promising male contraceptive devices currently being tested is the phaser. This is a small tube inserted into each vas deferens. The device has a small valve incorporated into its construction which is inserted in an "off" position preventing the flow of sperm. If the man wishes to have children, a small incision can permit the physician to switch the valve to an "on" or open position, thus allowing for the free flow of sperm.

If you recall, in a previous chapter, we specifically made reference to the nursing process and the steps involved in its utilization in situations requiring nursing actions. Applying this method to the area of family planning, we must become aware of the health status of the individual and of the whole family system, and of whether individuals are interested in birth control measures. This necessitates recognition of variables such as moral values, cultural background, and religious ascription as these influence the acceptance of family planning. At times, sex education, specifically knowledge of anatomy and physiology and the process of conception, is the basic information needed.

When giving contraception information, the nurse must always be cognizant of the preference of the couple, and the safety, efficacy, and expense of the method. The nurse also must realize that the right time to pursue the topic is whenever this information is requested. You may be asked about contraceptive devices in a variety of settings: the mother in early labor may decide that this is the time to discuss planning for a time lapse between children; you may be asked questions at a PTA meeting or in a pediatric or adolescent clinic. Whenever your advice is sought, you must be prepared with either current information or appropriate sources of referral.

Let us use the information about contraceptive devices in teaching one of our family models.

Jack Cummings, aged twenty-eight, and his wife Sandra, aged twenty-six, have been married for five and one-half years and have two little girls, aged four and two, and a one-year-old baby son. Jack is a mechanic for the local new car dealer, while Sandra is a full-time homemaker. The Cummingses live in a third-floor walk-up, five-room apartment. They have talked about the possibility of buying a home of their own.

You meet Mrs. Cummings and her two daughters in our combination GYN-family planning clinics, where she has come for her yearly checkup.

In this situation, which statement made by the nurse is a better one for initiating discussion regarding birth control measures?

A. "Why don't you let me tell you about birth control so that you won't have to have any more children."

Go to page 65 middle.

B. "With children so young you must be very busy. How do you manage to keep up with everything?"

Go to page 68 bottom.

Suppose Mrs. Cummings answers you by saying, "Yes, it wouldn't be so bad if I still didn't have two in diapers. . . . I don't know what I would do if I got pregnant again now."

This gives you the information that Mrs. Cummings would like to discuss birth control methods. Which of the following questions would be most appropriate for you to ask?

A. "Have you and your husband been doing anything to prevent you from becoming pregnant?"

Go to page 67 bottom.

B. "Would you like me to tell you about the various methods of birth control?"

Go to page 64 top.

Mrs. Cummings states that she tried the "pills" after her last pregnancy, but that with all she has to do with the house, children, etc., she can't seem to remember to take them when she is supposed to, so that she worries all the time.

You now can ask her, "Have you thought about any of the other methods of birth control?" and if she inquires as to what other methods there are available to her, you may then go on to explore these methods, such as the condom (rubber) and foam, the diaphragm, or the IUCD (often called the "coil" by women). Mrs. Cummings may or may not have heard of these methods so, once again, you wait for her to cue you in as to what type of information she needs. Let us go on with this situation and see what develops:

She replies, "I sort of know what those things are, but not really what is best." You offer to explain these methods to her and begin to discuss the uses of the condom or rubber prophylactic.

This method is effective in birth control because it _____
_____ .

prevents union of sperm and ova

Its effectiveness will be increased when _____
_____ .

used with a spermicidal agent

In addition, you should tell Mrs. Cummings that men often do not like this method since it interrupts the spontaneity of lovemaking.

It should be explained further that when a spermicidal agent is used in combination with a condom _____

another application of

_____ is necessary before a subsequent
act of intercourse.

    If she wants to douche after the last act of coitus, tell her to _____
_____ .

    The condom is applied prior to the actual insertion of the penis into the
vagina and removed immediately after ejaculation, to prevent the leakage of
semen. A new condom must be used before each act of intercourse.

    The second method of birth control that you discuss is the diaphragm.
It is preferred by some couples because it can be put into place any time prior
to intercourse and therefore does not interrupt the act of lovemaking.

    The diaphragm's effectiveness resides in the fact that it serves _____
_____
_____ .

    This rubber dome is used in conjunction with _____
_____ .

    If this device is inserted into the vagina more than 24 hours before
intercourse, another application of spermicidal agent is necessary at this time
and before each subsequent coital act. This device must be in place for a
period of at least _____
after intercourse. Douching before this time is contraindicated. After re-
moval, the diaphragm should be carefully washed, dried, lightly powdered,
and put away in its container.

    The IUCD is usually inserted on the third or fourth day of the
menstrual cycle. At the time of insertion, cramps, bleeding, or pain in the
back may be experienced. Bleeding may occur for a few days after insertion,
and the woman may have a heavier than normal menstrual period. The
woman should be cautioned also to check after each period for the string or
bead that she can feel in her vagina which will let her know that the device is
still in place, since some women reject it and expel it without their knowledge.

    Occasionally, the man may object to this device, as he can feel the bead
during coitus. The pregnancy rate will vary with the type of IUCD used; it is
between 1½ and 5 percent of users per year.

    You can then add, "Mrs. Cummings, if you choose to have an IUCD
inserted I will stay with you when you come back to have it inserted." The

---

(Answer column, right margin):

spermicidal agent

wait at least six to eight hours

to prevent union of sperm and ova

a spermicidal cream or gel

six to eight hours

thought of wearing this kind of device, especially if you tell her it may be painful initially, can be frightening, and it is important for her to know that there will be someone with her at this time.

You will tell her also that insertion of an IUCD is usually done on the

_____

_____ .

third to fourth day of the

menstrual cycle

Symptoms that may be experienced at this time are _____

cramps, bleeding, back pain

_____ .

The menstrual period may be _____

heavier than usual

_____ .

Further instructions that you will give Sandra relate to the necessity to

_____

check for the string/bead

after each period, since IUCDs have been known to be _____

rejected

by the woman without her knowledge.

Throughout your discussion with Mrs. Cummings, it is important for you to get feedback in her own words concerning her understanding of the various methods, of how they prevent pregnancy, how they are used, and how to care for them. You may then suggest that she take some of the pamphlets you have available, so she can show them to her husband in order for their decision to be a mutual one.

Our second family model consists of Barbara Young, a 19-year-old sophomore majoring in biology at a college 150 miles from her home town, and Bill Jones, with whom she has been going steady. Bill is a senior at the same college. Upon returning from summer vacation, Barbara and Bill decide to live together in an apartment off campus.

During the next clinic experience you meet Barbara, who has come to the clinic specifically for family planning information. After you introduce yourself to her and ask if she has any specific type of conception control in mind, she asks you about "the pill." Your first priority is to elicit the information and understanding she has about this method. During your discussion you find out that her knowledge is really scanty. All she really knows is that "you take a pill every day and you don't get pregnant."

Your response should be:

A. "You don't seem to understand what this is all about. I will give you the information you need."

B. "Yes. That's the idea. Maybe I can fill in with a little more information for you."

Go to page 68 top.

Go to page 64 middle.

At this time you would continue the discussion by explaining how "the pills" prevent pregnancy. Your explanation should include basic anatomy, physiology, and conception. Do not assume that just because Barbara is a biology major she must already have this information. It it is important that you assess the completeness and accuracy of her information and build on what she already knows and give credit and acceptance for her correct information.

You will want to inform Ms. Young of some of the common discomforts that may be experienced when the medication is started, plus the following side effects which should be reported immediately to the doctor. These side effects include: headaches, unusual swelling, skin rash, jaundice, or severe depression.

It also is important for Barbara to know that if she forgets to take the pill *one* day, she may take two the next day and continue as usual. However, should she miss two days or more, she should start taking the pills as soon as she remembers but also use another contraceptive method for the rest of that pill cycle.

Voluntary sterilization is an irreversible method of birth control which at present is gaining wide acceptance by both sexes as a means of preventing a pregnancy.

Whenever a man or a woman wishes to choose this method of pregnancy control, he or she is usually directed to seek medical advice and assistance about the availability of the procedure, the type of surgery that will be performed or indicated, and its expected results.

For a woman, the voluntary sterilization procedure that is performed is a tubal ligation. Generally, certain criteria are considered before this decision is made: the number of children the woman has borne; her age; in some cases, the husband's written consent will also be required. Nonhealth states, such as severe cardiac conditions or any other problem that may be aggravated by a pregnancy, are other situations that may indicate eligibility for this procedure.

In a tubal ligation, the woman is usually placed under general anesthesia. Two small incisions are made through the abdomen, and the fallopian tubes are cut and tied. This procedure produces permanent sterility and is irreversible since the chances of sewing the tubes back together and having them adequately resume their function as part of the female reproductive system are very poor.

A tubal ligation may also be done vaginally; however, this is not a popular surgical method at present. As technology improves, this procedure may be done under local anesthesia, so that there will be less discomfort for the patient.

The surgical method of birth control for the male is known as a "vasectomy." It is a relatively simple, hazard-free procedure and is generally carried out under local anesthesia. Two small incisions are made through the scrotum, and the vas deferens (the tubes through which the sperm must travel from the testes to the ejaculatory tract) are cut and ligated. Sterility usually is achieved about three months after this procedure is done, and it can be validated by submitting a semen sample for sperm count eight weeks after surgery.

Increasingly, these surgical measures of irreversible birth control are being sought out by both men and women as ways to limit the size of their families in a safe and reliable way. When information related to any of these procedures is requested of the nurse, it is important that the means and nature of these two forms of voluntary sterilization be explained and that their irreversible nature be clearly pointed out to the interested parties.

Principally, the couple must be able to work out their feelings about their sexuality, and they should be comfortable with the decision they have made. It is not unusual to find that once a couple has resorted to this means of birth control, they are able to relax and enjoy their sexual relationship without being subjected to the anxieties generated by the prospect of an unwanted pregnancy.

Answer *C*, "prolonged lactation," cannot be considered a highly effective method of birth control, since ovulation is *not* prevented. Although people for many years associated the delayed menses that often occurs with breast-feeding and the cessation of ovulation, studies have shown that there actually is no relationship between these events. Breast-feeding and pregnancy can occur simultaneously.

Return to page 54. Review the material and choose another response.

Good! By choosing *A*, "prevent union of sperm and ova," you have shown that you have clearly identified the action of the traditional methods of conception control. The condom, diaphragm, and spermicides prevent the ovum and sperm from uniting by creating a chemical or mechanical barrier, while rhythm ensures that the sperm and ovum do not unite because it requires abstinence during the fertile period of the female.

Turn to page 55 bottom and continue with the program.

Right! Your choice *C*, "prevent permanent implantation," shows that you recognize that IUCDs cause an enzymatic action preventing implantation and that oral contraceptives, by causing the endometrium to be out of phase, make it nonreceptive for implantation.

Turn to page 56 bottom and continue with the program.

Your choice of statement *B*, "Would you like me to tell you" . . . , **is indeed very** poor. This does not give Mrs. Cummings an opportunity to direct the discussion or **choose** the areas that she would like to pursue.

Review principles of teaching and interviewing techniques. Then return to page 58 and choose another response.

Correct! You were supportive of her but also indicated that her information was incomplete. You also recognized that a principle of teaching is to assess the level of a person's understanding.

Turn to page 61 and continue with the program.

If you chose *A*, you are wrong! IUCDs in no way prevent the union of sperm and ova. However, you did recognize the fact that oral contraceptives do prevent this from taking place. This indicates that you understand that the viscid cervical mucus caused by the oral contraceptives does indeed inhibit the entrance of sperm through the cervix.

Return to page 55 bottom. Review the material and choose another response from page 56.

Not so! The IUCDs do not prevent ovulation, *B*. Prevention of ovulation does occur when oral contraceptives are used correctly. However, this criterion does not apply to both these methods.

Return to page 55 bottom. Review the material and choose another response from page 56.

Your response, "Why don't you let me . . ." (statement *A*), is a poor one. By saying this you are making a judgment and imposing your ideas and values on Mrs. Cummings. Remember that birth control is a very personal matter and is influenced by religious and moral values. An abrupt approach will often cause embarrassment or resentment and close the area to further discussion.

Review the information on nursing intervention and your readings on interviewing and teaching principles, then return to pages 57 to 58 and reread the situation and statements.

You are quite right! In selecting *D*, "none of these," as your choice, you have indicated your understanding of the given criteria. Indeed neither coitus interruptus nor postcoital douche nor prolonged lactation can be thought of as being an effective method of contraception. These do not prevent the union of the sperm and ova, nor do they prevent ovulation, nor do they prevent permanent implantation. You have done a good job!

Turn to page 54 bottom and continue with the program.

Your answer, "prevent permanent implantation," *C*, indicates your lack of understanding of the meaning of the word "implantation" and the manner in which these methods prevent pregnancy from occurring. The use of traditional methods prevents the ovum from becoming fertilized.

Return to page 53. Review the material and choose another response from page 55.

Your answer, *A*, "coitus interruptus," shows that you are not aware of the limited effectiveness of this method. Remember that this method does not succeed in preventing the sperm from entering the vagina, and therefore it would not necessarily prevent the union of sperm and ova. It is important for you to remember also that it is difficult to control the exact time of ejaculation.

Return to page 54. Review the material and choose another response.

Your response, *B*, "prevent ovulation," is not correct. The traditional methods do not interfere with the hormonal balance controlling ovulation. Perhaps you had better review the menstrual cycle.

Return to page 53. Review the material and choose another response from page 55.

Excellent! In choosing statement *A*, you are asking Mrs. Cummings to share information and experience. This will give you much background information as to Mrs. Cummings' knowledge about birth control, the methods she has tried, and perhaps some of her ideas about prevention of pregnancies, allowing you to assess the situation. You can then use this information (assessment) as a basis to clarify and/or introduce new ideas and information. Let us follow this situation.

Turn to page 58 middle and continue with the program.

Your choice of statement *A*, "You don't seem . . . ," is a bad one. Although you recognized that Ms. Young's information is incomplete, you did not recognize the fact that you were being nonsupportive in your reply. By your emphasizing her lack of knowledge you were putting Barbara in the position of feeling rejected. A response such as this one has the tendency of shutting off receptivity to the information that you would want to convey.

Return to page 60. Review the material on interviewing skills and teaching principles and choose another response.

If you chose "postcoital douche," *B*, you do not have a clear understanding of the mechanism of irrigation. The introduction of fluid under pressure into the vagina after intercourse could aid in the propulsion of the sperm closer to the external os of the cervix. Therefore, the criterion of inhibiting the union of sperm and ova is not met.

Return to page 54. Review the material and choose another response.

Good opening! You supported the mother by accepting that things might be difficult and used an open-ended question. This allows Mrs. Cummings the freedom of continuing the discussion and of asking for help if *she* felt she needed it.

Turn to page 58 and continue with the program.

POST-TEST Indicate whether each statement is true or false by circling the appropriate letter. Then turn to page 71 and check how well you have done.

1. There is no special circumstance or setting that is necessary for family-planning teaching. T F

2. The nurse should choose the method of conception control based on her assessment of the woman and family. T F

3. It is not necessary for the nurse to get a feedback of understanding from the patient if she provides appropriate pamphlets. T F

4. The nurse should always start her explanations with the understanding that most patients have either partial or erroneous information and therefore must be given complete information immediately. T F

5. For maximum effectiveness, it is essential that a spermicidal preparation be used with the condom. T F

6. Spermicidal agents can be used alone or in conjunction with other methods. T F

7. A vaginal douche must always follow the use of a spermicidal agent. T F

8. Douching should be done immediately after intercourse when a spermicidal agent has been used. T F

9. The vaginal diaphragm can be removed two hours after coitus. T F

10. A woman has to be fitted only once for a diaphragm. T F

11. The IUCD prevents pregnancy by preventing ovulation. T F

12. The IUCD can be used by a woman who has never been pregnant. T F

13. The oral contraceptives can be taken by any woman. T F

14. The client should not be told about discomforts or side effects of the "pills" since many clients have a tendency to "imagine" these symptoms. T F

15. Oral contraceptives are contraindicated in breast-feeding mothers. T F

16. If the woman misses a day when using oral contraceptives she must stop using the pill and resume it after she has a menstrual flow. T F

17. The morning-after injection is one of the newest and best forms of contraceptive devices. T F

REFERENCES   1. Louis Hellman and Jack Pritchard: *Williams' Obstetrics,* Appleton-Century-Crofts, New York, 1971, p. 1100.

BIBLIOGRAPHY   Blake, Robert, Chester Insko, Robert Cialdini, and Alan L. Chaikin: *Beliefs and Attitudes About Contraceptives Among the Poor,* Monograph 5, Carolina Population Center, University of North Carolina at Chapel Hill, 1969.

Coutinho, M. Elsimar, et al., "Further Studies on Long-Term Contraception by Subcutaneous Silastic Capsules Containing Megestrol Acetate," *Contraception–An International Journal,* Vol. 5, pp. 389-393, May 1972.

Croxato, Horacio B., et al., "Contraceptive Action of Megestrol Acetate Implants in Women," *Contraception–An International Journal,* Vol. 4, No. 3, pp. 155-167, Sept. 1971.

Daves and Lesinski, "Mechanism of Action of Intra-uterine Contraceptives in Women," *Journal of Obstetrics and Gynecology,* Vol. 36, pp. 350-358, Sept. 1970.

de Souza, J. C. and M. Elsimar Coutinho, "Control of Fertility by Monthly Injections of a Mixture of Norgestral and a Long-Acting Extrogen: A Preliminary Report," *Contraception–An International Journal,* Vol. 5, pp. 395-399, May 1972.

Fuertes, Abelardo, et al., "Deaths Among Users of Oral and Non-oral Contraceptives," *Journal of Obstetrics and Gynecology,* Vol. 36, pp. 597-602, Oct. 1970.

Fischman, S. H., "Choosing an Appropriate Contraception," *Nursing Outlook,* Vol. 15, Dec. p. 28 ff., 1967.

Ganbrell, Richard D., "Immediate Post Partum Oral Contraception," *Journal of Obstetrics and Gynecology,* Vol. 36, pp. 101-106, July 1970.

Guttmacher, A. F., "Family Planning, the Needs and the Methods," *American Journal of Nursing,* Vol. 69, p. 1229 ff., June 1969.

Hellman, Louis and Jack Pritchard: *Williams' Obstetrics,* Appleton-Century-Crofts, New York, 1971.

Hubbard, Charles William: *Family Planning Education–Parenthood and Social Disease Control,* C. V. Mosby Co., St. Louis, 1973.

Hutcheson, Hazel, et al., "Georgia's Family Planning Program," *American Journal of Nursing,* Vol. 68, p. 332 ff., Feb. 1968.

Johnson, Dianne Schneider, "Conference Summary; Termination of Pregnancy: Current Status and Future Directions," *Contraception,* Vol. 5., p. 237 ff., March 1972.

Lane, M. E., "Emotional Aspects of Contraception," *Bulletin of the American College of Nurse-Midwives,* Vol. 15, p. 16 ff., Feb. 1970.

Manisoff, Miriam, "Counseling for Family Planning," *American Journal of Nursing,* Vol. 66, pp. 2671 ff., Dec. 1966.

——, "Family Planning Education for the Patient," *Bulletin of the American College of Nurse-Midwives,* pp. 67-73, Aug. 1968.

Ring, A. E., "Psychosocial Aspects of Contraception," *Bulletin of the American College of Nurse-Midwives,* Vol. 31, pp. 74-81, Aug. 1968.

Scutchfield, Douglas F., et al., "Medroxyprogesterone Acetate as an Injectable Female Contraceptive," *Contraception,* Vol. 3, p. 21, Jan. 1971.

Tatum, Howard S., "Intrauterine Contraception," *American Journal of Obstetrics and Gynecology,* pp. 1000-1023, April 1, 1972.

Wiedenbach, E., "The Nurses' Role in Family Planning," *Nursing Clinics of North America,* Vol. 31, pp. 355-365, June 1968.

PRETEST ANSWERS

1. Prevent pregnancy   2. a. Prevent union of sperm and ova   b. Prevent ovulation c. Prevent permanent implantation   3. F   4. T   5. F   6. F   7. F 8. F   9. T   10. T   11. T   12. F   13. F

POST-TEST ANSWERS

1. T   2. F   3. F   4. F   5. T   6. T   7. F   8. F 9. F   10. F   11. F   12. T   13. F   14. F   15. T   16. F 17. F

**UNIT I
EXAMINATION**

The following multiple-choice examination will test your comprehension of the material covered in the first unit of this program. Remember, you are not competing with anyone but yourself. Therefore, do not guess in order to answer the questions; if you are unsure, this means that you have not learned the content. Return to the areas that give you difficulty and review them, before going on with the examination.

Circle the letter of the best response to each question. After completing the unit examination, check your answers on page 332 and review those areas of difficulty before proceeding to the next unit.

1. When discussing concepts related to an "ideal" state of health, it is important to remember that health can be defined only in terms of:
    a. Absolute standards that must be met by everyone regardless of age, social position, or nationality
    b. A set of tenets postulating the complete physical and mental well-being of the individuals
    c. A comparative scale on which each individual's health can be measured in relationship to other individuals
    d. Individual differences, optimum capacities and potentials, and individuals' ability to establish a dynamic interaction with their internal and external environments

2. The principle of homeodynamics is predicated on the idea that
    a. The human organism is subject to environmental conditions over which it has no control
    b. The human organism is in a state of constant, simultaneous, and mutual interaction with its environment
    c. The human organism is directly responsible for effecting changes in the environment in order to maintain a constant static state
    d. None of these

3. Which of the following interactions best illustrates the dynamic relationships of stress adaptation?
    a. Stress ⟶ Stressor ⟵ Adaptation
    b. Stressor ⟵⟶ Stress ⟵⟶ Adaptation
    c. Stressor ⟶ Adaptation ⟶ Stress
    d. Adaptation ⟵⟶ Stressor ⟶ Stress

4. The utilization of the concept of stress adaptation in nursing:
    a. Has no bearing in identifying health status since individuals react differently to stress
    b. Implies that sources of stress vary and are interpreted differently by different individuals
    c. Is unreliable as a basis for identifying factors that will enter into care-planning considerations
    d. Is useful since once the source of the stress is identified, then the adaptation of all individuals can be predicted

5. The present trend in the provision of health care services for the consumer should be:
   a. Meeting crisis situations
   b. Providing the same kind of service throughout the country
   c. Meeting the specific needs of the community in which it is situated
   d. Providing the same level of care for all so that everyone achieves that same health status

6. Our definition of family implies that:
   a. Families are formed only through legal bonds
   b. There must always be a mother and a father present for a family to exist
   c. Families exist by recognition of the membership by society
   d. Families are formed through mutual recognition of relationships by their members

7. Within the same family:
   a. Roles may be shared and members may move in and out of one role
   b. Roles are static and are always occupied by the same individual
   c. Roles are assigned by the member who is in the power position
   d. Roles are occupied according to society's expectations

8. Which of the following categories does the text utilize throughout in identifying the roles various members of the family may occupy?
   a. Position
   b. Function
   c. Assigned
   d. Prescribed

9. When a stressor affects a single family member:
   a. Only that member needs to mobilize resources to effect adequate adaptation
   b. All family members must equally mobilize the same resources in order to effect adaptation
   c. No other member of the family system is affected
   d. Various members mobilize supportive resources in order to effect adaptation

10. In order to understand the specifics of a family system, it is important to be aware that this system:
    a. Is a functional unit and unique in its identity and goals
    b. Is a system that is able to function in isolation from other social factors
    c. Is an organizational hierarchy set up to rear children
    d. Is in operation only when a powerful stressor is introduced

11. The method that most effectively assists nurses in arriving at objective and logically sound conclusions is known as:
    a. Trial and error approach
    b. Random selection approach
    c. Unstructured thinking approach
    d. Problem-solving approach

12. The nursing process generally requires:
    a. Deciding first what the conclusion should be then gathering only the type of data that will support this conclusion
    b. Going through the steps of assessment, research, development of a hypothesis, and testing and evaluation
    c. Making a judgment as to the nature of the problem and testing this judgment through actual practice
    d. Making consistent attempts to arrive at solutions by engaging in different actions until the right one proves to be effective

13. In assessing the health of a family system, the interviewing nurse must take into consideration:
    a. Only the physiological factors and past medical history of the member affected
    b. The interactions and communication patterns of the various members, incorporating medical, cultural, educational, and economic background
    c. Only the immediately expressed physiological, cultural, and economic needs of the family
    d. That a single family member can give sufficient and significant information relating to the health of the family

14. Patterns of interpersonal relationships and methods of communication utilized by family members are:
    a. Of little value to the nurse establishing a health assessment
    b. Of value only in providing an understanding of roles
    c. Difficult to assess because they interfere with an objective appraisal
    d. Important in establishing the functioning of the family system

15. Susan Winters is at the family planning clinic for an initial visit. She is interested in discussing the advantages and disadvantages of the different methods of birth control. It is important that Susan understands that:
    a. Effective contraception is reversible when desired
    b. All modern methods of conception control are 100 percent effective
    c. There are no side effects from any of the available methods of conception control
    d. Only one member needs to be involved in the choice and utilization of conception control

16. The consistent use of oral contraceptives combining estrogen and progesterone throughout the cycle effectively meets which of the following criteria for conception control?
    a. Prevention of union of sperm and the ovum
    b. Prevention of ovulation
    c. Prevention of permanent implantation
    d. All of these

17. Economics, convenience, and side effects are factors that:
    a. Have no influence over the choice of contraceptives
    b. Are of importance only to the woman

    c. Do not have to be taken into account by the nurse

    d. Influence the type of contraceptive to be chosen

18. During your discussion with Susan, you clarify certain information. **When a spermicidal preparation is used, a douche may be taken after coitus without increasing the** risk of pregnancy:

    a. One hour later

    b. Immediately after coitus

    c. Three hours later

    d. Six hours later

UNIT II

ANATOMY OF THE MATERNAL ORGANS OF REPRODUCTION, AND FETAL GROWTH AND DEVELOPMENT

SUGGESTED BACKGROUND REFERENCES

The following list of suggested references includes content in the areas of anatomy and physiology which you should have mastered before advancing with this program. You already should have knowledge of the human organs of reproduction and of the ovarian cycle and its hormones, either through individual research or through a course in anatomy and physiology.

Chaffee, Ellen E. and Esther Greisheimer: *Basic Physiology and Anatomy,* 2d. ed., J. B. Lippincott Co., Philadelphia, 1969, Chap. 3, pp. 94-97; Chaps. 11-15, pp. 296-452; Chap. 19, pp. 546-568; Chap. 20, pp. 569-588.

Hellman, Louis M. and Jack Pritchard: *Williams' Obstetrics*, 14th ed., Appleton-Century-Crofts, New York, 1971, Sec. 2, Chaps. 2 to 8, pp. 19-236.

CHAPTER ONE

OBSTETRICAL LANDMARKS OF THE PELVIS

OBJECTIVES *Identify and locate the two innominate bones, the sacrum, and the coccyx, all of which make up the pelvis.*

Identify the four articulations of the bony pelvis.

Identify and locate the ischial tuberosities and the ischial spines.

Identify and locate the seven boundaries of the bony pelvis.

GLOSSARY *Linea terminalis:* Also known as the pelvic brim, is the ridge that circles the upper inner aspect of the innominate bone and is continuous with the sacral promontory
False pelvis: The area of the pelvis above the linea terminalis
True pelvis: The area of the pelvis below the linea terminalis
Pelvic inlet: The point at which the linea terminalis separates the true and the false pelvis
Pelvic outlet: The area enclosed by the symphysis pubis, the ischial tuberosities, and the coccyx
Pelvic axis: An imaginary line that may be plotted through the center of the true pelvis
Pelvimetry: Any method utilized to measure the diameters of the bony pelvis

PRETEST   Before you begin this chapter you may want to review the anatomy of the bony pelvis (pelvic bones and articulations). Below you will find a pretest. Fill in the spaces provided. The answers are on page 88. Depending upon your answers, you may be able to omit some of the information in the chapter. We will tell you on which page to begin your study.

1. The five bones of the pelvis are:

   a. _____

   b. _____

   c. _____

   d. _____

   e. _____

2. Identify the location of the pelvic bones you were able to name.

   a. _____

   b. _____

   c. _____

   d. _____

   e. _____

   _____

If you were able to answer questions 1 and 2 correctly, you may advance to page 82 middle.

3. Identify the location of:

   a. The ischial tuberosities _____

   _____

   b. The ischial spines _____

   _____

   _____

4. Identify and locate the articulations (joints) of the pelvis.

   a. _____

   _____

   b. _____

   _____

   _____

   c. _____

   _____

If you were correct, advance to page 83 bottom.

Since the mechanisms of labor are dependent upon the adaptation of the fetus to the maternal bony pelvis, it is essential that you be aware of the shape and diameters of the bony ring through which the fetus must pass during parturition.

The *bony pelvis* is made up of four fused bones: the two innominate bones (hip bones), the sacrum, and the coccyx. The following material will help you to identify these bones.

The *two innominate* bones are formed by the fusion of the *ilium*, the *ischium,* and the *pubic* bones. This fusion is completed between the ages of twenty and twenty-five. Both innominate bones are joined to the sacrum posteriorly, and they are joined to each other anteriorly at the symphysis pubis.

To locate these structures, you will need to refer to the illustration of the pelvis (see below). Carefully locate each of these bony structures so that you may identify how they function in forming the bony pelvis.

Let us begin by locating the three sets of bones that make up the innominate bone:

Directly anterior are the pubic bones. The pubic bones are fused laterally with the two ischia, completing the anterior portion of the bony pelvis.

The anterior portion of the pelvis consists of: the two _____   pubic bones;

_____ and the two _____ .   ischia

The two ischia and the pubic bones make up the part of the pelvis that

is located _____ .   anteriorally

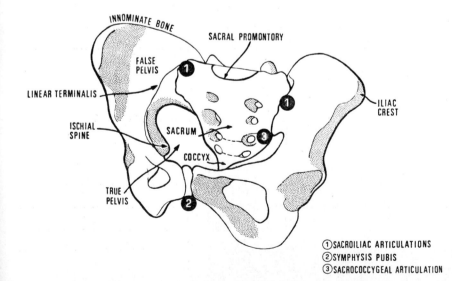

①SACROILIAC ARTICULATIONS
②SYMPHYSIS PUBIS
③SACROCOCCYGEAL ARTICULATION

This is a drawing of the pelvis. You will notice that certain sections have been labeled. As you progress into the program, study each part and check the location of the bone or articulation with the information provided.

The two ilia, which form the sides of the pelvis, are fused to the two ischia.

The two ilia are fused at the sides of the _____ .   ischia

In the pelvis, the bones located directly anterior are the _____   pubic
bones.

The pubic bones are joined to the two _____ .   ischia

The two ischia are joined laterally to the two _____ .   ilia

Now let us locate the sacrum and coccyx in relation to the innominate bones. The ilia join the sacrum, which is below the lumbar spine, at the back of the pelvis. The coccyx, which is the lowermost portion of the spine, is joined to the bottom of the sacrum completing the back of the bony pelvis.

The posterior portion of the pelvis is made up of the _____   sacrum;
and the _____ .   coccyx

The sacrum is joined at the sides to the _____ .   ilia

The tail, or lowermost portion, of the spine, which completes the posterior of the bony pelvis, is the _____ .   coccyx

The pelvic bones are joined by four *articulations* (joints) consisting of fibrocartilage. They become softened during pregnancy, allowing for some degree of mobility; this is one of the causes of back and leg discomfort.

These articulations are:

1. The symphysis pubis

2. The sacroiliac articulation

3. Two sacrococcygeal articulations

The *symphysis pubis* is the articulation that unites the two pubic bones. The *sacroiliac articulations* are located at the junctures of the ilia and the sacrum. The *sacrococcygeal articulation* joins the sacrum to the coccyx.

The tail of the spine or the coccyx is joined to the sacrum by the
_____ articulation.   sacrococcygeal

The four joints joining the bones of the pelvis soften during pregnancy. These joints consist of _____ .   fibrocartilage

Directly anterior, the joint joining the two pubic bones is known as the

_____ .   symphysis pubis

Posteriorly the ilia are joined to the sacrum by the _____ joints.

sacroiliac

The coccyx and the sacrum are united by the _____ articulation.

sacrococcygeal

At this time, let us identify and locate the *ischial tuberosities* and the *ischial spines.* The tuberosities of ischia (ischial tuberosities) are the lower, posterior protuberances of the ischia. It is these protuberances on which the body rests when in a sitting position. They serve as a landmark for making pelvic measurements. The ischial spines extend from the center of the posterior margin of each ischium and are of great obstetrical importance since a line drawn between them is the shortest diameter of the pelvic cavity. The spines can be palpated on pelvic or rectal examination and are used as a landmark to determine the descent of the fetus into the pelvic cavity during parturition.

The ischial tuberosities are _____ _____ _____ _____ .

the lower posterior protuberances of the ischia on which the body rests when sitting

These serve as _____ _____ .

landmarks for pelvic measurements

The ischial spines extend from _____ _____ _____ .

the center of the posterior margin of each ischium

Their importance as obstetrical landmarks lies in the fact that the distance between them is the _____ _____ .

shortest diameter of the pelvic cavity

Now that you are cognizant of the construction of the bony pelvis, let us continue to demarcate further the boundaries of the passage (bony pelvis) through which the passenger (fetus) must travel during the birth process.

On the pelvic drawing (Figure 1, page 81) you will find labeled boundaries and important obstetrical areas. As you study the program, check your understanding with the drawing.

Let us now proceed to identify and locate the boundaries of the bony pelvis and their functions. These boundaries are:

a. Linea terminalis
b. False pelvis
c. True pelvis
d. Inlet
e. Outlet
f. Pelvic cavity
g. Pelvic axis

The *linea terminalis*, also called the *pelvic brim*, is a ridge that circles the upper, inner aspect of the innominate bones and is continuous with the sacral promontory. (The sacral promontory is the upper anterior portion of the body of the first sacral vertebrae and projects forward into the pelvic cavity.)

This ridge separates the true pelvis from the false pelvis and forms the *pelvic inlet.*

The *true pelvis*, which is below the pelvic brim, is demarcated by the ridge called the _____ or

_____ .

linea terminalis;

pelvic brim

The true pelvis is the bony canal thru which the fetus must pass during parturition. The true pelvis contains the reproductive organs, bladder, and rectum and supports the muscles of the pelvic floor.

The true pelvis is important because it is the canal (bony passage) through which the _____ must pass during the birth process. Within the true pelvis are found the _____ organs, the _____ , and the _____ .

fetus;

reproductive;

bladder; rectum

The *false pelvis* is found above the pelvic brim (inlet) and helps to support the growing uterus during pregnancy. The false pelvis serves to

_____

and is located above the _____

_____ .

support the growing uterus;

inlet or linea terminalis

The inlet or pelvic brim is usually heart-shaped (gynecoid) in the female, and its *transverse diameter* is greater than its anterior-posterior diameter.

The gynecoid pelvic brim has a _____ diameter _____ than its _____

_____ .

transverse;

larger; anterior-posterior

diameter

The outlet of the pelvis has as its boundaries the symphysis pubis anteriorly, the ischial tuberosities at the sides, and the coccyx posteriorly. The *anterior-posterior* diameter of the outlet is longer than the transverse diameter, thus making it the longest diameter of the outlet.

The longest diameter of the pelvic outlet is its _____ _____ diameter.

anterior-posterior

The *pelvic axis* is an imaginary line through the center of the true pelvis and is the direction the fetus must follow during parturition. The pelvic cavity is the space between the inlet, on top, and the outlet, at the bottom, and between the anterior, posterior, and lateral walls of the pelvis. It is wide at the top; it is funnel-shaped at the ischial spines due to the muscles of the pelvic floor.

The imaginary line that passes through the true pelvis and is the direction the fetus must follow during parturition is called the pelvic _____ .

axis

The space between the inlet and the outlet of the bony pelvis is known as the pelvic _____ .

cavity

In looking at the shape of the pelvic cavity, the top is found to be _____ while the shape at the ischial spines is _____ like.

wide; funnel

The portion of the pelvis which is located above the pelvic brim is called the _____ . Below the pelvic brim, also called the _____ , is the portion of the pelvis known as the _____ pelvis.

false pelvis;

linea terminalis;

true

From the preceding description of the pelvis, it is clear that the longer diameter of the pelvic outlet (anterior-posterior) lies almost at right angles to the longer diameter of the inlet (transverse). Therefore, in order to traverse the pelvic cavity during the birth process, the baby's head must rotate in making its descent through this bony passage. When the head of the baby enters the true pelvis, its long diameter (suboccipitobregmatic) conforms to the longer diameter of the inlet, and then as it moves down through the pelvic cavity, it must rotate so that its long diameter lies along the anterior-posterior axis to conform with the longer diameter of the pelvic outlet through which it must pass to emerge. This is known as internal rotation. It will be discussed in further detail in the portion of the program devoted to the normal birth process.

The longer diameter of the pelvic outlet is the _____ diameter, which lies almost at _____ angles to the longer diameter of the inlet or the _____ diameter.

anterior-posterior;

right;

transverse

It becomes apparent that the baby's head must _____   rotate;
since its longer diameter must conform to the longer diameter of the inlet. As
the baby moves down through the pelvic cavity, its head must once again
_____ , so that now its longer diameter lies _____   rotate; anterior
_____ . In this way the head of the fetus conforms to the _____   posterior; longer;
diameter of the_____outlet.   pelvic

     This movement is known as _____ rotation.   internal

POST-TEST   Match the terms in the left column with the appropriate definitions in the right column. Complete each series and then turn to page 88, check your answers, and follow the directions.

Series 1

a. Innominate bones

b. Pubic bones

c. Ischia

d. Ilia

e. Sacrum

f. Coccyx

1. Joined to the pubic bones to complete the anterior portion of the bony pelvis

2. Tail of the spine

3. Composed of three sets of bones making up part of the bony pelvis

4. Bones that form the most anterior portion of the bony pelvis

5. Forms the lateral part and is fused at the back with the sacrum

6. Joined to the coccyx to form the back of the bony pelvis

Series 2

g. Symphysis pubis

h. Sacroiliac

i. Sacrococcygeal

j. Fibrocartilage

k. Ischial spines

l. Ischial tuberosities

7. Substance forming the articulation

8. Joins the sacrum and coccyx

9. Joins the two pubic bones

10. Joins the sacrum and ilia

11. The shortest diameter of the pelvis

12. Serve as a landmark for pelvic measurements

In the specific areas with which you had difficulty, return to the material and review.

BIBLIOGRAPHY
Chaffee, Ellen and Esther Greisheimer: *Basic Physiology and Anatomy,* 2d ed., J. B. Lippincott Co., Philadelphia, 1969.

Hellman, Louis and Jack Pritchard: *Williams' Obstetrics,* 14th ed., Appleton-Century-Crofts, New York, 1971.

PRETEST ANSWERS

1. and 2.   a.   Ischium—anterior portion   b.   Ilium—sides of the pelvis   c.   Pubic bone—directly anterior   d.   Sacrum—posterior portion of pelvis   e.   Coccyx—lowermost posterior portion or tail of the pelvis   3.   a.   Lower posterior projection of the ischia   b.   Extend from the center posteriorly on each ischium   4.   a.   Symphysis pubis joins the pubic bones   b.   Two sacroiliac joints join the sacrum on either side to the ilia   c.   Sacrococcygeal joints join the sacrum and the coccyx

POST-TEST ANSWERS

Series 1   a.   3   b.   4   c.   1   d.   5   e.   6   f. 2

If you did not correctly answer any of the preceding please review the material on pages 81 and 82.

Series 2   g.   9   h.   10   i.   8   j.   7   k.   11   l.   12

If you did not correctly answer any of the preceding please review the material on pages 82 and 83.

CHAPTER TWO

DIAMETERS OF THE PELVIS AND PELVIC MEASUREMENTS

OBJECTIVES   *Identify three diameters of the inlet and their critical measurements.*

Identify two diameters of the outlet and their critical measurements.

Identify the important midpelvic diameter and its critical measurement.

GLOSSARY   *Conjugata vera:* A measurement of the distance between the top of the symphysis pubis and the sacral promontory

Diagonal conjugate: A measurement of the distance between the undersurface of the symphysis pubis and the sacral promontory

Transverse diameter: A measurement of the distance across the pelvic brim; the largest diameter of the pelvic inlet

Bi-ischial diameter: A measurement of the distance between the two ischial tuberosities

Interspinous diameter: A measurement of the distance between the two ischial spines

Gynecoid pelvis: A heart-shaped, normal female pelvis

Platypelloid pelvis: A flat pelvis with a narrow anterior-posterior diameter of the inlet and a wide outlet

Android pelvis: A triangular, masculine-type pelvis

Anthropoid pelvis: An oval female pelvis

PRETEST   In the spaces provided, fill in the word or words that best complete(s) the statements. Then turn to page 97 and check your answers.

1. Pelvimetry is the measurement of the _____

   _____ .

2. There are three groups of diameters of the pelvis. These three groups of diameters are

   a. _____

   b. _____

   c. _____

3. The shortest anterior-posterior diameter of the pelvic inlet is the _____

   _____ .

4. The distance between the undersurface of the symphysis pubis and the sacral promontory is called the _____ .

5. The greatest width of the pelvic inlet is the _____ .

6. The shortest diameter of the pelvic outlet is the _____ between the

   _____

   _____ .

7. The longest diameter of the pelvic outlet is the _____

   _____ .

8. Generally types of pelves are classified as falling into one of four categories according to their shapes. These categories are:

   1. _____

   2. _____

   3. _____

   4. _____

You already are aware that, during normal parturition, the fetus (passenger) must be able to enter the inlet of the true pelvis, pass through the pelvic cavity in the direction of the pelvic axis, and pass through the pelvic outlet. In order to assess the adequacy of the size of the mother's pelvis (passage), you must know some of the important diameters and their critical measurements.

Pelvimetry is the measurement of the diameters of the pelvis; it can be done manually by vaginal examination, by x-ray, and by sonic waves. Early in the antepartum period, pelvimetry usually is done by vaginal examination. It may be repeated later in pregnancy, if a very large baby is estimated, or during parturition, if there is no progress during active labor. At these times, x-ray or sonic waves give a more accurate measurement.

The diameters of the pelvis are classified as follows:

1. The *inlet diameters*, made up of:
    a. The conjugata vera
    b. The diagonal conjugate
    c. The transverse diameter

2. The *outlet diameters* or:
    a. The bi-ischial or intertuberous diameters
    b. The anterior-posterior diameter

3. The *midpelvic diameter*, which is also known as the interspinous diameter

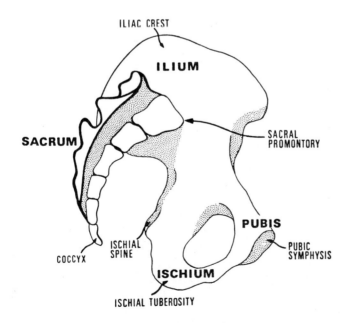

Pelvis—side view.

Pelvimetry is a method utilized to _____ the _____ of the _____ . This may be done either _____ by_____ examination, by _____ , or by_____ .

Early in the antepartum period, this measurement usually is done by means of a _____ examination. However, if the processes of labor are prolonged, or if the baby's size is estimated to be too large in proportion to the size of the maternal pelvis, _____ or _____ wave methods may be used since these are _____ _____ methods of arriving at a measurement.

There are three main diameters of the pelvis, classified as the _____ diameters; they are the_____ , the _____ and the _____ _____ .

The outlet diameters are composed of the _____ or _____ diameters, and the _____ _____ diameter, and the midpelvic diameter is the _____ diameter.

The following material goes into greater description of these quite important obstetrical landmarks.

INTERNAL PELVIC INLET MEASUREMENTS

The *true conjugate* (conjugata vera or C.V.) is the shortest anterior-posterior diameter of the pelvic inlet. It is measured from the top of the symphysis pubis to the sacral promontory and must be estimated or measured by x-ray. A C.V. of less than 10 centimeters is considered critical.

The *diagonal conjugate* (C.D.) is the distance between the undersurface of the symphysis pubis and the sacral promontory. This diameter can be measured by introducing the fingers of the examiner's hand into the vagina until the middle finger reaches the sacral promontory. The point at which the examiner's hand reaches the symphysis is marked with a finger of the other hand and the distance is measured after the hand is withdrawn. The C.D. is approximately 1.5-2.0 centimeters longer than the C.V. and therefore can be used to estimate the length of the true conjugate. A C.D. of less than 11.5 centimeters is considered critical.

The greatest width of the inlet, the *transverse diameter*, is measured horizontally across the pelvic brim and at right angles to the C.V. A transverse diameter of less than 12 centimeters is considered critical.

Answer column (right margin):

measure;

diameters; pelvis;

manually; vaginal;

x-ray; sonic waves

vaginal;

x-ray;

sonic; more accurate

inlet;

conjugata vera;

diagonal conjugate; transverse

diameter

bi-ischial;

intertuberous; anterior-posterior;

interspinous

⬇

The anterior-posterior diameter of the inlet which must be estimated or measured by x-ray is known as the _____ . The anterior-posterior diameter of the inlet which can be measured manually and which is used to estimate the C.V. is known as the _____ . The true conjugate is measured from the _____ to the _____ . The critical diameter of the C.V. is _____ .

The C.D. is measured from the _____ to the _____ . The critical measurement of the diagonal conjugate is _____ .

The greatest width of the pelvic inlet is the _____ diameter. The critical measurement of the transverse diameter is _____ .

true conjugate (conjugata vera) (C.V.);

diagonal conjugate (C.D.);
top of symphysis pubis;
sacral promontory;
10 centimeters
bottom of the symphysis pubis;
sacral promontory;

11.5 centimeters
transverse;
12 centimeters

INTERNAL PELVIC OUTLET DIAMETERS

The shortest diameter of the pelvic outlet is the distance between the inner surfaces of the ischial tuberosities. This diameter is called the *bi-ischial diameter*, also known as the *intertuberous diameter* and abbreviated as T.I. The critical measurement for the bi-ischial diameter is 10 centimeters.

The longest diameter of the pelvic outlet is the *anterior-posterior diameter*, measured from the lower margin of the symphysis pubis to the tip of the sacrum. The critical measurement of this diameter is 10.5 centimeters.

The shortest diameter of the pelvic outlet is the _____ diameter. The intertuberous diameter is measured between the _____ of the _____ . The critical measurement of the T.I. is _____ .

The longest diameter of the pelvic outlet is the _____ diameter.

The critical measurement of the anterior-posterior diameter of the pelvic outlet is _____ .

bi-ischial (intertuberous) (T.I.);

inner surfaces;
ischial tuberosities;
10 centimeters
anterior-posterior;

10.5 centimeters

Diameters of the midpelvis cannot be measured accurately manually and must either be estimated by feeling the prominence or slope of the *ischial spines* or measured by x-ray.

The distance between the ischial spines is the shortest diameter of the pelvis. The critical measurement of this *interspinous diameter* is 8.5 centimeters. A small interspinous diameter may be evidence of midpelvic contraction and can prevent a vaginal delivery. A contracted pelvis means that one or more of its diameters are shortened enough to interfere with the normal mechanism of labor, but this may not necessarily prevent a vaginal delivery.

The shortest diameter of the pelvis, found in the midpelvis, is the

distance between the_____ . The   ischial spines;

critical interspinous diameter is _____ .   8.5 centimeters

Delivery may be, and frequently is, accomplished even though the pelvis may not be within the normal limits of shape or size. A small baby can be delivered through a small pelvis, and a very large baby sometimes cannot be delivered through what may be considered a normal pelvis. The type of delivery always depends upon the adaptation of the passenger (fetus) to the passage (pelvic cavity).

The pelves of all women differ; no two are alike. These differences are caused by many things: disease, nutrition, heredity, injury, and development. In 1930, Caldwell and Moloy classified pelves according to the type of posterior and anterior segments at the pelvic inlet.[1] There are four types of pelves: the *gynecoid*, the *anthropoid*, the *android*, and the *platypelloid*. The gynecoid or normal female pelvis is somewhat heart-shaped and is found in 42 percent of women; the anthropoid is oval shaped and is found in 23 percent of white women and 40 percent of nonwhite women. The android or masculine-type pelvis is triangular at the inlet and narrowed at the outlet and midplane and is found in 32 percent of white women and 15 percent of nonwhite women. The platypelloid or flat pelvis has a short anterior-posterior inlet diameter and is wide at the outlet. This type is found in 3 percent of white women and 2 percent of nonwhite women. In most women, there is a combination of these basic types.

The type of delivery to follow the processes of labor is always depen-

dent upon the adaptations of the _____ to the _____   baby; pelvic

cavity.

Since types of female pelves _____ due to several   differ;

factors such as_____ , _____ , _____ ,   disease; nutrition; heredity;

_____ , and development, a classification of pelvis types   injury

became an important means of ensuring a healthy delivery.

There are _____ types of pelvic configurations or shapes. The_____ or normal female pelvis; the anthropoid or_____ ; the _____ or masculine type, which is _____ at the inlet and _____ at the outlet and midplane; and the _____ or flat pelvis, which has a short _____ inlet diameter and a _____ outlet diameter.

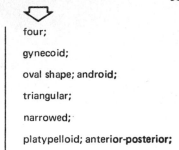

four;

gynecoid;

oval shape; android;

triangular;

narrowed;

platypelloid; anterior-**posterior**;

wide

An understanding of the anatomy of the female bony pelvis is essential in assessing the type and course of delivery processes and as a means of diagnosing the appearance of stressors that may become high-risk situations for both the mother and the baby. Thus, it is important that you study this area thoroughly, since once you have mastered it you will be able to comprehend how the baby passes through the birth canal as it is born.

POST-TEST Indicate whether each statement is true or false by circling the appropriate letter. Then turn to page 97 and see how well you have done.

1. Pelvimetry can be done only through vaginal examinations. T F

2. The conjugata vera is a diameter of the pelvic outlet. T F

3. A conjugata vera diameter measurement of less than 10 centimeters is considered critical. T F

4. The diagonal conjugate measures the distance between the lower edge of the symphysis pubis and the sacral promontory. T F

5. The greatest width of the pelvic inlet is the transverse diameter. T F

6. The distance between the ischial tuberosities represents the longest diameter of the pelvic outlet. T F

7. The critical measurement of the anterior-posterior diameter is 8.5 centimeters. T F

8. A gynecoid pelvis is the normal female pelvis. T F

9. Poor nutrition, genetic factors, injury, and other conditions produce differences in types of pelves. T F

10. Type of delivery always depends on the adaptations between the fetus and the bony pelvis. T F

In the specific areas with which you had difficulty, return to the material and review.

REFERENCES

1. Louis Hellman and Jack Pritchard, *Williams' Obstetrics,* 14th ed., Appleton-Century-Crofts, New York, 1971, p. 313.

BIBLIOGRAPHY

Fitzpatrick, Elise, Sharon Reeder, and Luigi Mastroianni: *Maternity Nursing,* 12th ed., J. B. Lippincott Co., Philadelphia, 1971.

Hellman, Louis and Jack Pritchard: *Williams' Obstetrics,* 14th ed., Appleton-Century-Crofts, New York, 1971.

Ziegel, Erna and Carolyn C. Van Blarcon: *Obstetric Nursing,* 6th ed., The Macmillan Co., New York, 1972.

PRETEST ANSWERS

1. Diameters of the pelvis   2. The three diameters of the pelvis are: a. The inlet diameters   b. The outlet diameters   c. The midpelvic diameter   3. Conjugata vera (true conjugate) (C.V.)   4. Diagonal conjugate   5. Transverse diameter   6. Distance between the inner surfaces of the ischial tuberosities   7. Anterior-posterior diameter   8. The four types of pelves are: 1. The gynecoid   2. The anthropoid   3. The android   4. The platypelloid

POST-TEST ANSWERS

1. F   2. F   3. T   4. T   5. T   6. F   7. F   8. T   9. T   10. T

CHAPTER THREE

ANATOMY OF THE UTERUS

OBJECTIVES *Identify the four distinct areas of uterine demarcation.*

Identify the four ligaments that support the uterus and/or its portions.

GLOSSARY *Corpus:* The triangular body of the uterus
Fundus: The rounded portion of the uterus located above the fallopian tubes
Isthmus: The section of the uterus where the cervix joins the body
Cervix: The neck or lowermost part of the uterus
Internal os: The opening of the cervical canal leading into the uterine cavity
External os: The opening of the cervical canal leading into the vagina
Broad ligaments: Folds of peritoneum extending from each side of the uterus to provide support; also dividing the pelvic cavity into the anterior and posterior portions
Cardinal ligaments: The supporting structures found at the lowermost portion of the broad ligaments; made up of dense connective tissue
Round ligaments: Cords of connective tissue extending from the corpus to the labia majora
Uterosacral ligaments: Supporting structures that extend from the cervix to the fascia of the sacral vertebrae

PRETEST   In the spaces provided, fill in the word or words that best complete(s) the statements. Then turn to page 104 and check your answers.

1. The female organ of menstruation and reproduction is the _____ .

2. This organ is located within the _____ cavity.

3. Identify the four areas into which the uterus has been anatomically divided:

    a. _____

    b. _____

    c. _____

    d. _____

4. Name the four ligaments that support the uterus:

    a. _____

    b. _____

    c. _____

    d. _____

The uterus, or female organ of menstruation and reproduction, is a hollow, muscular organ shaped much like a pear. It is located in the pelvic cavity between the rectum and the urinary bladder, and it is partially covered by peritoneum. In spite of the fact that, in its nonpregnant state, it is of a small size, weighing approximately 2 ounces, this organ is capable of great growth.

Anatomically, the uterus has been divided into four distinct areas of obstetrical significance. The *corpus*, or triangular body, of the uterus is the largest part. The rounded portion, or the *fundus*, is located above the insertion of the fallopian tubes, which extend from either side of the upper portion of the corpus. The *cervix*, or neck, of the uterus is separated from the main body by a narrowing called the *isthmus*. The cervix has two openings, the internal os, which leads to the uterine cavity, and the external os, which opens into the vagina. (See page 101 bottom.)

The products of conception are contained, until birth, in the _____. This female organ of reproduction serves also as the organ of _____. Anatomically, this organ is divided into _____ areas, which are the _____, the _____ , the _____ , and the _____ .	uterus; menstruation; four; corpus; fundus; cervix; isthmus
The uterus is located in the _____ cavity, between the _____ and the _____ . It is a pear-shaped organ partially covered by _____ .	pelvic; rectum; urinary bladder; peritoneum
The large portion of the uterus located below the insertion of the _____ is called the _____ ; its neck, called the _____ , is separated from the larger body by the _____ .	fallopian tubes; corpus; cervix; isthmus
The opening between the neck of the uterus (the _____) and the uterine cavity is the _____ ; the opening leading into the vagina is called the _____ _____ .	cervix; internal os; external os

The uterus is supported by a number of ligaments that consist mainly of peritoneum. The *broad ligaments* extend from each side of the uterus in a winglike fashion and divide the pelvic cavity into two portions, anterior and posterior. At the lowermost or base portion of the broad ligaments, the *cardinal ligaments,* made up of dense connective tissue, may be found, providing an additional source of support for the uterus.

The *round ligaments,* which resemble fibrous cords, extend from either side of the corpus immediately below the fallopian tubes, through the inguinal canal, to the upper section of the labia majora; these function primarily in maintaining the fundus in a forward position.

Finally, the set of ligaments that serve to support the cervix are the *uterosacral ligaments,* which extend from the posterior cervical aspect to the fascia of the sacral vertebrae.

The uterus is supported by _____ that extend from
either side of this organ. Consisting of _____ , these winglike
structures divide the_____ cavity into two portions,
_____ and _____ portions. This set of
ligaments is known as the_____ .

At the base of these ligaments, the_____ ligaments
may be found. These are made up of dense _____
_____ and serve to provide additional_____
to the _____ .

The round ligaments extend from _____
_____ of the _____ , and serve to maintain the fundus
in a _____ position.

ligaments;

peritoneum

pelvic;

anterior; posterior;

broad ligaments

cardinal;

connective tissue;

support;

uterus

either

side; corpus;

forward

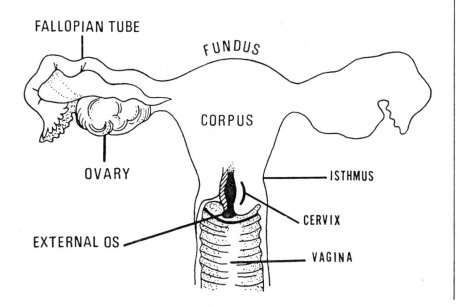

Uterus.

Supporting the _____ and extending from the posterior cervical aspect are the _____ ligaments, completing the supportive structure that aids in maintaining the female reproductive organ in place within the pelvic cavity while at the same time ensuring its position.

cervix;

uterosacral

POST-TEST   Match the items in the left column with the definitions in the right column. Then turn to page 104 and see how well you have done.

1. Corpus _____
2. Fundus _____
3. Isthmus _____
4. Cervix _____
5. Internal os _____
6. Broad ligaments _____
7. Uterosacral ligaments _____

a. Ligaments supporting the cervix
b. Opening into the uterine cavity
c. Opening into the vaginal canal
d. Triangular body of the uterus
e. Located above the insertion of the fallopian tubes
f. Extend from each side of the ovary
g. Extend from either side of the corpus
h. Neck of the uterus
i. Narrowing above the neck of the uterus

In the specific areas with which you had difficulty, return to the material and review.

BIBLIOGRAPHY   Chaffee, Ellen and Esther Greisheimer: *Basic Physiology and Anatomy,* 2d ed., J. B. Lippincott Co., Philadelphia, 1969.

Hellman, Louis and Jack Pritchard: *Williams' Obstetrics,* 14th ed., Appleton-Century-Crofts, New York, 1971.

PRETEST ANSWERS

1. Uterus   2. Pelvic   3. a. Corpus   b. Fundus   c. Isthmus   d. Cervix
4. a. Broad ligaments   b. Cardinal ligaments   c. Round ligaments   d. Utero-sacral ligaments

POST-TEST ANSWERS

1. d   2. e   3. i   4. h   5. b   6. g   7. a

CHAPTER FOUR

GROWTH AND DEVELOPMENT OF THE FETUS

OBJECTIVES   *Identify the two genetic characteristics and the pattern of growth that are established as a result of fertilization.*

Identify the three periods of growth.

Identify the three parts of the decidua.

Identify the three germinal layers and their major functions.

Identify the six functions of the amniotic fluid.

Identify the process of placental development and the five functions of the placenta.

Identify the five fetal circulatory structures.

Identify major developmental characteristics during the period of growth.

GLOSSARY   *Gamete:* The sex cell, a sperm or an ovum
Haploid: Half the number of chromosomes of the organism
Diploid: The full complement of chromosomes

Mitosis: A process of cell division into two equal parts

Endometrium: Inner lining of the uterus

Decidua: Enriched endometrium

Decidua vera: Lining of the uterus but not in contact with the implanted ovum

Decidua basalis: Lining of the uterus forming the base for the implanted ovum

Decidua capsularis: Lining of the uterus over or covering the implanted ovum

Morula: The ovum after it has differentiated into a mulberry-shaped cluster of cells

Trophoblast: Term referring to an ovum as it is ready to implant

Germinal layers: Embryonic tissues that form the basis of all body structures

Entoderm: Inner germinal layer

Mesoderm: Middle germinal layer

Ectoderm: Outer germinal layer

Amnion: Inner fetal membrane

Chorion: Outer fetal membrane

Placenta: Organ of transfer between the maternal and fetal systems

Hydrostatic wedge: Amniotic fluid inside the membranes acting as a dialator

Trimester: A division of pregnancy, e.g.: first trimester, the first three months; second trimester, the next three months; third trimester, the last three months

PRETEST   In the spaces provided, fill in the word or words that best complete(s) the statements. Then turn to page 119 and check your answers.

1. At the time of fertilization, the number of chromosomes is restored to the _____ number.

2. The type of cell division that begins after the sperm and ovum unite is _____ .

3. The period of the embryo begins at the_____week and lasts until the _____ week.

4. After fertilization of the ovum takes place, the endometrium is termed the _____ .

5. The three germinal layers are the _____ , _____ , and _____ .

6. The germinal layer from which the skin arises is the _____ .

7. The digestive and respiratory tracts arise from the germinal layer, the _____ .

8. List the five functions of the placenta.

   _____

   _____

   _____

   _____

   _____

9. In the fetal circulation there are five fetal structures that are necessary during intrauterine life; they are:

   _____

   _____

   _____

   _____

   _____

10. The structure of the fetal organs and systems during the first trimester is _____ .

11. The soft, downy hair covering the fetal body is called _____ .

12. The fetus is considered viable at _____ weeks or_____ grams.

13. At term, the fetus usually weighs approximately_____pounds.

The process of growth and development of the fetus takes place within the maternal body; the fetus is dependent solely on the mother to provide the necessary elements for growth. Thus, there is a constant interaction between the two systems as they adapt reciprocally to one another while at the same time achieving their own homeodynamic states.

This chapter discusses the patterns of growth of the fetus and the specific needs that are present.

Fertilization occurs when the spermatozoa deposited in the vagina travel to the outer third or distal end of the fallopian tube and engulf the ovum, allowing for penetration of the ovum by one sperm, resulting in the union of the two gametes.

As a result of fertilization, certain characteristics are established. Each gamete has a haploid number of chromosomes (23 chromosomes); at the time of union, this number is restored to the *diploid number* or a total of 46 chromosomes. Another genetic characteristic that is established is the *sex* of the offspring. This is dependent upon whether the sperm contained an X chromosome, resulting in a female, or a Y chromosome, resulting in a male.

The pattern of growth established as a result of the union of the two gametes is a sequence of *mitotic divisions.* This division increases the number of cells while maintaining a constant number of chromosomes in each cell because each chromosome divides in half during each cell division.

When the ovum and the sperm unite, the fertilized ovum (also called zygote) has 46 chromosomes, which is a _____ number.

> diploid

One of the chromosomes carried by the sperm determines the _____ of the offspring.

> sex

Following fertilization, the zygote begins to have an increased number of cells because of a sequence of _____ .

> mitotic divisions

The period of growth from fertilization until full term is divided into three parts corresponding to certain occurrences. The first period is the *period of the ovum*, which occurs from the time of fertilization until the process of implantation is completed, which takes two weeks. Following the period of the ovum is the *period of the embryo*, lasting until the eighth week of gestation. This is the time when the major structures and organs are laid down. The *period of the fetus* follows and lasts until full term. It is the time of maturation of all the structures and organs.

The first two weeks from fertilization until implantation is completed are termed the period of the _____ . The period in which the organs and structures are laid down is termed the period of the _____ .

> ovum;
>
> embryo;

The growth period from eight weeks until term is called the period of the

_____ .

fetus

    Naegele's formula[1] is used to estimate the date when the baby is due. Add seven days to the first day of the last menstrual cycle, subtract three months, and add a year and that is the expected date of confinement. For example: If the mother's last menstrual period started on June 14, 1973, that would be

      6/14/73

add seven days

      6/21/73

subtract three months

      3/21/73

add a year

      3/21/74

This would make her estimated date of confinement (EDC) March 21, 1974. This is the easiest way of determining the approximate due date, as people do not often know the time of conception, which knowledge is necessary in order to count up 280 days or 40 weeks, which is the period of gestation.

    What is the EDC for a mother whose first day of her last menstrual period was October 15, 1973? _____

July 22, 1974

    Let us review what happens to the fertilized ovum. The place where the ovum was fertilized was the _____

distal end

of the fallopian tube, and it then takes three to four days to travel to the uterus.

    The ovum is propelled by the cilia and the peristaltic waves of the fallopian tube. During this time, the number of cells increases by _____

mitotic division

_____ so that the ovum is filled with a cluster of cells. The cluster is often described as mulberry-shaped and is termed a *morula.*

    Now, within the uterine cavity, the morula floats freely for two to three days. As fluid collects within the morula, the cells are massed to one side of the morula. An outside layer, called the trophoblastic layer, surrounds the morula. This layer is capable of breaking down the endometrium. At this time the name of the morula changes to *trophoblast*. It takes about a week for the trophoblast to burrow completely into the endometrium. This is the process of *nidation* or implantation.

This ends the period of the _____ . The morula appears as a _____

_____ .

ovum;

mulberry-shaped cluster of cells

Travel time of the ovum along the tube is _____

_____ , and it is propelled by

_____ and _____ .

three-four days;

cilia; peristalsis

Once in the uterus, the morula _____

_____ .

floats for two-three days

At the time of implantation, the morula now is called the

_____ .

trophoblast

The process of nidation is complete in _____ .

a week

At the time of implantation, the endometrium becomes hyperemic (very vascular) and is now termed the *decidua*. The decidua is divided into three parts according to the location of the ovum. The part of the decidua which is not in contact with the ovum is termed the *decidua vera*; it lines most of the uterus. At the site of implantation, the part of the decidua under the ovum, forming a base, is termed the *decidua basalis*. As the ovum burrows in, part of the decidua closes over or encapsulates the ovum, so this part of the decidua is termed the *decidua capsularis*.

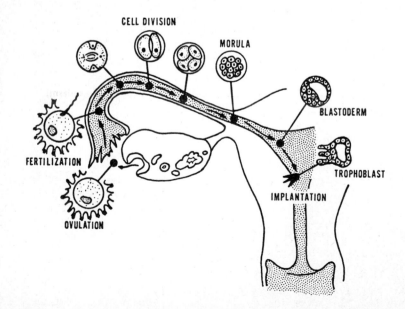

Implantation.

As nidation occurs, the endometrim is called the _____
and is divided into three _____ .

  The part that lines most of the uterine cavity is called the _____
_____ , and the part underneath the ovum is termed
the _____ . The section directly
over the implanted ovum is the _____ .

  As the ovum begins to implant, the structure now is called a
_____ .

decidua;

parts

decidua vera;

decidua basalis;

decidua capsularis

trophoblast

  It has two differentiated areas: the cells that have massed together
forming the embryonic mass or disc, and the outside layer of cells, termed the
trophoblastic layer.

  The *embryonic disc* develops into special structures: the *amnion* (the
innermost fetal membrane), the *yolk sac* (a temporary structure), the *body
stalk* (which becomes the umbilical cord), and the *three germinal layers*
(which give rise to the organs and structures of the body).

  The three germinal layers are the *ectoderm,* the *mesoderm,* and the
entoderm. The major structures formed from the outer layer, the ectoderm,
are the *skin* and the *nervous system.* Also derived from the ectoderm are the
epithelium of the nasal and oral passages, hair, nails, sebaceous and sweat
glands, salivary and mucous glands, and enamel of the teeth.

  The major structures formed from the middle layer, the mesoderm, are
the *circulatory, urinary,* and *reproductive systems*; the *muscles*; and the
bones. The mesoderm also is responsible for the lining of the pericardial,
pleural, and peritoneal cavities; ligaments and tendons; and areolar tissue. The
inner layer, the entoderm, develops into the two major structures, the
digestive tract and *the respiratory tract.* The entoderm also is the basis of
the thymus, thyroid, bladder, and urethra.

  The three germinal layers are the _____ , _____ ,
and _____ . The outer layer, which gives rise to the skin and nervous
system, is the_____ . The layer that gives rise to the muscles,
bones, and circulatory system is the _____ . The inner layer,
which becomes the digestive tract and the respiratory tract, is the_____ .

ectoderm; mesoderm;

entoderm;

ectoderm;

mesoderm;

entoderm

  Some of the cells of the embryonic disc which separate off from the
amnion, a thin, tough, transparent membrane surrounding the developing
embryo. This membrane is nonvascular and has no nerve innervation. The
amniotic sac holds fluid called *amniotic fluid* within it. This fluid amounts to
500-1,000 cubic centimeters at term. The amniotic fluid serves six functions:

1. Provides even pressure on the developing embryo, thus allowing for further molding of body structure

2. Protects the fetus from jolts

3. Permits fetal movements

4. Maintains constant temperature of the fetus

5. Provides fluid that the fetus drinks (up to 500 cubic centimeters per day at term)

6. Provides a hydrostatic wedge during childbirth

The fetus is surrounded by fluid called _____ _____ . When there are direct blows near the fetus, the fluid serves to_____ . The fluid allows for freedom of_____ . Since the fetus is floating in the fluid, the pressure on every fetal part during development is _____ . The fluid maintains a relatively constant environment by regulating the _____ . The fluid may provide some nourishment, since the fetus _____ it. During childbirth, the amniotic fluid serves as a _____ .

amniotic fluid;

protect it;

movement;

even;

temperature;

drinks;

hydrostatic wedge

While the inside of the ovum has been differentiating, the outside layer, the trophoblastic layer, also has been undergoing change. At the time of implantation, the trophoblastic layer proliferates, developing chorionic villi on its entire surface. These villi invade the decidua and tap the maternal blood vessels, making pools, called *lacunae* which are filled with blood. As the villi continue to grow the maternal arterioles are tapped and form maternal lakes around the villi in the intervillous spaces.

As growth of the embryo takes place, the decidua capsularis becomes very stretched and thin and is unable to provide sufficient nourishment for the chorionic villi. Thus the villi begin to degenerate and become the smooth *chorionic membrane*, also called the chorionic laeve or the chorion. The chorionic membrane (chorion) surrounds the outer aspects of the amniotic membrane (amnion). However, the villi in the decidua basalis continue to grow and proliferate, taking on a bushy appearance; at this time they are known as *chorionic frondosum*. The *chorionic frondosum* together with the *decidua basalis* form the *placenta*.

The outside of the ovum, called the _____ , begins to grow and develop the _____ .

trophoblastic layer;

villi

As these villi tap the maternal vessels, the spaces thus formed are called
_____ . When the growing villi invade the maternal arterioles, the blood-filled spaces are known as _____
_____ . The degenerating villi form a smooth membrane known as the _____ .

lacunae;

maternal lakes;

chorion

(chorionic laeve)

(chorionic membrane)

At the end of the first three months of gestation, the placenta is completely functioning and the only further placental growth is in actual size. The placenta serves as an organ of transfer between the mother and the fetus. Specifically, the five major functions of the placenta are:

1. *Nutrition:* Carbohydrates, fats, proteins, water, inorganic salts, calcium, phosphorous, and iron are transported from the mother to the fetus.

2. *Excretion:* Fetal waste materials are transported to the maternal circulation.

3. *Respiration:* Oxygen is transported from maternal to fetal circulation, and carbon dioxide diffuses from fetal to maternal circulation.

4. *Barrier:* Large molecules cannot pass through the semipermeable membrane of the placenta. Therefore, the blood cells of the fetus and mother cannot cross this barrier and mix. Other large particles, such as bacteria, also are prevented from crossing the placenta to the fetus.

   During the first six months of pregnancy, the inner lining of the villi contains special cells (Langhan's cells) that function to prevent the passage of *Treponema pallida* (which cause syphilis). Small molecules such as viruses, some drugs, and antibodies are able to cross.

5. *Synthesis:* By the end of the first trimester, the placenta is completely responsible for the production of estrogen, progesterones, and chorionic gonadotrophin. It is also thought to produce some adrenocorticosteroids.

The placenta is a completely functioning organ by the end of the
_____ . The
placenta allows for the transfer of nutrients, thus providing for fetal
_____ .

first trimester (first three months of pregnancy);

nutrition

The passage of wastes from the fetus to the mother meets the fetal need for _____ . The exchange of gases through the placenta provides for fetal _____ . The semipermeable nature of the placenta allows it to function as a _____ .

excretion;

respiration;

barrier

Since the placenta takes over the function of production of estrogen and progesterone, it is said to _____ .

synthesize

Since the placenta functions as the respiratory organ for the fetus and the fetal lungs are not functioning for respiration, there are five special fetal circulatory structures (see page 115 bottom):

1. *Umbilical vein:* A structure that brings highly oxygenated, nutrient-rich blood to the fetus from the placenta

2. *Ductus venosus:* A special structure that allows the major portion of the blood to enter the inferior vena cava from the umbilical vein and bypass the liver

3. *Foramen ovale:* An opening between the right and left atria allowing most of the blood to be shunted directly into the left atrium

4. *Two umbilical arteries:* Branches of the hypogastric arteries which carry deoxygenated blood back to the placenta

5. *Ductus arteriosus:* A special structure that joins the pulmonary artery to the aorta, allowing most of the blood to bypass the lungs and go directly into the aorta

The two umbilical arteries and the one umbilical vein are covered by a white, gelatinous substance called Wharton's jelly, forming the umbilical cord. At term, the cord is 2 feet long and ½ inch thick.

Let us review:

The structure that brings food from the placenta to the fetus is the _____ . The blood that comes from the placenta is rich in _____ and _____ _____ .

umbilical vein;

nutrients; highly

oxygenated

Blood enters the inferior vena cava through a structure called the _____ . Blood returns to the placenta by means of the _____ .

ductus venosus;

umbilical arteries;

Blood is shunted from the right atrium to the left atrium through the _____ . Most of the blood that

foramen ovale;

circulates through the pulmonary artery is shunted through a special structure in the aorta. This is the _____ .

⟱

ductus arteriosus

The special structures found in fetal life change at the time of birth. As the umbilical cord is cut, blood must circulate through the lungs in order for it to become oxygenated. A flap falls over the foramen ovale so that the blood in the right atrium now goes to the right ventricle and through the pulmonary artery. Here, the ductus arteriosus contracts so that the blood continues on its way to the lungs. The ductus venosus also contracts, and the umbilical vein and arteries are only vestiges of the former structures.

As we proceed, the major developmental characteristics of the fetus will be discussed by trimesters.

The first trimester is the period from the time of conception through the twelfth week of gestation. During the embryonic stage, *rudimentary fetal organs* and systems appear and, as early as the fourth week of life, the heart begins to pulsate and other major structures can be identified. By the end of the twelfth week, other systems such as the alimentary tract and excretory and nervous systems have differentiated sufficiently to begin functioning. The fetus at this time is approximately 3 inches long and weighs close to 1 ounce.

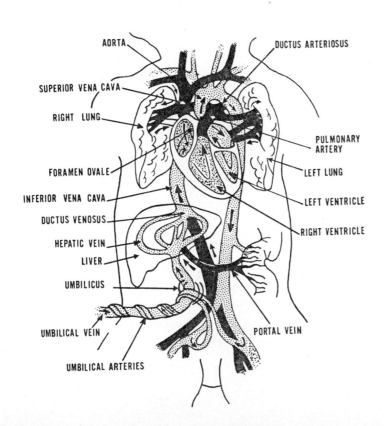

Fetal circulation.

During the first trimester, fetal organs and systems begin to develop; however, these are _____ . The heart begins to pulsate on or around the _____ week of life.

By around the twelfth week of gestation, the systems that begin to function are the _____ , the _____ , and the _____ , systems.

At this point, the weight of the fetus is approximately _____ and its length is about _____ .

rudimentary;
fourth
alimentary; excretory;
nervous
1 ounce;
3 inches

During the second trimester, or the period from the twelfth week through the twenty-fourth week of gestation, the organs that have begun to develop earlier now continue to become highly specialized systems. By the twentieth week, fetal movements are strong enough to be felt by the mother. This awareness of fetal life by the mother is called *quickening.* By this time, *lanugo,* a fine, downy hair, now covers the fetal body, and *vernix caseosa,* a white, cheeselike substance, covers its skin. It is during this trimester that minerals such as calcium and iron, essential nutrients for fetal development, begin to be stored. Toward the end of this trimester the fetus is 12 inches long and weighs 1½ pounds.

The second trimester of pregnancy is the period of time from the _____ week through the _____ week of gestation. Organs and systems now begin to become quite _____ in their functioning. By the twentieth week, fetal movements are strong enough to be _____ by the _____ . This is called _____ .

The fine, downy hair covering the fetal body is known as _____ , while the skin is covered by a white, cheeselike substance called _____ .

During this trimester, that is the _____ trimester, two important minerals or nutrients are stored in the _____ body. These two minerals are _____ and _____ .

twelfth; twenty-fourth;
specialized;
felt; mother;
quickening
lanugo;
vernix caseosa
second;
fetal;
calcium; iron

The third trimester, beginning at the twenty-fourth week and ending at the fortieth week of gestation, marks the final maturational process for the baby.

At 28 weeks of life, the fetus weighs about 2½ pounds or 1,000 grams, and the systems have developed sufficiently so that the fetus is considered to be *viable,* that is, able to survive if born at this time.

After 36 weeks, fat storages increase and the fetus begins to take on a more rounded shape. At term, or the point at which the pregnancy is ended by a normal delivery, the baby usually will weigh 7¼ pounds and measure 20 inches in length.

The twenty-fourth to the fortieth week of life marks the_____   third;

trimester of fetal development. At 28 weeks, the fetus weighs _____   1,000;

grams, and, if born, it would be considered to be_____ ,   viable;

that is, able to _____ if _____ at this time.   survive; born;

Fat storages increase after _____ weeks, giving the fetus its   36;

_____ shape.   more rounded

At term, or the point at which the pregnancy is ended, the baby's

weight is usually_____ while its   7¼ pounds;

length measures _____ .   20 inches

The total process of conception has taken a short time when compared with the total developmental processes that occur within a period of 40 weeks. Indeed, the origin and development of human life is a marvelous occurrence which, when reflected upon, may be thought of as being one of the major miracles of nature.

POST-TEST Indicate whether each statement is true or false by circling the appropriate letter. Then turn to page 119 and check how well you have done.

 1. At the time of fertilization the diploid number of chromosomes is restored. T F

 2. Meiosis takes place after fertilization occurs. T F

 3. If the sperm has a Y chromosome, the offspring will be a male. T F

 4. The period of the ovum extends through the first three months. T F

 5. The decidua vera lines the uterine cavity but does not come into contact with the implanted ovum. T F

 6. Part of the entoderm develops into the nervous system. T F

 7. The mesoderm forms the skin. T F

 8. The amniotic fluid provides protection for the fetus. T F

 9. The placenta is formed by the fusion of the amnion and the decidua basalis. T F

10. The placenta provides for the exchange of maternal and fetal blood. T F

11. Small molecules such as viruses are able to cross the placental barrier. T F

12. The foramen ovale is the opening between the pulmonary artery and the aorta. T F

13. In the fetal circulation there are two umbilical arteries and one umbilical vein. T F

14. The umbilical arteries bring highly oxygenated and nutrient-rich blood to the fetus. T F

15. The organs of the fetus are present in rudimentary form during the first trimester. T F

16. The soft, downy hair covering the fetal body is called lanugo. T F

17. The fetus is considered viable at 28 weeks or at 1,000 grams. T F

In the specific areas with which you had difficulty, return to the material and review.

REFERENCES
1. Ernestine Wiedenbach: *Family-Centered Maternity Nursing,* 1st ed. G. P. Putnam's Sons, New York, 1958, p. 38.

BIBLIOGRAPHY

Batsone, Gifford, Blair Alastair, and Jack Slater: *A Handbook of Pre-Natal Paediatrics,* J. B. Lippincott Co., Philadelphia and Toronto, 1971.

Corner, George W.: *Ourselves Unborn,* Yale University Press, New Haven, 1945.

Greene, John W., John L. Durring, and Kaighn Smith, "Placental Function Tests," *American Journal of Obstetrics and Gynecology,* Vol. 92, pp. 1030-1057, 1965.

Langman, Jan: *Medical Embryology,* Williams and Wilkins Co., Baltimore, 1963.

Levine, Louis: *Biology of the Gene,* C. V. Mosby Co., St. Louis, 1969.

Moore, Mary Lou: *The New Born and the Nurse,* W. B. Saunders Co., Philadelphia, 1972.

Montagu, M. F. Ashley: *Prenatal Influences,* Charles C. Thomas, Springfield, Ill., 1962.

PRETEST ANSWERS
1. Diploid   2. Mitotic   3. Second; eighth   4. Decidua   5. Entoderm, mesoderm, ectoderm   6. Ectoderm   7. Entoderm   8. Nutrition, respiration, excretion, barrier, production of hormones   9. Ductus venosus, foramen ovale, ductus arteriosus, umbilical vein, and two umbilical arteries   10. Rudimentary   11. Lanugo   12. 28 weeks or 1,000 grams   13. 7 to 7½

POST-TEST ANSWERS
1. T   2. F   3. T   4. F   5. T   6. F   7. F   8. T   9. F   10. F   11. T   12. F   13. T   14. F   15. T   16. T   17. T

The following multiple-choice examination will test your comprehension of the material covered in the second unit of this program. Do not guess at the answers; if you need to do this then you have not learned the content. Return to the program and review areas that give you difficulty, before going on with the examination.

Circle the letter of the best response to each question. After completing the unit examination, check your answers on page 332 and review those areas of difficulty before proceeding to the next unit.

1. The innominate bones are formed by the:
   a. Pubis, sacrum, ilium
   b. Coccyx, ischia, and ilium
   c. Sacrum, ilium, ischia
   d. Ilium, ischium, and pubis

2. The coccyx and the sacrum:
   a. Form the lowermost part of the spine
   b. Are fused and join the pubic bone
   c. Are part of the ischial spine
   d. Form the inlet to the true pelvis

3. The fundus is:
   a. The largest part of the uterus
   b. The neck of the uterus
   c. The rounded part of the uterus above the fallopian tubes
   d. The body of the uterus

4. The sacroiliac articulations are found between the:
   a. Symphysis pubis and the sacrum
   b. Ischium and the ilium
   c. Sacrum and the ilium
   d. Coccyx and the sacrum

5. The symphysis pubis is a:
   a. Bone
   b. Articulation
   c. Ossification
   d. Ligament

6. Lowest posterior protuberances of the ischia on which the body rests are the:
   a. Ischial spines
   b. Ischial ligaments
   c. Ischial tuberosities
   d. Ischial articulations

7. The shortest diameter of the pelvic cavity is marked by the
   a. Linea terminalis
   b. Bi-ischial diameter
   c. Diagonal conjugate
   d. Ischial spines

8. The false pelvis is located:
   a. Above the pelvic inlet
   b. In the middle of the pelvic cavity
   c. At the pelvic outlet
   d. At the bottom between the anterior and posterior walls

9. When the mother goes for her initial prenatal visit, a clinical evaluation of her pelvis is done, and an actual measurement may be done by digital examination of the:
   a. Transverse diameter of the pelvic inlet
   b. Transverse diameter of the pelvic outlet
   c. Transverse diameter of the midpelvis
   d. Transverse diameter of the false pelvis

10. An important diameter of the pelvic inlet which cannot be measured manually but must be estimated using the distance between the lower edge of the symphysis pubis and the sacral promontory is the:
    a. True conjugate
    b. Diagonal conjugate
    c. Bi-ischial diameter
    d. Intercristal diameter

11. The measurements that are most important in evaluation of the pelvis and estimation of its adequacy are:
    a. Interspinous and external conjugate
    b. Intercristal and intertuberous
    c. Diagonal conjugate and interspinous
    d. Diagonal conjugate and intertuberous

12. Following fertilization, the diploid number of chromosomes are restored and:
    a. Meiosis and cell differentiation begins
    b. Sex characteristics are established with further division into haploid number of cells
    c. Mitotic division begins and sex characteristics are established
    d. Each gamete divides into two and then fusions occur and produce 48 chromosomes

13. At the tenth week of pregnancy, the period of growth is that of the:
    a. Zygote
    b. Ovum
    c. Embryo
    d. Fetus

14. If the first day of the last menstrual period of the mother's was on September 10, then her EDC would be:
    a. May 6
    b. May 10
    c. June 10
    d. June 17

15. Implantation of the fertilized ovum in the uterine lining begins about which day after conception?
    a. Third
    b. Fourth
    c. Seventh
    d. Eleventh

16. The portion of the fertilized ovum responsible for implantation is the:
    a. Trophoblast
    b. Amnion
    c. Embryonic disc
    d. Entoderm

17. One of the main functions of the amniotic fluid is to:
    a. Prevent improper nidation
    b. Maintain constant fetal temperature
    c. Prevent fetal wastage
    d. Act as a catalyst for absorption of electrolytes

18. The placenta is formed by the:
    a. Chorionic villi that atrophy and unite with the decidua capsularis
    b. Chorionic villi that penetrate the decidua capsularis
    c. Chorionic villi that unite with the decidua vera
    d. Chorionic villi that unite with the decidua basalis

19. The umbilical cord contains which of the following structures:
    a. One artery, two veins, and Wharton's jelly
    b. One artery, one vein, and Wharton's jelly
    c. Two arteries, two veins, and Wharton's jelly
    d. Two arteries, one vein, and Wharton's jelly

20. During the fifth lunar month, the mother asks, "What does my baby look like now?" You would answer:
    a. "Your baby is almost completely formed now, but its sex is not yet determined."
    b. "Your baby is about 8 inches long, and soon his heart will begin to beat."
    c. "Your baby looks like a real baby now; vernix caseosa, a white, cheeselike substance, is covering the skin; hair is appearing on the head; and you may feel that the baby is moving, if you haven't already felt it."
    d. "Your baby is completely formed now except for the toenails and fingernails, and it has lots of hair."

UNIT III
THE PREGNANCY EXPERIENCE

CHAPTER ONE

SIGNS AND SYMPTOMS OF PREGNANCY

OBJECTIVES *Differentiate between grava and para.*

Identify eight presumptive signs of pregnancy.

Identify six probable signs of pregnancy.

Identify the three positive signs of pregnancy.

Identify two differences between biological and immunological pregnancy tests.

GLOSSARY *Grava:* Relating to pregnancy
Para: Relating to a woman who has delivered an infant of viable age
Presumptive signs: Related to symptoms usually identified by the mother which indicate pregnancy
Probable signs: Related to those signs found by an examiner which indicate pregnancy
Positive signs: Related to those findings that confirm pregnancy
Amenorrhea: Relating to the absence of menses
Frequency: Relating to the need to void often
Quickening: Relating to the mother's experience of the first fetal movement
Linea nigra: Darkened line from the symphysis pubis to the umbilicus
Striae gravidarum: Reddish stretch marks often seen on the abdomen, thighs, and breasts of the pregnant woman
Chloasma: Mask of pregnancy; darkened pigmented areas on the face
Hegar's sign: A clinical finding, the softening of the isthmus
Goodell's sign: A clinical finding, the softening of the cervix
Immunological pregnancy test: A chemical reaction which uses the antigen antibody response to chorionic gonadotrophins in the urine
Biological pregnancy test: A procedure utilizing animals whereby urine containing chorionic gonadotrophins is injected into the animal and characteristic changes are found
Colostrum: A precursor of breast milk

PRETEST   In the spaces provided, fill the word or words that best complete(s) the statements. The answers are on page 136. Depending upon your answers, you may be able to omit some of the information in the chapter. We will tell you on which page to begin your study.

1. A primigravida is a _____

     _____ .

2. A nullipara is a _____

     _____

     _____ .

3. A woman in her second or any subsequent pregnancy is known as a

     _____ .

If you have answered the preceding questions correctly, begin this chapter on page 129.

4. The following symptoms of pregnancy can be identified as either probable or presumptive; place an *A* next to those that are *probable signs* and a *B* next to those that are *presumptive signs.*

     Breast changes   _____

     Changes in the size of the abdomen   _____

     Cessation of menses   _____

     Positive pregnancy tests   _____

     Skin changes   _____

5. Hegar's sign, a probable sign of pregnancy, is _____

     _____ .

6. Pregnancy tests depend upon the secretion of_____

     _____ in the urine of a pregnant woman.

7. The reddened lines on the mother's abdomen which occur as a result of adrenal cortical action are called _____ .

8. Chloasma is also known as the _____ and

     can also be caused by _____ .

9. An immunological pregnancy test utilizes the urine of a pregnant mother and

     _____ in order to check for pregnancy.

10. The three positive signs of pregnancy are:

    a. _____

    b. _____

    c. _____

    _____

11. These occur during the _____ trimester.

If you have answered the preceding questions correctly, begin this chapter on page 133.

A planned, wanted pregnancy is a joyful, exhilarating experience looked upon by the parents as a happy event expected to fulfill many of their wishes and dreams. Nonetheless, coupled with the gratification and excitement brought about by the news, conflicting feelings arise. *Ambivalence* towards the pregnancy takes over when the parents must deal with the reality and not the dream. The once hoped for, wished for, occurrence is no longer an abstraction; it a concrete, awesome responsibility that, in subtle ways, begins to introduce stressors within the family, calling upon its members to mobilize their adaptive resources.

It has been said that pregnancy is a psychological crisis brought about by a physiological process.[1] Yet, the interdependence of these two factors, that is, the biological and psychological components, makes it difficult to identify at what point one can determine a clear-cut cause and effect relationship.

From the moment the pregnancy is confirmed, psychological stresses produced by the threat of physiological alterations begin to operate. Although the addition of a new member was planned, doubts begin to appear characterized by conflicting thoughts such as, "I want it but not now," or, "I want it but will I be able to?" Furthermore, changes are anticipated in the way roles are perceived or have been occupied up to now, and these changes are looked upon with feelings of insecurity and uncertainty.

As the pregnancy progresses, unanticipated difficulties emerge. With each trimester, alterations take place which touch upon every aspect of the family's life-style. It is a source of wonder that, in 280 days, individuals are successful—barring complications—in coping with such complex stressors and thus harmoniously adapting to such great variations.

The following material will serve to identify the major psychological, physiological, and social changes that take place during the maternity cycle.

When the history of the mother is taken upon her first visit to the antepartum clinic, it is important that her obstetrical status be determined. The term that indicates the number of pregnancies a woman has had is *gravida;* a nongravid woman is not pregnant whereas a gravid woman is pregnant. A primigravid woman would be a woman who is pregnant for the first time; this condition often is abbreviated as Gravida I. A woman who is pregnant a second time or any time thereafter is a multigravid woman, e.g., Gravida II, Gravida V.

The term *para* indicates that a pregnancy ended after the point at which the fetus was viable; the baby may or may not have been born alive. The woman who is nulliparous, Para 0, is one who has not produced a child of viable age, whereas a multiparous woman is one who has delivered two or more children of viable age.

A mother who is pregnant for the first time is a _____ woman. A mother who is pregnant for the third time is a _____ woman.

primigravid;

multigravid

A mother who has two living children is a _____   multiparous
woman.

When you see Gravida I, Para 0 written, this means that the mother is
_____   pregnant for the first time;
and has_____ .   no children of viable age

When a mother comes to an antepartum clinic, her obstetrical status
Gravida III, Para I indicates that this is her _____   third pregnancy;
_____ and she has _____   delivered one child of viable age
_____ .

The information about the woman's obstetrical status is an important
part of the nursing assessment. This knowledge can provide clues about the
present physiological and psychological state of the mother and about her
response to this present pregnancy.

There are specific physiological signs and symptoms experienced by the
mother when pregnancy occurs. These signs often indicate that the pregnancy
has already begun, although positive confirmation does not occur until the
sixteenth to the twentieth week of gestation.

These signs and symptoms are classified as *presumptive, probable,* and
positive signs. The presumptive signs appear at various times during the first
trimester and are for the most part subjective. Although the probable signs
also occur at various times during the pregnancy, they are usually identified
only by the obstetrical examiner. Both the presumptive and the probable
signs can be caused by physiological alterations other than pregnancy; this
makes the confirmation of pregnancy difficult.

The positive signs, however, occur only in pregnancy and appear late, so
that the mother is halfway through the pregnancy before these can be
identified.

It is important for the nurse to recognize the diagnostic limitations of
presumptive and probable signs of pregnancy. Also, she must be supportive of
the couple who are anxiously awaiting confirmation of their impending
parenthood.

The *presumptive* signs of pregnancy are:

1. *Amenorrhea:* Earliest and most important sign in women of
   childbearing age who usually have regular menstrual cycles or
   have had intercourse without the use of contraceptives.

2. *Breast changes:* Increased size and feeling of fullness in early
   pregnancy. After the second month, nipples become more
   pronounced, the areola becomes darker, and the veins under
   the skin become more transparent. Montgomery's tubules enlarge, and colostrum may be expressed after the tenth week.

3. *Nausea and/or vomiting:* Often termed "morning sickness." Appears in about 50 percent of pregnant women about the fourth week of pregnancy and disappears spontaneously by the end of the first trimester.

4. *Frequency:* Begins in the early weeks because of the pressure of the hyperemic uterus, and lasts until the end of the first trimester, when the growing uterus moves into the abdominal cavity.

5. *Quickening:* First fetal movements felt by the mother, occurring between the sixteenth and the nineteenth weeks of gestation.

6. *Skin changes: Linea nigra*—darkening of the line between the umbilicus and the symphysis pubis.

   Striae gravidarum—reddish stretch marks that may occur on the abdomen, thighs, and breasts.

   Chloasma—mask of pregnancy—irregular darkly pigmented areas on the face.

7. *Fatigue:* Periods of lassitude and drowsiness during the first trimester.

8. *Chadwick's sign:* Bluish purple discoloration of the vaginal mucosa.

Let us review:

Those signs of pregnancy which, for the most part, are subjective are called _____ signs.   presumptive

While observing and interviewing a pregnant woman in clinic, you obtain the following information:

"My period is eight weeks late!" This is termed _____ .   amenorrhea

"I can't understand why my breasts hurt." This may indicate

_____ .   breast changes

"All I want to do is sleep." This is an indication of _____ .   fatigue

"Can you tell me where the Ladies Room is; I can't seem to be far from one lately." This probably is an indication of _____ .   frequency

"Is there a soft drink machine around? I couldn't eat a thing for breakfast, I felt so sick." This is called _____ .   morning sickness

During the pelvic examination, the doctor notes that the vaginal mucosa is purplish in color. This is called _____ .   Chadwick's sign

While the doctor is doing the physical examination, you notice a darkened vestigial line on the woman's lower abdomen; this is called the

_____ .

linea nigra

You are aware also of darkly pigmented areas on the woman's forehead and cheeks, commonly called _____ or the _____

_____ .

chloasma; mask of pregnancy

Fetal movement felt by the mother later in pregnancy is called

_____ .

quickening

The probable signs of pregnancy are those that are determined by a medical person upon examination. Some of these signs are also present in conditions other than pregnancy.

The probable signs of pregnancy are:

1. *Enlargement of the abdomen:* Occurs after the third month as the growing uterus moves up into the abdominal cavity.

2. *Changes in internal organs: Small increase* in the size of the *uterus* due to increased vascularity although for the first trimester it remains a pelvic organ. The most important uterine change is *Hegar's sign,* which occurs about the sixth week of pregnancy and is a softening of the isthmus of the uterus. *Goodell's sign,* which is a softening of the cervix, occurs about the beginning of the second month of pregnancy.

3. *Ballottment:* Occurs between the fourth and fifth months of pregnancy; the small fetus, suspended in a relatively large volume of amniotic fluid, will rebound when the uterus is sharply tapped by the finger of the examiner.

4. *Braxton-Hicks contractions:* Irregular uterine contractions that begin early in pregnancy and usually are not felt by the mother until about the seventh month of pregnancy.

5. *Outlining of the fetus* by abdominal palpation late in pregnancy.

6. *Pregnancy tests:* Based on the secretion of chronic gonadotrophins in the urine of a pregnant woman found as early as ten days after the last menstrual period. After the first trimester, the level of chorionic gonadotrophins begins to drop and the tests become increasingly unreliable. The *immunological* pregnancy tests combine a urine specimen of the pregnant woman with substances that, in the case of pregnancy, will produce an

antigen antibody reaction. The results of these tests are available within five minutes to two hours.

The *biological tests,* in which the urine is injected into various kinds of animals, take anywhere from 12 hours to five days for a report.

Hormone-induced withdrawal bleeding is sometimes used as a pregnancy test since bleeding usually will not occur if a pregnancy exists.

Let us review:

Those signs usually found by the examiner which may indicate pregnancy are termed _____ signs.

probable

After the third month of pregnancy, the uterus moves into the abdominal cavity causing an enlargement of the _____ .

abdomen

About the sixth week of pregnancy, the softening of the isthmus which occurs is called _____ sign.

Hegar's

The phenomenon of the rebounding of the fetus in response to a tap on the uterus is termed _____ .

ballottment

The irregular contractions of the uterus which occur throughout pregnancy are called _____ contractions.

Braxton-Hicks

Late in pregnancy, by abdominal palpatation the examiner is able to outline the shape of the _____ .

fetus

The secretion of chorionic gonadotrophins in the urine of a pregnant woman is the basis for _____ .

pregnancy tests

You now are aware of the presumptive and probable signs of pregnancy and realize that they can occur at different times during the antepartum period. The *positive* signs of pregnancy, however, do not occur until after the sixteenth week of pregnancy. These signs are evidence of pregnancy and pregnancy alone; they are: *hearing and counting of the fetal heart rate* with the use of a fetascope; *movements of the fetus felt by the examiner*; and *roentgenographic or sonographic examination*, which shows fetal structure. With the use of new devices such as the doptone and the fetal cardiogram, it now is possible to detect fetal heart rate as early as twelve weeks of pregnancy.

Those signs that clearly prove the presence of a fetus are called _____ signs.

positive

The fetascope, fetal cardiogram, and doptone make it possible to hear and count the _____ .

A roentgenogram will clearly show the _____ _____ .

The examiner, by placing his hand on the mother's abdomen, is now able to feel _____ .

During your Ob-Gyn experience in a group-practice office, you once again meet Bill and Jean Garry, our third family model, who have made an appointment because Jean believes she is pregnant.

In taking the history, you learn that Jean's *last menstrual period* (LMP) was seven weeks ago and that she normally has a 28-day cycle. She complains of *sore breasts,* occasional *nausea* upon rising, and a feeling of *tiredness* which she explains is probably due to the fact that she has been getting up several times during the night *to void.* Her past medical history reveals no significant problems.

The foregoing signs and symptoms are_____ signs of pregnancy.

Jean seems to chatter on and on while continuously playing with the catch on her purse. Bill can't seem to keep his pipe lit. You are aware that this is a stressful situation and attempt to lower the *anxiety* level by helping them to *verbalize their feelings.* You elicit the information concerning Jean's apprehension about the physical examination and their desire to have the fact of the pregnancy confirmed since they have been trying to have a child for six months.

You assure Jean that *you will be with her* during the examination and *explain exactly what the doctor will do.*

Your presence with Jean will serve to provide_____ and to _____ state.

As you finish your explanation, Jean is called into Dr. Franklin's office. You instruct her *to void*, and you save a specimen of the urine for any tests ordered. You ask her to remove all of her clothes and provide her with an examining gown.

You then assist Jean onto the examination table, *draping her properly.* The doctor does a complete physical, including a breast examination. He then instructs you to prepare Jean for a pelvic examination, pap smear, and gram stain.

A *pap smear* is a cytological examination of cervical cells which assists in determining the normality of these cells and/or any deviations present. A gram stain is also done at this time to rule out presence of the veneral disease gonorrhea.

You tell Jean to place her legs on the stirrups as you carefully *drape* her, to keep her buttocks on the examination table, and to *relax* her abdomen by taking deep abdominal breaths.

After the examination, Dr. Franklin tells Jean that he thinks she is pregnant but that to be sure he wants to do a pregnancy test. Since an *immunological pregnancy test* is being done, you can use the urine specimen already obtained. (For some other types of pregnancy tests, usually those done on animals, a first voided morning specimen must be used and the woman must be instructed not to take any medication the previous night.)

A positive result of an immunological pregnancy test is a ＿＿＿＿＿ ＿＿＿＿＿＿＿＿＿＿＿＿＿＿＿＿＿.

probable sign of pregnancy

At this time, Dr. Franklin has confirmed Jean's pregnancy to the anxiously waiting Garrys. He then asks you to set up an appointment for Jean's prenatal blood work, chest x-ray, and dental examination.

POST-TEST Indicate whether each statement is true or false by circling the appropriate letter. Then turn to page 136 and check how well you have done.

1. A primigravid woman has been pregnant more than once.   **T F**

2. A multigravid woman is a woman who is pregnant for the first time.   **T F**

3. Hegar's sign is a positive sign of pregnancy.   **T F**

4. Amenorrhea is a presumptive sign.   **T F**

5. The three positive signs of pregnancy can be determined by the tenth week of gestation.   **T F**

6. The probable sign of nausea and vomiting appears early in the first trimester.   **T F**

7. Breast changes are one of the early presumptive signs.   **T F**

8. Frequency is a probable sign of the second trimester.   **T F**

9. Goodell's sign is the softening of the isthmus of the cervix.   **T F**

10. The linea nigra is the darkened line from the umbilicus to the symphysis pubis.   **T F**

11. Chadwick's sign is the bluish discoloration of the vagina.   **T F**

12. Ballottment occurs between the fourth and fifth months of pregnancy.   **T F**

13. Braxton-Hicks contractions are positive signs of pregnancy.   **T F**

In the specific areas with which you had difficulty, return to the material and review.

REFERENCES   1. Gerald Caplan: *Concepts of Mental Health and Consultation: Their Application in Public Health Social Work,* U.S. Children's Bureau, Washington, D.C., 1959, p. 46.

BIBLIOGRAPHY   Caplan, Gerald: *Concepts of Mental Health and Consultation: Their Application in Public Health Social Work,* U.S. Children's Bureau, Washington, D.C., 1959.

Hellman, Louis and Jack Pritchard: *Williams' Obstetrics,* 14th ed., Appleton-Century-Crofts, New York, 1971.

PRETEST ANSWERS   1. Woman experiencing her first pregnancy   2. Woman who has never had a child of viable age   3. Multigravida   4. B, A, B, A, B   5. Softening of the isthums of the uterus   6. Chorionic gonadotrophins   7. Striae gravidarum   8. Mask of pregnancy; anti-ovulatory pills   9. Chorionic gonadotrophins   10. a. Hearing of the fetal heart rate   b. Outlining the fetal skeleton   c. The examiner feeling fetal movements   11. Second

POST-TEST ANSWERS   1. F   2. F   3. F   4. T   5. F   6. F   7. T   8. F   9. F   10. T   11. T   12. T   13. F

CHAPTER TWO

THE PREGNANCY CYCLE DURING THE FIRST TRIMESTER

OBJECTIVES   *Identify the major task of the first trimester.*

Identify the major maternal physiological changes of the first trimester.

Identify the major psychological adaptations of the family in the first trimester.

Identify the cardinal danger signs of pregnancy.

Identify role changes of the parents during the first trimester.

Identify nutritional needs during the first trimester.

Identify the common discomforts associated with the first trimester.

Identify nursing intervention during the first trimester.

GLOSSARY   *Corpus luteum:* The ovarian follicle, once the ovum is released; the corpus luteum produces estrogen and progesterone

PRETEST   In the spaces provided, fill in the word or words that best complete(s) the statements. Then turn to page 155 and check your answers.

1. The major task of the first trimester is _____ _____ .

2. Although weight gain during pregnancy varies with individuals, the usual weight gain during the first trimester is _____ .

3. At the time of conception, estrogen and progesterone are secreted by the _____ .

4. During the first trimester, the secretion of estrogen and progesterone is taken over by _____ _____ .

5. The changes in the uterine cells which take place during the first trimester are _____ _____ .

6. Breast changes in the first trimester are due to _____ _____ .

7. During the first trimester, the breasts may secrete a substance that is known as _____ .

8. Fatigue of the mother during the first trimester is caused by_____ _____ _____ _____ .

9. If the mother experiences palpitations during the first trimester, it is considered to be a _____ .

10. The need for caloric intake during the first trimester is directly related to the mother's _____ and _____ .

11. The protein intake of the pregnant adult is _____ _____ . In the pregnant adolescent it is _____ _____ .

12. The mood changes experienced by the mother during the first trimester are due in part to _____ changes.

13. During the first trimester, the father often assumes the _____ and the _____ roles.

14. In order to work through her feelings about the new mother role, the woman must first work through _____ _____ .

15. The man also must deal with role changes due to the pregnancy; he must work through his feelings about _____ _____ .

The period of gestation and the alterations it brings about may be better understood when the cycle is broken down into trimesters. At the end of each of these periods, definite fetal changes have taken place which have produced adaptive responses in the physiological makeup of the mother and, by implication, in the psychosocial aspects of family life.

Generally, *trimesters* can be defined more clearly when they are related to the major tasks that are accomplished by the end of each of these cycles.

During the first trimester, the *major task confronting the family is the acceptance of the pregnancy.* The family experiences joy and anticipation and also the directly opposite feelings of fear, panic, and commitment to a long-term responsibility, thus giving rise to the *ambivalence* experienced at this time. This conflicting interplay of emotions may become another of the many stresses that are to affect both parents as the pregnancy progresses.

The mother usually is the first to suspect that a pregnancy is in progress, and it is, therefore, up to her to seek confirmation. Undoubtedly, being the first to possess this information places her in the *power role,* for she decides if, when, where, and how to tell the father and/or other family members.

Amenorrhea generally is the *first indication* to the mother that she may be pregnant. Once the pregnancy is certain, conflicting feelings arise. With the awareness that a new life has been conceived, the initial parental response is one of pride; the couple may view the event as proof of their virility and fertility.

The task of accepting the reality of the pregnancy becomes further complicated by the fact that few visible physiological changes can be determined. For example, *weight gain* is *minimal,* ranging from *0 to 3 pounds*; it is of interest to note that, at times, in order to prove the existence of the pregnancy, the mother may begin to eat in excess. Although *nausea and vomiting* may be present (a symptom often regarded as positive proof), this lacks the finality of concrete evidence such as the sensation of actual movement of the fetus.

About *50 percent* of all pregnant women experience nausea and vomiting during the first trimester. This is thought to be due partly to hormonal changes and psychological reactions. To alleviate this *common discomfort* of early pregnancy, the mother can be advised to eat dry crackers or toast and jelly before arising and to take small frequent meals of solids, desisting from liquids at mealtime, also limiting fats and increasing **carbo**hydrates in the diet.

The major task of the first trimester is to _____ _____.   **accept the pregnancy**

Nonetheless, this vague pattern of symptoms cannot mask the major physiological alterations that are in progress.

It may be said that the *major changes* beginning to take place are those affecting the *endocrine system.* "The presence of the growing fetus and the hormonal changes of pregnancy are major factors in the mother's physiological adaptive response to her pregnant state."[1]

As the ovum implants, the chorionic villi begin to secrete *chorionic gonadotrophic hormone.* The leuteotrophic activity of this hormone stimulates the *corpus luteum* to secrete *estrogen* and *progesterone*; these hormones are secreted up to the seventh and twelfth weeks of gestation, respectively, by the corpus luteum. At the end of these two periods, the *production* of these *hormones* is taken over completely by the *placenta.*

The high levels of estrogen and progesterone during pregnancy are the cause of one of the first presumptive signs noticed by the mother. This is

_____ .

> amenorrhea

The normal weight gain of the first trimester is usually _____

> 0-3

pounds.

The nausea and vomiting of pregnancy found in about 50 percent of all pregnant women is thought to be due to_____

> increased hormones;

_____ and _____ .

> psychological factors

Amenorrhea, nausea, and weight gain, often interpreted by the mother as positive signs of pregnancy, are in actuality called _____

> presumptive

signs.

The hormone secreted by the chorionic villi found in the urine of pregnant women is the basis for _____ .

> pregnancy tests

This hormone is_____ .

> chorionic gonadotrophin

The corpus luteum is stimulated to secrete_____ and

> estrogen; progesterone; chorionic gonadotrophin

_____ by the_____ .

By the end of the first trimester, the placenta is solely responsible for the secretion of _____ and _____ .

> estrogen; progesterone

The presence of estrogen and progesterone is crucial to the progression and viability of the pregnancy. *Estrogen,* primarily responsible for *uterine changes,* brings about an *increase in the number, size, and weight of uterine cells* and *glands* and in the amount of fluid, protein, and enzyme activity the uterus contains. In addition, this hormone is directly responsible for the typical enlargement of the *female external genitalia* at this time, because of the *increased vascularity* that it produces.

This increased vascularity of the vaginal mucosa is referred to as

_____ .

> Chadwick's sign

Around this time, the cervical mucus glands proliferate, producing a mucus plug that seals off the cervix preventing any infection from entering the uterus.

The growth of the uterus is the primary cause for the common complaint of discomfort associated with the excretion of urine. As the uterus enlarges, it creates pressure on the bladder and stretches the neck of the urethra. This decreases the capacity of the bladder and stimulates nerve endings responsible for urination; as a result, *urgency* and *frequency* occur.

Progesterone, on the other hand, is instrumental in generating the development of *the decidua,* which in turn provides nourishment to the implanted embryo for approximately the first five weeks of gestation. Throughout the pregnancy, this hormone is responsible for depressing *contractability* and *mobility* of the *uterus,* thus being instrumental in preventing ejection of the products of conception.

The concurrent actions of *estrogen* and *progesterone* upon breast tissue are responsible for the changes that affect these glands in preparation for lactation. As with the uterus, these hormones act on the breast by increasing *size, vascularity,* and *glandular secretion* as well as producing skin changes. These alterations become the factors underlying the *common complaint of soreness of the breasts* which is found at this time. *Colostrum,* or the *precursor of milk* in the mother, may be expressed from the breast at this time.

Changes in uterine size and in the number of cells are directly affected by the action of the hormone _____ .

> estrogen

The increased size of the external genitalia is evidence of _____ _____ .

> increased vascularity

Any infection is prevented from traveling up into the uterus by the _____ .

> mucus plug

Frequency is the result of pressure on the bladder and neck of the urethra by _____ .

> the growing uterus

Progesterone is responsible for the development of the lining of the uterus now called _____ .

> decidua

The products of conception are kept within the uterus because of decreased contractability and mobility due to the action of _____ .

> progesterone

The changes in the vascularity and size of the mammary glands are due to the combined effects of _____ and _____ .

> estrogen; progesterone

Colostrum is the _____ .

> precursor of milk

This may be expressed from the breasts beginning early in the _____ .

> first trimester

The high levels of *estrogen* present in the bloodstream stimulate an increase in the secretion of *adrenocorticosteroids* which in turn have the effect of *decreasing basal metabolic activity or rate* (BMR). This is generally thought to be the cause of the diabetogenic effect that may be found in some pregnancies and the source of the feeling of *fatigue* that is so often expressed by pregnant women.

Thus, in early pregnancy, estrogen increases the secretion of _____ causing a decreased _____ .

adrenocorticosteroids;

BMR

Coupled with these alterations of the endocrine system, circulatory changes begin to take place. An increase in blood plasma volume begins at this time, proceeding at a faster rate during the second trimester, slowing somewhat during the third trimester, and reaching its peak several weeks before term. Although the number of erythrocytes present in the circulatory system increases, it is never in direct proportion to the increased levels of blood plasma; thus lower hemoglobin and hematocrit level readings result. Expanding *circulatory volume* coupled with neurosensory changes are the causes of *palpitations,* a frequent symptom at this time.

During the first trimester, there are circulatory changes related to

_____

_____ , an increase that rapidly progresses during the

_____ reaching its peak at a slower

rate by _____ . The number of _____

never increases in direct proportion to _____ ;

this results in low _____ and _____ .

Common symptoms of palpitation are the result of _____

_____ and _____

_____ .

increased blood plasma volume;

second trimester;

term; erythrocytes;

plasma volume;

hematocrit; hemoglobin

expanding circulatory volume;

neurosensory changes

Nutritional requirements during the first trimester have been the subject of intense research. Almost daily, new studies point to health problems being created or eliminated by the presence or absence of certain nutrients. Nevertheless, the evidence regarding nutritional effects on the fetus and the welfare of the pregnancy is inconclusive. Generally, it is felt that need for *caloric intake* is individualized and is determined by the *degree of activity* in which the mother is engaged and by the presence or absence of marked weight gain or loss. However, the need for *protein intake* is markedly *increased* by 10 grams per day because of needs created by the growth and maintenance of the fetus and the formation of maternal tissue such as breast and uterus.

The need for addition of *calcium,* an essential mineral at this time, can be met easily by the consumption of one quart of milk or its equivalent amount of milk products daily, since this particular food item is the best available source of this nutrient.

The nutritional needs of the *pregnant adolescent* at this time, however, require that the intake of *protein* be increased to more than 65 grams per day. The need for a change in carbohydrate and fat intake is directly related to prescribed weight levels. *Calcium* requirements of pregnant adolescents can be met easily by the intake of five glasses of milk or the equivalent per day.

All other nutritional requirements are met if the mother continues to consume adequate daily amounts of the foods in the *basic four food groups*, that is, meats, vegetables and fruits, milk and milk products, and breads and cereals.

The caloric intake of the pregnant woman should be determined and evaluated in terms of her ＿＿＿＿＿＿＿＿＿＿ and ＿＿＿＿＿＿＿＿＿＿ .

weight; activity

Because there is a great increase of cell development, it is necessary for the normal pregnant adult to increase her intake of protein by ＿＿＿＿＿＿ grams per day.

10

Because of her own growth as well as the growth of the fetus, the pregnant adolescent needs a greater amount of ＿＿＿＿＿＿＿＿＿＿ .

protein;

The requirement for calcium per day can be supplied by＿＿＿＿＿＿＿＿

intake of five glasses of milk daily

＿＿＿＿＿＿＿＿＿＿＿＿＿＿＿＿＿＿＿＿＿＿＿＿＿＿＿＿＿＿＿

or its equivalent.

The importance of antepartum care must be communicated and constantly stressed since this has been the most important single factor contributing to the reduction of morbidity and mortality rates. The promotion of maternal-child health begins with early medical assessment and is continued with monthly visits to the antepartal center during the first seven months of gestation. These visits increase in frequency; there are biweekly visits after the seventh month and weekly visits during the ninth month as term approaches.

Antepartum care has contributed significantly to the ＿＿＿＿＿＿＿＿

reduction of morbidity and

＿＿＿＿＿＿＿＿＿＿＿＿＿＿＿＿＿＿＿＿＿＿＿＿＿＿＿＿＿＿＿

mortality rates

＿＿＿＿＿＿＿＿＿＿＿＿ .

This care should begin _____ .

Scheduling of antepartal visits should be _____

_____ during the first seven months then increase to

_____ until the _____

_____ when the visits should be made every _____ .

It is important for the mother to have good and continuing care during the antepartal period. Young women should be encouraged to seek medical confirmation of the pregnancy as soon as they suspect the possibility. It is only through this continuity of care that an appropriate regimen of care and guidance, teaching, and, when needed, appropriate referrals, can be carried out.

The mother who does not attend a prenatal clinic or see her obstetrician may fall into the category of high risk because meaningful symptoms of problems are unrecognized or ignored. It is essential that, during an early visit, the mother be informed of problems that can occur at various times during the pregnancy and that must be reported immediately to a physician. These symptoms are called cardinal danger signs and are:

1. Bleeding from the vagina

2. The escape of fluid from the vagina (this not to be confused with the normal increased vaginal discharge often found during pregnancy)

3. Abdominal pain

4. Dizziness or blurring of vision

5. Chills and elevated temperature

6. Persistent and severe vomiting (not the common nausea and vomiting of early pregnancy)

7. Persistent headache

8. Edema of face and fingers

It is important for a mother to have continuous medical care during her pregnancy. This care includes physical management, _____ ,

_____ , and referrals.

Mothers should be taught the difference between normal discomforts of pregnancy and the _____ .

Signs and symptoms falling under the _____

category are usually referred to as being the cardinal danger signs and include:

1. _____   bleeding from vagina;

2. _____   fluid from vagina;

3. _____   abdominal pain;

4. _____   dizziness or blurring of vision;

_____

5. _____   chills and elevated temperature;

_____

6. _____   persistent severe vomiting;

7. _____   persistent headache;

8. _____   edema of face and hands

In addition to informing the mother about these important symptoms, the nurse should be evaluating the family in order to set realistic long- and short-term goals for their guidance and teaching.

There are many areas that cause concern to parents when they hear confirmation of the pregnancy. Their fears may be influenced by stories that they have heard from friends and relatives. For instance, the woman may have heard that she must not work any longer than the fourth or fifth month of gestation. However, it now is well understood that as long as the *type of employment* does not cause *undue fatigue or strain* and the woman is able to have rest periods, she can continue at her job as long as she is in good health. *Traveling,* too, has often been considered inadvisable. Physicians now feel that *travel is not contraindicated* except near *term* and then only because the woman should be near to her own physician or clinic at this time. If car travel is desired, it is recommended that the woman get out and walk around every hour or so.

Advice about the continuity of employment is dependent upon whether

_____   it causes undue fatigue or strain;

_____ . Traveling is _____   not contraindicated;

except near _____ .   term

Many women ask about *maternity clothes.* In this area women are very lucky. The normal styles are such that there often is no need for this added expense. It is suggested only that the clothing be *comfortable, loose,* and of the weight that is suited to the climate.

Bathing and good hygiene are recommended throughout pregnancy. The mother may notice *changes* in *glandular secretions* which may affect the texture of the skin; this is an increased activity of sebaceous glands. Also there may be increased perspiration. During the last months of pregnancy, the mother's size and altered center of gravity make *tub bathing* awkward; thus sponge baths or showers are recommended at this time.

Women are very surprised to learn that they can continue to participate in all of the *activities* that they did before pregnancy. *Swimming, bowling,* and *gardening* during pregnancy, for instance, are no longer frowned upon. It is only recommended that the activity be stopped *before fatigue occurs.*

Sexual intercourse, in the healthy mother, is not curtailed during the early months of pregnancy. The couple's sexual activity will depend upon the woman's level of desire. This may be different at different times during the pregnancy. It should be carefully explained that *coitus will not cause harm* to the mother or the baby.

Douching, however, should be *refrained from.* It is unnecessary and could cause problems. If there is a normal increased vaginal discharge, the mother should be advised to bathe more frequently. *Cathartics* and *enemas* also are *contraindicated* during pregnancy unless specifically ordered by the physician.

Breast care can begin early in pregnancy. A *good, supporting* bra can help with the discomfort caused by the growing breasts. If the mother intends to breast-feed, she will be advised late in pregnancy how to begin to prepare her breasts for this.

When she asks questions relating to sexual activity, the mother should be told that intercourse is _____ by   not curtailed;

the pregnancy and that coitus _____ cause   will not

harm to the mother or the baby.

Pressure of increased vaginal discharge requires _____   frequent bathing

_____ .

Maternity clothes should be _____   loose and comfortable

_____ .

Activities are carried out as normal and should be limited only when

_____ .   fatigue occurs

Concomitant with these changes, *social* and *psychological adaptations* are required on the part of the mother and father. How the pregnancy is perceived is directly related to the interaction of many factors that eliminate or reinforce old psychological conflicts or even create new ones.

The subtle physiological changes in the woman, as well as the *mood swings* due in part to hormonal alterations, become apparent at this time and often will cause the man to feel at a loss. At first, he may accept the demands made upon him and he will be in the supportive and companionship roles. As this behavior of the woman persists, such acceptance may become a difficult task and tension may arise causing him to wish to abdicate these roles.

The couple's attitudes toward childbearing and rearing are influenced primarily by their early parent-child relationships and experiences. For the woman, the pregnancy brings about readjustments in role and behavior patterns which, up to now, she *did not have to deal with* and which tend to bring into focus her past experiences and relationships with her own mother. It is at this time that she must separate and sort out her past "little girl" role in relation to her mother from her own role as a mother. This, in turn, leads her to incorporate some of the positive aspects of her mother's occupation of the role and eliminate the negative ones. If she has not known a mother, the task of acceptance of her new role may be complicated by fantasies related to the child: she may, for example, transfer to the child all of her emotions related to the absent mother. Lack of resolution of this fantasy may lead to many problems in later years.

For the man, there is the beginning of a recognition of the new role that he will be asked to fulfill. His feelings about the father role are closely identified with his perception of how his father portrayed the role. He must begin to deal with and accept the positive aspects of his father's role occupation and reject the negative aspects in order for him to begin to identify with this role. As he begins to accept the pregnancy as a fact, the stress increases, creating an ambivalence of feelings.

Psychological vacillations due partially to hormonal changes are maternal _____.   mood swings

Because of demands made upon him, the father often must assume the _____ and _____ roles.   supportive; companionship

To achieve the task of the first trimester, the woman must work through her _____.   identification with her mother

To achieve his new role successfully, the father must work through his feelings about his identification with _____.   his father

While the parents-to-be are experiencing these new feelings, their patterns of adaptation also are undergoing change, so that their mutual relationship also must undergo change in order to deal with these new stresses.

Once this major task has been completed successfully in a previous pregnancy, the parents are able to handle it rather quickly during subsequent pregnancies. However, during subsequent pregnancies, they have to work through their feelings about being the parents of more than one child.

In a one-parent family, the mother does not have the support of the father, and the stress of dealing with the feelings alone is greatly magnified. Her feelings of aloneness and often desertion add other problems.

Where there are other children in the family, it is unusual for them to be informed about the pregnancy in the first trimester. However, if the sibling is an adolescent and he or she is informed, many problems may arise. There may be feelings of peer embarrassment, fear of parental rejection, or jealousy. There also may be feelings of acceptance and anticipation or any combination of any of these feelings.

A thorough, sensitive, and objective nursing assessment, which will bring into focus the needs of the family at this time, is essential in assisting families toward the adjustments and adaptations necessary for the acceptance of the reality of the pregnancy.

Through successful utilization of interviewing techniques, the nurse can become a valuable therapeutic agent, aiding family members in the completion of this essential task.

Let us see how one of our family models reacts to the events of the first trimester.

During your antepartal clinic experience, you meet Sandra Cummings and her active two-year-old. She seems delighted to see you and happily tells you about the family's recent move to a three-bedroom house in a new development and about how well her eldest daughter is adapting to the new school. She sheepishly smiles when she tells you that she really didn't intend to be back so soon but thinks she is pregnant. She has just missed her second period and feels nauseated in the morning. You are still with Sandra when the pregnancy report confirms her suspicions.

Sandra smiles and says, "I know I should be happy, but well, I'm not really sure . . . I guess it will work out as soon as I get used to the idea."

In your assessment of Sandra's response you recognize:

A. Sandra is really very depressed over the pregnancy and is rejecting it.

Go to page 152 top.

B. Sandra is verbalizing uncertainty as evidence of the early ambivalence of pregnancy.

Go to page 151 top.

C. Sandra is nonfeeling about the pregnancy and this should be referred to the psychiatric social worker.

Go to page 153 top.

Let us go on. Before Sandra's physical examination, you weigh her; check her blood pressure; and check her urine for sugar and albumin, which is done during each antepartal visit. Sandra looks at the scale and remarks about her 2-pound weight loss. Based on this response, you ask her if her nausea has interfered with her eating. She tells you, "It is pretty bad, but usually passes by late morning. And I have a snack then. It really is hard having to get up and get breakfast for the kids and Jack, you know."

Since you are aware of the need for good nutrition in early pregnancy, your approach would be:

A. "I know how difficult it must be for you, but breakfast is the most important meal of the day. You might try to get your breakfast before the children descend on you or wait until after Jack leaves for work."

Go to page 151 bottom.

B. "I know how difficult it must be for you. You might try some tomato juice to settle your stomach and when the nausea passes, try to be sure to include some of the basic four food groups. This might also be a good time to get in some extra milk in cocoa and protein in bacon and eggs."

Go to page 152 bottom.

C. "It must be hard to fix breakfast for the family when you are feeling so ill. Have you tried a soda cracker before getting out of bed in the morning, followed by small frequent meals that are low in fat and high in sugar content. It is a good idea also to alternate dry foods with liquids."

Go to page 153 bottom.

The next time you meet Sandra in the clinic a month later, you are glad to meet Jack, who has come along to take care of the youngest child while Sandra has her examination. You find yourself talking to Jack in the waiting room while Sandra is having her dental checkup. Jack seems at ease with you and his son, and you soon find yourselves in conversation. You ask, "How are things going at home?" Jack smiles and says, "As hectic as usual." You ask what he means. "Well," he says, "kids running in the back door and out the front, school car pools, diapers, shopping, church activities, and trying to look for another job to supplement my income . . . and besides that, Sandra seems so tired all the time. Is everything all right with her? How come she gets up so many times at night to go to the bathroom? I am really concerned that something might be wrong with her kidneys."

After assessing Jack's reply, which of the following responses would be most appropriate to meet his immediate need?

A. "Sandra's being tired all the time and her need to urinate so often are all normal events at this time and are caused by hormonal changes taking place due to the pregnancy. Both should subside in another three to four weeks. You might be able to remember that this happened with her other pregnancies as well."

Go to page 153 middle.

B. "It must be difficult for you to have to worry about so much happening at home and in addition to have to work two jobs."

Go to page 152 middle.

C. "Don't you remember that these things happened with all the other pregnancies? By the way, have you and Sandra thought about family planning after this baby is born?"

Go to page 151 middle.

Good! You recognized and identified the ambivalence that Sandra verbalized. You also remembered that this is very common and normal in early pregnancy.

Turn to page 149 bottom and continue with the program.

Your response, "Don't you remember . . . ," shows that you have not identified the priority of needs exhibited by Mr. Cummings. By selecting this response, you have not utilized your nursing assessment abilities or your interpersonal relationship techniques. Look at it this way: Aren't you being judgmental? Also, you have assumed that previous experiences are always learning experiences, and in the process of doing so, you may have succeeded in belittling Mr. Cummings and thus cutting off any further communication.

When you return to the situation, listen to what is being said and what is really being asked of you. Then, choose another response from page 150.

Your choice, which recommended breakfast as the most important meal of the day, is not valid in this situation. Although you showed some understanding of Sandra's difficulties, you have not assessed correctly. What are the factors that contributed to Sandra's weight loss and what can you suggest to help?

Return to page 140-144. Review the material and choose another response from page 149.

If you chose, "Sandra is really very depressed . . . ," you did not remember the kinds of feelings that the mother can experience during the first trimester.

Review the material and choose another response from page 149.

———————————————

Although your response, ". . . it must be difficult for you . . . ," indicates your awareness of how situations at home affect family relationships and roles and shows that you have recognized the significance of the husband in relation to the pregnancy, you have not identified the response that would best meet his primary need at this time.

At times it may appear that exploration of feelings is most important, but in communications one must be a good listener if one is to detect the primary concern. As you return to the situation, *listen*. What is Jack asking for?

Return to the situation and choose another response from page 150.

———————————————

Your choice suggesting tomato juice, etc., is incorrect. Your understanding of Sandra's difficulties is good. You recognized that Sandra's nausea is part of her nutritional problem . . . but your guidance is invalid even though you showed awareness of the need for increased protein and calcium.

Return to page 140-144. Review the material and choose another response from page 149.

Your response, "Sandra is nonfeeling...," is incorrect. You have identified Sandra's response as pathological and have made an incorrect assessment. This shows that your understanding of the normal reactions during the first trimester is erroneous.

Return to page 149. Review the material and choose another response.

On selecting the response, "...all are normal events...," you have clearly demonstrated your ability to differentiate between situations requiring a direct explanatory response and those needing further exploration. This is a very good selection, for it indicates that you have acquired a sophistication in clearly assessing a situation and utilizing meaningful approaches.

You also have showed good recognition of the need to make sure that the father knows and understands the normal changes that the mother is experiencing.

Advance to page 154 and take the post-test.

Good assessment of the situation. You gave the mother support by identifying her difficulty. You have assessed Sandra's major problem as nausea. You have intervened appropriately by utilizing information about dietary means of dealing with the nausea of early pregnancy. When this is not effective, antiemetic agents such as Bendectin may be prescribed. It is essential, however, to keep in mind that drugs should be used minimally during pregnancy.

Turn to page 150 and continue with the program.

POST-TEST Indicate whether each statement is true or false by circling the appro**priate le**tter. Then turn to page 155 and check how well you have done.

1. The major task of the first trimester is acceptance of the pregnancy. T F

2. The weight gain during the first trimester should be dependent on the needs of the developing fetus only. T F

3. The chorionic villi secrete estrogen and progesterone beginning at the first week of pregnancy. T F

4. The uterine cells increase both in size and in number. T F

5. The breasts become sore due to the increased vascularity. T F

6. Cardiac palpitations may occur and increase blood volume in pregnancy. T F

7. Fatigue is a normal phenomenon during the first trimester. T F

8. If the mother experiences mood swings, these are always signs of psychiatric problems. T F

9. Nausea and vomiting are uncommon symptoms of pregnancy. T F

10. Amenorrhea, nausea and vomiting, and weight gain are presumptive signs of pregnancy. T F

11. There are no significant changes of nutritional requirements during the first trimester. T F

12. Headache and abdominal pain are symptoms to be expected with any pregnancy. T F

13. The pregnant woman should not continue with any employment after the fifth month of gestation. T F

14. Sexual activity does not have to be curtailed during pregnancy. T F

15. During the first trimester, the expectant couple go through the process of reidentification with their own parents. T F

In the specific areas with which you had difficulty, return to the material and review.

REFERENCES   1. Arthur C. Guyton: *Medical Physiology,* 2d ed., W. B. Saunders Co., Philadelphia, 1964.

BIBLIOGRAPHY   Apgar, Virginia, "What Every Mother-To-Be Should Know," *Today's Health,* Feb. 1966, p. 35 ff.

———, "Drugs in Pregnancy," *The American Journal of Nursing,* Vol. 54, pp. 104-105, March 1965.

Bibring, Gretel, "Recognition of Psychological Stress Often Neglected in OB Care," *Hospital Topics,* Sept. 1966, pp. 100-103.

Clark, Ann, "The Beginning Family," *The American Journal of Nursing,* Vol. 66, pp. 802-805, April 1966.

Colman, Arthur and Libby L. Colman: *Pregnancy, the Psychological Experience,* Herder and Herder, New York, 1971.

Colman, Arthur, "Psychological State During First Pregnancy," *American Journal of Orthopsychiatry,* Vol. 39, pp. 788-797, June 1969.

Guyton, Arthur C.: *Medical Physiology,* 2d ed., W. B. Saunders Co., Philadelphia, 1964.

Horsley, J. S., "The Psychology of Normal Pregnancy," *Nursing Times,* March 25, 1966, p. 400 ff.

Kitlinger, Sheila: *The Experience of Childbirth,* Penguin Books, Harmondsworth, Great Britain, 1967.

Mayer, Jean, "Some Aspects of the Relation of Nutrition and Pregnancy," *Postgraduate Medicine,* Vol. 33, pp. 277-282, March 1963.

Moore, M. L., "The Mother's Changing Needs," *Briefs,* Vol. 32, p. 79, May 1968.

Mowrer, Ernest R., "The Differentiation of Husband and Wife Roles," *Journal of Marriage and the Family,* Vol. 31, p. 539 ff., Aug. 1969.

Meeloo, Joost, "Mental First Aid in Pregnancy and Childbirth," *Child and Family,* Vol. 5, Fall 1966.

Warrick, Louise H., "Femininity, Sexuality and Mothering," *Nursing Forum,* Vol. 8, No. 2, p. 212 ff., 1969.

Williams, Robert E. M.: *Textbook of Endocrinology,* 3d ed., W. B. Saunders Co., Philadelphia, 1965.

PRETEST ANSWERS   1. Acceptance of the pregnancy   2. 0-3 pounds   3. Corpus luteum   4. Chorionic villi of the placenta   5. Increases in the size and number of cells   6. Estrogen and progesterone   7. Colostrum   8. Decreased basal metabolic rate (BMR) as a result of high estrogen levels   9. Normal phenomenon   10. Weight and activity   11. (Increased by) 10 grams per day to 65 grams per day; further increased   12. Hormone   13. Supportive and companionship   14. Identification with her own mother   15. His identification with his father

POST-TEST ANSWERS   1. T   2. F   3. F   4. T   5. T   6. T   7. T   8. F   9. F   10. T   11. F   12. F   13. F   14. T   15. T

CHAPTER THREE

THE PREGNANCY CYCLE DURING THE SECOND TRIMESTER

OBJECTIVES *Identify the major task of the second trimester.*

Identify the major psychological adaptations of the family during the second trimester.

Identify the major maternal physiological changes during the second trimester.

Identify the common discomforts of the second trimester.

Identify the nutritional needs of the mother during the second trimester.

Identify the role changes of the parents during the second trimester.

Identify nursing intervention during the second trimester.

GLOSSARY *Hematenics:* Drugs that contain iron supplements

PRETEST   In the spaces provided, fill in the word or words that best complete(s) the statements. Then turn to page 169 and check your answers.

1. The major task that the parents must accomplish **during the second trimester is**

    _____

    _____ .

2. The psychological response of the woman **during this time is very much involved** with _____ .

3. Sexual desires of the woman may _____ or _____ .

4. Role changes of the father occur in direct relation to _____ .

5. The maternal weight gain during the second trimester is usually about _____ _____ but is dependent upon _____ _____ .

6. The basal metabolic rate _____ during the second trimester.

7. The primary source of the hormones necessary to the maintenance of the pregnancy is the _____ .

8. The term describing the first movement of the fetus felt by the mother is

    _____ .

9. The reddish streaks that may appear on the abdomen, thighs, **and breasts are called** _____ and are due to _____

    _____ .

10. The maternal blood volume during the second trimester _____ .

11. Physiological anemia of the second trimester is due to_____

    _____

    _____

    _____ .

12. The mother may complain of heartburn; this is due to_____

    _____ .

13. Common discomforts of the digestive tract at this time are _____ ,

    _____ , and _____ .

14. Alterations in the urinary system may result in_____ .

15. The vitamins that should be increased by dietary or supplemental means are

    _____ , _____ , _____ , and

    _____ .

16. The mineral being stored in great quantities in this trimester is _____ .

During the second trimester, the couple are confronted with the *task* of having to *define and establish their own roles as parents,* a significant step that is made possible by the fact that it is at this time that the baby is conceptualized as reality as he begins to stir and give positive evidence of his presence.

The quiet months of the second trimester allow for the completion of the tasks that began during the first three months of the pregnancy: the *reidentification of roles* and the resolution of old *conflicts* with the couple's *own parental figures.* Positive characteristics related to the "mother-father" roles are incorporated while those that were identified as negative are eliminated; thus, the couple begin to *identify their future roles* within the family structure in a new light. It may be said that, in effect, new identities are shaped out of old relationships and through a kind of resocialization process based on the remodeling of what the couple perceives as being the ideal parent state.

Although this process may not be quite completed during this time, the importance of its accomplishment before the birth of the baby cannot be diminished if successful adaptation is to be ongoing, for lack of resolution of old conflicts and/or the inability to identify the essential components built into a parent role will present the couple with serious stressors that may affect the family system in later years.

The myriad emotional changes taking place at this time—many of which are sometimes attributed to the various *hormonal alterations* going on within the woman[1]—are reflected in the complexity of her behavior; this, for the most part, tends to leave the man bewildered. As the pregnancy progresses, the *woman becomes increasingly preoccupied with herself* and engages in *constant introspection.* She is subject to *fantasies* related to the fact that for the first time the changes within herself cannot be controlled by her; they are being generated by the still strange creature growing within her. As these events develop, the woman may shift her previous dependence on her mother to the father-to-be. *Dreams* and sudden mood swings, *because of their alien character,* are often perceived as dangerous and frightening. Old wives' tales of "evil eye" become fraught with reality. Pervading the woman's psyche, these feelings and beliefs become sources of the sometimes extravagant demands made on the man to satisfy needs that at other times might have been thought of by the couple as being foolish and superstitious.

The major task for the parents to work through during the second trimester is that of _____   establishing their parental roles

_____ .

The woman's almost complete absorption with herself and her inability to control the many changes occurring within may lead her to _____   dream;

and _____ .   fantasize

At this time she becomes more dependent on _____ .   the father

More and more, the *urgency and frequency of requests* requiring constant indulgence on the part of the man become sources of *stress* which, when not explained to him, may threaten his security as well as the stability of the family life. *Sexual activity* and desires may *vary* and may place the man in the position of having to either increasingly satisfy the woman's drive or adjust to constant rejection. Not understanding the reasons for her behavior and confronted with emotional changes of his own, the man may seek refuge outside of the home. Alternatively, he may sublimate his sexual drive by acquiring a hobby through which he can prove his masculinity.

This latter possibility may serve a twofold purpose, for as well as proving his maleness, the involvement with a new creative activity may serve as a symbolic expression of his childhood fantasies in which he too could be pregnant, while at the same time it gives vent to his feelings of jealousy and frustration at his inability to experience the movement of the new life which he has created.

The psychological impact of the pregnancy on the father at this time is heightened by the *demands in role changes* made upon him, and he may need to redesign and readjust the nature of some of the roles that he has up to now occupied. As the woman's dependency upon him increases, he is placed in situations in which he has to be a *supportive* and understanding companion, having to reassure the woman constantly.

He also may be required to handle tasks that were previously within her domain, such as shopping and housework. In a psychological sense, he may find himself being *stripped* in subtle ways of his *power role,* since all of the couple's activities are increasingly being centered on the woman and dictated by her condition.

Explanation concerning the reasons for the mother's behavioral changes will help to alleviate the father's _____. | stress

Sexual desires on the part of the woman may _____ | increase;

or _____ . | decrease

The father may meet some of his own needs through _____ . | hobbies

The mother's constant need for understanding and reassurance often places the father in a continuing _____ role. | supportive

To the woman, the second trimester becomes a period where perception of *body image* alterations begin to occur. Physiological changes taking place at this time seem to enhance the feeling that the internalized picture of the self no longer matches the reflection in the mirror, and there is a constant *need* to have the *father reassure her* of her beauty and sexual appeal. The abdomen begins to enlarge and there is an additional *weight gain of about 11 pounds* due to the products of conception, some fluid retention, and fat and protein storage.

With the enlargement of the baby, *metabolic rate* is *increased.* This process begins on or around the sixteenth week of gestation and is believed to be due to hyperplasia of the thyroid as the gland is under the influence of estrogen **and** possibly of progesterone.

The usual weight gain during this trimester is _____ .

11 pounds

This weight gain is due to _____ ,

products of conception;

_____ , _____ , _____ .

fluid; fat; protein

As a direct result of fetal growth, the *uterus* continues to *enlarge* and moves into the abdominal cavity, and the *placenta,* the vital life-sustaining organ for the fetus, is at this time *completely functioning* as the primary source of the hormones necessary to maintain the viability of the pregnancy. *Quickening,* or *the first fetal movement felt by the mother,* occurs during this time. As previously stated, it may be said that this event is the first concrete validation for the woman of the reality and individuality of the baby.

The prominent skin changes that are commonly present at this time are thought to be due to hormonal influences. *Striae gravidarum,* the reddish, slightly depressed, irregularly curved streaks that appear in the skin of the abdomen, upper thighs, and buttocks, are the result of the hyperactivity of the adrenal cortex, representing one of the effects of the increased secretion of the adrenocortical hormone during pregnancy.

In addition, there are discolorations and changes of skin pigmentation due to deposits of melanocytes in other areas of the body. The *linea nigra,* or the thin brownish-black line extending from the umbilicus to the symphysis pubis, appears; *chloasma gravidarum,* or the *mask of pregnancy,* distinguished by typical brownish, irregularly shaped blotches of pigment over the cheeks, bridge of nose, or forehead is common.

The areolae, or pigment area around the nipples of the breast, become more deeply pigmented; the *Montgomery follicles,* hypertrophied sebaceous glands scattered throughout the areolae, become more prominent at this time, and the nipples themselves enlarge, becoming deeper in color and more erectile. Striations similar to those present on the abdomen, thighs, and buttocks may develop on the breasts as they too enlarge in preparation for lactation.

Vascular spiders, or small red elevations of the skin which are usually found on the neck, upper chest, and arms, appear at this time. It is thought that these skin changes are due primarily to the high levels of estrogen present in the blood.

These changes of skin pigmentation which are so prominent and common during the second trimester are generally thought to be brought about by the melanocyte-stimulating effect of estrogen and progesterone. With the exception of the striae, which may become silvery in color, they usually disappear.

Quickening is _____ the first fetal movement felt by

_____ . mother

Hyperactivity of the adrenal cortex is thought to cause the skin change

called _____ striae gravidarum

Other skin changes that occur during this trimester are _____ , chloasma;

_____ , _____ vascular spiders; linea

_____ and _____ nigra; deeper areola pigmentation

_____ .

Should a mother show concern about these skin changes, she could be

told that they all will disappear except the _____ striae gravidarum

_____ .

Circulatory changes that began to occur during the *first* trimester

continue, with significant and rapid expansion of _____ blood plasma;

_____ volume followed by a lower hemoglobin. A lower

hemoglobin is due to the fact that the _____ do not erythrocytes

increase in direct proportion to the increased volume of plasma. A hemo-

globin count of 11 grams or above is considered adequate at this time.

The volume of circulating erythrocytes is one cause of the increased
demand for iron in the woman's diet. It is important to note that iron
requirements during a normal pregnancy not only are dictated by maternal
needs but also are based on the fixed *iron demands of the fetus*. The high
level of iron needed at this time can be supplied easily by adequate dietary
intake of meats and by supplemental chemotherapeutic addition of any of
the hematenics commonly used.

The changes that occur in the circulatory system during the second

trimester are due to the increase in _____ plasma volume;

and _____ . erythrocytes

This alteration sometimes has the effect of lowering the mother's

_____ . hemoglobin

It is necessary, therefore, to increase the mother's intake of _____ . iron

A hemoglobin level of 11 grams is considered to be _____ normal

at this time.

Concomitantly, changes in the digestive system become sources of discomfort to the mother. As the uterus rises into the abdominal cavity, the stomach and intestines are displaced. Gastric secretion and intestinal motility are altered, and it is thought that some women experience a decrease in the secretion of hydrochloric acid as well, prolonging the emptying time of the stomach. Mothers' common complaint of *heartburn* usually is the result of the rebound of acid secretions into the lower portion of the esophagus and of the altered position of the stomach. Because of these digestive difficulties, it should be recommended that the pregnant woman avoid fatty, fried, and highly spiced foods in her daily diet. Also, lying down immediately after meals should be discouraged.

The large amounts of progesterone secreted by the placenta produce a generalized relaxation of the smooth muscles of the intestinal tract, altering muscle tone and peristaltic activity and thus the frequency of emptying time of intestinal contents. These events lead to the common complaints of *constipation* and *flatulence.* Such conditions can be alleviated somewhat by diet and activity. No cathartics should be used unless prescribed.

The rise of the uterus into the abdominal cavity causes discomfort by displacing the _____ and _____ .   stomach; intestines

The delayed emptying of the stomach contents and the reverse peristalsis result in the common complaint of _____ .   heartburn

Constipation and flatulence are due to the altered intestinal _____   tone;
and _____ .   peristalsis

Alterations affecting the urinary system are related primarily to the increased blood volume being filtered by the kidneys. *Glycosuria* may be present due to hormonal activity preventing the *reabsorption of glucose* by the kidney tubules. In addition, the effects of the pressure exerted on the kidneys by the pregnant uterus and the effects of high levels of progesterone seem to be the factors producing dilatation of the ureters, thus being the frequent causes of the urinary stasis that may be found at this time, and thus affecting urinary output. This situation often results in urinary tract infections such as cystitis.

Glycosuria during pregnancy may be due to lowered _____   kidney reabsorption
_____ .

Ureteral dilatation and decreased muscle tone result in urinary _____ and may be a cause of increased _____   stasis; urinary tract
_____ .   infections

The calorie intake during the second trimester usually is *increased* by

200 calories over the normal average requirement for the nonpregnant adult. Women who are less active, however, may require no increase whereas more active ones may need a greater caloric intake. This points to the fact that the rate of weight gain should be the indicator used in estimating the number of calories that can be consumed.

The pregnant teen-ager, on the other hand, may require an increase of up to 400 calories over the normal requirements for this age group. Again, however, weight gain and the quality of the individual's nutritional pattern should be the criteria guiding estimates of caloric needs.

Other important nutrients that need to be considered are *vitamin A,* usually increased to 6,000 units; thiamine, needing to be increased to 1.0 grams; riboflavin, increased to 1.6 grams; niacin, increased up to 17 milligrams in pregnant adults and up to 18 milligrams for pregnant adolescents. *Ascorbic acid,* playing a vital role in tissue structure, needs to be increased to 100 milligrams. Vitamin C is extremely important at this time for both maternal and fetal welfare. In addition, it assists in overcoming the hyperemic, hemorrhagic conditions affecting the mother's gums at this time. Finally, the needs for vitamin D are easily met with the recommended consumption of milk each day.

Needs for *protein* and *calcium* are continuously being met by the consistent intake of milk that began during the first trimester. The importance of calcium for the development of fetal skeletal structure is to be stressed, particularly with mothers who may have difficulty drinking the recommended amounts of milk. It is important to clarify the misconceptions that a tooth is lost for each baby.

It will be noted that, at this time the amount of iron supplied by dietary intake seems to be insufficient to meet the demands imposed by the pregnancy, so that, as previously stated, supplemental iron may be needed in the form of hematenics.

As previously stated, *iron* is a most essential mineral that begins to be stored in great quantities at this time; therefore it is necessary that its intake be increased to 18 milligrams per day in order to meet the _____ | fixed iron demands;

_____ of the fetus and the |

needs created by increased _____ . | blood volume

Adequate, well-planned nutritional intake is crucial if the needs of both the fetus and the mother are to be met. Careful attention should be given to dietary patterns of mothers during the second trimester, since it is at this time that the greatest rate of growth occurs.

Nutritionally, the mother's calorie intake is dictated by her _____ , | age;

_____ , and _____ . | weight; activity

Vitamin C should be increased in the mother's diet as it is necessary for the development and maintenance of _____ and _____ tissues.

maternal; fetal

The daily requirement for vitamin D in the mother's diet can be met by her consumption of _____ or its equivalent.

one quart of milk

Calcium is needed for the development of the _____ _____ .

fetal skeleton

It may be necessary for the mother to supplement her dietary iron intake with a _____ .

hematenic

The second trimester, devoid of all of the earlier physical discomforts, and with its validation of the presence of a new, unique life in the process of growing yet not imminent in its arrival, provides the couple with a quiet period during which they may reevaluate their life-styles. They must adjust themselves to changes in roles and prepare for the coming event, adapting, it is hoped, to the various stressors that appear in the form of the many psychological, physiological, and social alterations that a pregnancy brings about.

In the following situation, Bill and Jean Garry arrive at Dr. Franklin's office on time for one of Jean's antepartum checkups. While she is changing into an examination gown, you approach Bill and ask, "How is the prospective father doing?" to which he replies, "I guess all right . . . although a little confused at times. At the beginning Jean and I talked to each other a lot about her being pregnant, but lately it sometimes seems like she is preoccupied with herself and seems to be far away. Other times I can't seem to be able to keep up with all of the things she wants me to do."

You respond by saying, "You must be really busy."

Bill answers, "Yes, I really keep hopping and I have just completed my new darkroom, too, and am beginning to develop my own prints."

From Bill's response you identify:

A. That Bill is very unsure about wanting the baby and now wishes that it wasn't so because he would rather be involved with his photography and darkroom.

Go to page 166.

B. That Bill is unsure about this new change in Jean and the extent to which he has to assume the supportive role. He is looking for explanations and support.

Go to page 167.

C. That Bill is upset with all of this strange behavior of Jean's and really wants you to talk to her and explain that pregnancy is normal and that this erratic behavior is uncalled for.

Go to page 165.

If you have identified Bill's asking you to talk to Jean about her erratic behavior, you really missed the point of Bill's remarks. You were able to see that Bill is concerned about Jean's behavior but you did not sort out the rest of what he was saying. You do not seem able to identify normal psychological changes that occur during the second trimester.

Return to pages 158 and 164. Review the material and choose another response.

If you chose *A*, "That Bill is very unsure . . . ," you misinterpreted the feeling that Bill was verbalizing. He did not give any indication that he wishes they weren't going to have a baby.

Return to pages 158 and 164. Review the normal psychological changes of the second trimester, then reread the situation and see if you can identify what Bill is really asking of you.

By choosing *B*, you have shown that you are able to identify Bill's primary need: that of explanation and support. You have seen the need for explanation of the normal maternal psychological changes of the second trimester and for support that he is being a good husband. You also may have identified Bill's hobby as being an important creative outlet for him at this time.

Advance to page 168 and take the post-test.

POST-TEST Indicate whether each statement is true or false by circling the appropriate letter. Then turn to page 169 and check how well you have done.

1. The parents' task of the second trimester is to identify their own roles.   T   F

2. During this time, the mother becomes quite involved with others.   T   F

3. Dreams and fantasies often are sources of maternal fears during this trimester.   T   F

4. Sexual activity always is diminished at this time.   T   F

5. During this trimester the father's role in relationship to the mother's remains static.   T   F

6. The mother's weight gain at this time is entirely due to excessive eating.   T   F

7. During this trimester the placenta functions as the main source of hormones.   T   F

8. Chloasma gravidarum are the brown lines extending from the umbilicus to the symphysis pubis.   T   F

9. All maternal skin changes are permanent and cannot be reversed.   T   F

10. A hemoglobin of 11.5 is considered abnormal during pregnancy.   T   F

11. Hematenics may be prescribed as supplements to dietary iron intake.   T   F

12. Heartburn is a common complaint of the second trimester.   T   F

13. Cathartics always are used to relieve constipation caused by hormonal action on the bowel.   T   F

14. Urinary stasis results from ureteral dilatation.   T   F

15. An increased intake of calcium by the mother is needed for fetal skeletal development.   T   F

16. Dental caries may result when the fetus depletes maternal calcium storages.   T   F

In the specific areas with which you had difficulty, return to the material and review.

REFERENCES   1. Arthur Coleman and Libby Coleman: *Pregnancy, the Psychological Experience,* Herder and Herder, New York, 1971, p. 10.

BIBLIOGRAPHY   Colman, Arthur and Libby Colman: *Pregnancy, the Psychological Experience,* Herder and Herder, New York, 1971.

Cooper, Lenna F., et al.: *Nutrition in Health and Disease,* 14th ed., J. B. Lippincott, Philadelphia, 1963, Chaps. 10, 11, and 12.

Davis, Edward M. and Reva Rubin: *DeLee's Obstetrics for Nurses,* 18th ed., W. B. Saunders Co., Philadelphia, 1966.

Deutsch, Helene: *The Psychology of Women—Volume II, Motherhood,* Grune and Stratton, New York, 1945.

Down, Florence, "Maternal Stress in Primigravidas As a Factor in the Production of Neonatal Pathology," *Nursing Science,* Vol. 2, p. 348 ff., Oct. 1964.

Hellman, Louis and Jack Pritchard: *Williams' Obstetrics,* 14th ed., Appleton-Century-Crofts, New York, 1971.

Kitzinger, Sheila: *An Approach to Antenatal Teaching,* National Childbirth Trust, London, 1968.

Meek, Lucille, "Maternal Emotions and Their Implications in Nursing," *R.N.,* Vol. 32, pp. 38-39, April 1969.

Rubin, Reva, "Basic Maternal Behavior," *Nursing Outlook,* Vol. 9, p. 683 ff., Nov. 1961.

———, "The Cognitive Style of Pregnancy," *American Journal of Nursing,* Vol. 70, p. 502, March 1970.

Stone, Anthony R., "Cues to Interpersonal Distress Due to Pregnancy," *American Journal of Nursing,* Vol. 65, p. 88 ff., Nov. 1965.

PRETEST ANSWERS   1. Identification of their own parental role   2. Herself   3. Increase; decrease   4. The mother's changes   5. 11 pounds; diet, activity, and previous weight   6. Increases   7. Placenta   8. Quickening   9. Striae gravidarum; hormonal influences   10. Increases   11. Increase of blood plasma greater than the increase in red blood cells   12. Reflux of gastric contents   13. Constipation, heartburn, and flatulence   14. Cystitis   15. Vitamins A, B, C, and D   16. Iron

POST-TEST ANSWERS   1. T   2. F   3. T   4. F   5. F   6. F   7. T   8. F   9. F   10. F   11. T   12. T   13. F   14. T   15. T   16. F

CHAPTER FOUR

THE PREGNANCY CYCLE DURING THE THIRD TRIMESTER

OBJECTIVES *Identify the three major tasks of the third trimester.*

Identify the major psychological adaptations of the family during the third trimester.

Identify the major maternal physiological changes during the third trimester.

Identify the seven major discomforts of the third trimester.

Identify role changes of the parents during the third trimester.

Identify nursing intervention during the third trimester.

PRETEST   In the spaces provided, fill in the word or words that best complete(s) the statements. Then turn to page 182 and check your answers.

1. The three main tasks to be accomplished during the third trimester are _____
    _____
    _____ , _____
    _____ ,
    and _____
    _____ .

2. **As the expected day of confinement becomes imminent, the couple experience** feelings of _____ and _____ .

3. The roles that the couple share during this time are the _____ and _____ roles.

4. The usual weight gain during the third trimester is _____ **pounds.**

5. Maternal dyspnea during the third trimester is caused by _____
    _____ .

6. The blood volume is greatest between the _____ and _____ weeks.

7. Hypotensive syndrome is due to _____
    _____ .

8. In the primigravida, the fetus moves down into the true pelvis about the _____
    _____ week; this is known as _____ .

9. Frequency reoccurs during the third trimester because of _____
    _____ .

10. Hemorrhoids and varicosities often occur at this time because of _____
    _____
    _____ .

11. The softening of the fibrocartilage in the pelvic articulations is one of the causes of the mother's _____ .

It has been said that the third and last trimester is the "climax of the pregnancy 'trip' "[1] The reality of the baby is inescapable, and the couple at this time feel pride, joy, fulfillment, and expectation, at times counterbalanced by fears, anxieties, and anticipation of the approaching unknown events of delivery.

To the couple this is a period when important tasks such as *acceptance of bodily and psychological image changes, acceptance of the reality of the baby,* and *preparation for the advent of a new family member* must be accomplished.

To the woman, this is an increasingly anxious and uncomfortable stage; yet frustrations and annoyances stemming from the effects that a now quite rapidly growing fetus has on her body seem to be balanced by the special prerogatives with which her pregnant state has invested her. Clearly in a *dominant position and therefore in the power role,* she relishes the little special attentions bestowed upon her.

As the expected date of delivery nears, *fears* and *anxieties* related to the *well-being* of the *baby* and of *herself* begin to emerge. More and more, thoughts related to the unknown events of labor and delivery and to the effects that the culmination of the pregnancy will have on the adaptive resources of the couple occupy their time and conversation. Indeed, there are important things for which to prepare during these last three months.

The three major tasks of the third trimester are _____   accepting image changes;

_____ , _____   accepting baby as a reality;

_____ , and   preparing for the new member

_____ .

During the third trimester, the mother is in a _____   power
role.

The fears and anxieties now experienced by the mother are concerned with _____ and with the _____ .   herself; baby

During this stage, the couple's main concern is the baby. Final preparations for its advent into the family are being made. The fascinating topic of naming it represents the couple's final struggle to accept its reality as an individual; thus the naming of the baby is an activity that serves the important function of helping the family prepare for the new arrival.[2]

The anxieties and other feelings toward the unknown events assist the couple in *sharing* and working together to meet the challenge that will soon be foisted upon them. Emerging from the intense, at times separate, reveries of their inner worlds, they now seek each other to provide practical solutions to the potential difficulties of labor and delivery. The *sharing* of the *com-*

panionship and supportive roles at this time becomes a primary source of strength to the couple.

The many visible physiological alterations that have been ongoing give added support to the woman's feeling that her body has altered greatly from her perception of herself during her prepregnancy state. With an additional weight gain of 11 pounds and an increased amount of fluid retention of still another 2 to 3 liters, the woman's body has grown even larger and more cumbersome. The changes taking place are contemplated, at times, in almost disbelief. To the man, they may represent the pride of knowing that the awkward figure who is his companion is carrying the proof of his masculinity, or, strongly reacting to the visible alterations, he may be repelled by the large proportions of the abdomen and swollen breasts.

To the woman, her disproportionate figure leads her to the belief that she is carrying more than one baby, adding to the fears and anxieties generated by the nearing expected date of delivery.

Evidence of their acceptance of the baby as an individual is shown by the parents when they select _____.

a name

During the third trimester, the support and companionship roles are

_____.

shared

The mother's ability to accept her changes in bodily appearance accomplishes the task of _____

acceptance of body image

_____.

The husband may see the changes in his wife's body as proof of his

_____.

masculinity

The now quite voluminous uterus places pressure on the diaphragm, abdominal organs, and ribs, widening the thoracic cage and giving rise to dyspneic episodes when the mother is supine. These discomforts, coupled with increased fetal activity, are often the factors responsible for mothers' common complaints of *insomnia*.

During this trimester, circulatory changes related to increased plasma volume reach their peak and seem to level off. The heart, which has become quite enlarged because of the demands made upon its capacity by the increased volume of blood plasma it has had to handle, is displaced upward and to the left and has been caused to shift anteriorly by the added pressure of the uterus. Blood volume, which was greatest during the twenty-fifth to thirty-seventh weeks of gestation, diminishes around the thirty-eighth to fortieth weeks. During this trimester, the mother should be prevented from assuming a supine position since it produces arterial changes in maternal circulation leading to the development of *hypotensive syndrome.*

The now quite enlarged uterus consistently compresses the return venous system, the inferior vena cava, thus reducing cardiac filling and decreasing cardiac output. In addition, the uterine pressure on the aorta produces significant changes in arterial pressure; in the presence of this systemic hypotension, uterine arterial pressure is markedly decreased; thus, lying on the back could prove to have quite deleterious effects on both the mother and the baby.

Insomnia of the third trimester may be caused by _____ and _____ .

> dyspnea; fetal movements

Because of the increased blood volume and diaphragmatic changes, the heart is displaced _____ _____ .

> upward and to the left

The increased blood volume of the twenty-fifth to thirty-seventh weeks at the thirty-eighth week begins to _____ .

> diminish

Hypotensive syndrome can be precipitated if the mother is placed in a _____ .

> supine position

On or about the thirty-sixth week of gestation, *lightening,* or the descent of the fetal head into the pelvic inlet, occurs in a majority of primigravidas, thus relieving some of the dyspnea.

As pressure is added, the bladder becomes displaced and irritated and *frequency* and *urgency* of urination appear. The dropping of the enlarged pregnant uterus produces pressure on the pelvic organs and thus on the hemorrhoidal veins, causing obstruction of venous return which in turn occasionally produces *hemorrhoids,* which may become painful. These, however, soon disappear, and they become asymptomatic after delivery. Application of soothing ointments and warm compresses may be suggested as means of overcoming the hemorrhoids.

Lightening, which occurs in the primigravida during the last month of pregnancy, happens when _____ _____ .

> the fetus moves into the true pelvis

Increased pressure of the pregnant uterus on the bladder and on the venous system causes _____ , _____ , and _____ .

> frequency; urgency; hemorrhoids

Occasionally, *varicosities* of the lower extremities may appear and may become prominent as the pregnancy progresses. The pressure of an enlarged pregnant uterus on the pelvic veins, together with reduced efficiency of venous return during advanced pregnancy stages, cause interference with circulatory processes, thus producing stasis of blood in the lower extremities. These events also contribute to the development of the dependent edema frequently found at this time. Weight increases and prolonged standing may exaggerate these conditions. These symptoms may be alleviated by encouraging periodic elevation of the legs, elimination of constriction created by external sources such as clothing, and periods of rest.

Stasis of blood in the lower extremities may cause the mother to develop _____ and _____ .

edema; varicosities

Dependent edema of the lower extremities is due to _____ _____ .

pressure on the pelvic veins

Added weight and _____ aggravate this condition.

prolonged standing

Guidance to alleviate these circulatory problems should include instructions about _____ , _____ , and _____ .

clothing; elevating legs; resting at frequent periods

Added sources of discomfort are the *back and pelvic* aches that become more prominent during this trimester as a result of the softening of the sacroiliac and pelvic joints; these complaints may become aggravated following excessive weight lifting, bending, or exercise. Normally, these discomforts may be alleviated by wearing a light maternity girdle and by eliminating undue strain and fatigue. Alternating periods of rest and sleep with exercise should be encouraged at this time.

The third trimester of pregnancy presents the couple with the need to modify previous patterns of sexual behavior, and their physician will advise them of any need to abstain from sexual intercourse during the last three weeks of gestation.

As the inevitable climax of delivery nears, the woman may begin to wish for the signs of labor. The mild, intermittent, spontaneous uterine contractions known as "Braxton-Hicks" are accentuated and add to the sense of imminence experienced by the woman, prompting her to seek constant reassurance from the man regarding plans and preparations for their trip to the hospital.

The more prominent back and pelvic discomfort of the third trimester is due to _____ as well as to weight gain and excessive _____ .

softening of the joints; exercise

In the last weeks the couple's sexual activity may be _____

Braxton-Hicks contractions are _____ and

_____ tightening and relaxing of the uterine muscles.

The imminence of delivery may cause the woman to demand reassurance from the father about his plans for _____

_____ .

modified

mild;

intermittent

going to the hospital

The end of the third trimester is the culmination of the pregnancy experience. Psychologically, it has served the woman in preparing her to separate physiologically from the baby by giving birth, and it has aided the man in readying his adaptive responses for the new responsibilities of fatherhood. If this is the first child, it has aided the couple in understanding the changes that their relationship will undergo as a new member is added to the family.

For the multiple family, the new baby is generally a source of excitement; other children in the family anxiously await the arrival of a new "little brother or sister," each of them having his own expectations, feelings, and plans regarding the meaning and impact of this event.

Now let us see how two families experience the events of the third trimester.

Sandra Cummings arrives at the antepartum clinic for her scheduled visit. She is in her eighth month of pregnancy and, as you interview her, she tells you that she is "getting tired of the whole thing; sometimes I get the feeling that I am going to be pregnant for the rest of my life; none of my clothes fit me anymore and Jack says he won't let me buy new dresses until I lose all of this weight. I guess my figure doesn't resemble the girl he married."

Which of the following choices best illustrates what is going on with Sandra and Jack?

A. Sandra and Jack seem to be arguing over financial expenses.

B. She is rejecting the baby; this is an abnormal process at this time particularly since she has had previous pregnancies.

C. The couple is having difficulty accepting body image alterations.

Go to page 178 top.

Go to page 179 middle.

Go to page 180 top.

The physical examination reveals Sandra's and the baby's health statuses to be good. A clinic appointment is made for two weeks hence.

Sandra is 15 minutes late for her next appointment; she is accompanied by Jack, who apologetically tells you that they had gone on a shopping spree during which Sandra bought a new maternity outfit and cosmetics to be used during her hospital stay and they both chose and bought a new bassinet and completed the baby's layette. Indeed, the couple seem to be glowing over their achievements of this day and to be quite excited over Jack's creativity in designing and furnishing the new nursery in their recently bought home.

You recognize that both Jack and Sandra have done much in accepting body image changes brought about by the pregnancy. Their interaction of today reveals that another major task of the third trimester has been accomplished.

Which of the following choices identifies this task?

A. Preparing for the baby's arrival

Go to page 178 middle.

B. Adjusting to parental role changes

Go to page 180 middle.

C. Accepting the reality of the pregnancy

Go to page 179 top.

The next situation deals with Bill and Jean Garry. If you recall, Jean has been under the care of her private obstetrician, Dr. Franklin. She is in her thirty-sixth week of pregnancy and therefore is making weekly prenatal visits.

As you greet her, you notice that she looks tired and that there are deep circles under her eyes. When you inquire how she has been doing during the past week, she tells you that she has not been sleeping very well; she finds it difficult to breathe easily while in bed and, once awake, she begins to wonder about what labor and delivery will be like.

Based on the preceding situation, your plan of nursing intervention to meet Jean's needs would include which of the following choices?

A. Providing information relating to the importance of sleep at this time and suggesting that taking short naps in the afternoon would be helpful.

Go to page 179 bottom.

B. Providing information that will clarify to Jean the fact that shortness of breath is quite common with lying flat on the bed; suggesting that sleeping on several pillows frequently helps; allowing for expression of feelings and concerns regarding labor and delivery.

Go to page 178 bottom.

C. Giving guidance about the amount of daily exercise that will help her sleep better; teaching Jean how to deep-breathe; providing reassurance that she has nothing to fear about the normal processes of labor and delivery.

Go to page 180 bottom.

In choosing *A,* you said that Sandra and Jack were arguing. Is this the major theme? Is Jack's limiting the purchase of new dresses related to financial difficulties or is it communicating something else?

Return to page 173. Review the material and choose another response from page 176.

Excellent! Your identification of choice *A* as the task that has been completed indicates that you remember the importance of accepting and preparing for the arrival of a new member into the family.

Turn to page 177 and continue with the program.

In selecting statement *B,* you have evidenced ability to carry out accurate assessment of Jean's needs and at the same time institute therapeutic nursing intervention. Not only have you been able to allay fears and anxieties that may be related to the fact that she is not able to breathe easily, but also you are suggesting how she may remedy the problem. Also, you have addressed yourself to what seems to be another of Jean's main concerns at this time: her fears and anxieties related to what will be occurring during labor and delivery. By allowing her to express herself, you are opening additional channels of communication whereby she may be able to identify the particular concerns and worries that are affecting her, and thus you will be able to provide additional guidance.

Advance to page 181 and take the post-test.

Your choice of statement *C,* "accepting the reality of the pregnancy," is wrong. This is a very early task of pregnancy which obviously has been accomplished by the couple because they have been involved in activities that have indicated their acceptance of the reality of the baby.

Return to page 172. Review the material and choose another response from page 177.

In choosing statement *B,* you have said that Sandra is rejecting the baby in spite of the fact that she has gone through this process twice before. Your interpretation is wrong. Can you think why? Isn't it quite normal at this time for a woman to be tired of the pregnancy? Does that in itself imply that Sandra is *rejecting* the baby?

Return to page 173. Review the material and choose another response from page 176.

Choice *A,* "providing information about the importance of sleep," although always useful, is not the best possible approach to meeting Jean's needs at this time. This information is not addressing itself to what seems to be the major difficulty. You have not made an accurate assessment of the problem; thus your intervention measures are not therapeutic.

Return to page 177. Examine the situation more carefully and choose again. You may need to review content relating to the needs that appear during this trimester.

The selection of statement *C* is quite correct. You have been able to identify the fact that at this time the couple is dealing with the acceptance of major body image alterations that seem to be taking place at a very rapid pace during this time. It is important that Sandra and Jack be assisted in completing this major task of the third trimester so that your nursing intervention measures should be geared toward providing them with support and continue to allow them to express their feelings at this time.

Turn to page 176 bottom and continue with the program.

In choosing *B,* that is, "adjusting to parental role changes," as being the task that has been accomplished, you have forgotten that this was a step that should have begun at the end of the first trimester and should have been completed during the second trimester. Although it is true that role changes and adjustments occur throughout the pregnancy and even after the new member has arrived, this is not a major task of this stage in Sandra's pregnancy.

Return to page 172. Review the material and choose another response on page 176.

In choosing statement *C,* you have not identified the specific needs Jean has expressed; in fact, have you really *listened* to her? First, by telling Jean that exercises will enable her to sleep better, you are acting under false assumptions. Second, although teaching deep breathing may be a part of prenatal instruction, it is not done to relieve the discomforts of which Jean is complaining. Finally, you are falsely reassuring her that there will be no complications during labor and delivery, while at the same time you are denying her feelings and thus closing any further means of communications with her.

Return to page 177. Reexamine the situation more carefully and choose another response. You may need to review the content relating to the needs that appear during this trimester as well as the type of nursing intervention measures that must be instituted when problems arise.

POST-TEST Indicate whether each statement is true or false by circling the appropriate letter. Then turn to page 182 and check how well you have done.

1. The only task the expectant couple must achieve during the third trimester is the acceptance of the reality of the baby. T F

2. During this time, the mother assumes the power role. T F

3. The primary sources of normal fears and anxieties experienced at this time relate to the couple's relationship. T F

4. The responsibility for the accomplishment of the tasks during this trimester rests primarily with the mother. T F

5. During this time, the father may react either negatively or positively to bodily changes taking place in the mother. T F

6. Fetal activity often results in maternal insomnia at this time. T F

7. The supine position is the most comfortable resting position for the mother at this time. T F

8. If the mother develops urgency or frequency, this is a sign of flatulence. T F

9. Lightening occurs when the fetus drops into the true pelvis. T F

10. Dependent edema of the lower extremities is a dangerous sign. T F

In the specific areas with which you had difficulty, return to the material and review.

REFERENCES   1. Arthur Colman and Libby Colman: *Pregnancy, the Psychological Experience,* Herder and Herder, New York, 1971, p. 51.

BIBLIOGRAPHY   Caplan, Gerald C.: *Concepts of Mental Health and Consultation: Their Application in Public Health Social Work,* U.S. Children's Bureau, Washington, D.C., 1959.

Colman, Arthur and Libby Colman: *Pregnancy, the Psychological Experience,* Herder and Herder, New York, 1971.

Fitzpatrick, Elise and J. Eastman Nicholson: *Obstetrics for Nurses,* 19th ed., J. B. Lippincott Co., Philadelphia, 1960.

Flanagan, Geraldine L.: *The First Nine Months of Life,* Simon and Schuster, New York, 1962.

Hellman, Louis M. and Jack Pritchard: *Williams' Obstetrics,* 14th ed., Appleton-Century-Crofts, New York, 1971.

Wiedenbach, Ernestine: *Family-Centered Maternity Nursing,* 2d ed., G. P. Putnam's Sons, New York, 1967.

PRETEST ANSWERS   1. Acceptance of psychological and body image changes; acceptance of the reality of the baby; preparation for the arrival of the baby   2. Anticipation and fear   3. Companionship and supportive   4. 11   5. Pressure of the fundus on the diaphragm   6. Twenty-fifth and thirty-seventh   7. Pressure on the inferior vena cava   8. Thirty-sixth; lightening   9. Pressure of the uterus on the bladder   10. Decreased venous return due to pressure on the pelvic vessels   11. Backache

POST-TEST ANSWERS   1. F   2. T   3. F   4. F   5. T   6. T   7. F   8. F
9. T   10. F

CHAPTER FIVE
CHILDBIRTH EDUCATION

OBJECTIVES   *Identify the need for childbirth education.*

Identify the five factors influencing the perception and response to pain.

Identify the main characteristics of the Read and Lamaze methods of childbirth education.

Identify the two objectives of childbirth education.

Identify the nursing assessment of the needs of the family in relation to childbirth education.

PRETEST   In the spaces provided fill in the word or words that best complete(s) the statements. Then turn to page 189 and check your answers.

1. The need met by childbirth education is _____

    _____ .

2. Five factors that can influence the perception of pain are: _____ ,

    _____ ,

    _____ , _____ ,

    and _____ .

3. The Read and Lamaze methods of childbirth education provide_____

    and _____ and _____

    _____ .

4. The objectives of childbirth education are to _____

    _____ and _____ .

5. Classes in childbirth education provide information about _____

    _____ , _____

    _____ , _____ ,

    _____ , _____ , _____

Throughout the centuries, women have been taught to think of their destiny in terms of their future roles as mothers and thus to look forward to the unique experience of giving birth. Surrounding these expectations, however, is the mythology created by old wives' tales, misinformation, and gross exaggerations. Birth often is depicted as a terrible ordeal soon to be forgotton once the newborn is held. Even in modern times these ideas continue to receive reinforcement from literary works, cinema, television, and stage productions. The fantasies related to parturition become stressors that heighten the degree of stress (normally brought about by the pregnancy) that results from the many complex alterations taking place within the family.

This preconditioning often makes labor and delivery more difficult and fearful. But these effects often can be alleviated by providing accurate information about the childbirth process. This is the basis of childbirth education programs.

The subject of pain has been the topic of continued scientific research and investigation. *Pain* produces *stress,* which affects the whole homeodynamic system's functioning. A painful stimulus such as boiling water spilled on your finger produces a strong stimulus that travels from the periphery to the central nervous system where the message is analyzed by the *sensory discrimination system* and a reaction is initiated, such as pulling your finger away from the source of the boiling water.

The system responsible for minimizing or maximizing the response to a stimulus is the *motivational affective system.* It has been demonstrated that the interpretations of and reactions to pain can be altered. Thus, the painful stimulus may be ignored, as often occurs when an athlete playing hockey is injured in the leg and continues to play without perceiving the painful stimulus. The opposite response may occur when a young child falls and skins his knee and becomes almost overwhelmed by the painful stimulus.

The preceding examples illustrate that the psychological processes underlying the motivational affective system can influence the perception of pain. In the first example, there was an *altered focus of attention*—on winning rather than on the painful stimulus. Interpretations of and responses to painful stimuli are altered also by *learned behavior or conditioning.* Other psychological factors that can affect the perception of stimuli are: *social expectations, fear and anxiety,* and the feeling of *aloneness and isolation.*

Pain affects the _____   whole homeodynamic system's
_____ .   functioning

The type and source of the painful stimulus is identified by the _____ system.   sensory discrimination

The motivational affective system either _____ or   minimizes;
_____ the response to the stimulus.   maximizes

Some of the factors responsible for altering the perception of pain are:

_____ , _____ ,

_____ , _____ ,

and _____ .

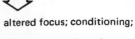

altered focus; conditioning;

social expectations; fear;

isolation

This theoretical framework related to pain underlies the development of both the Read and the Lamaze methods of education and their application to labor and delivery. The significant difference between these two approaches to childbirth education is one of methodology rather than of objective. Primarily, both of these schools of thought have as their goal the eradication of negative attitudes toward the processes of parturition and the promotion of health for the mother and the neonate.

The provision of information about the labor process provides positive expectations and decreases the fear and anxiety as the couple learn about and understand the stages of labor. The provision of emotional support by the father and the staff eliminate the mother's isolation.

In the Read method, the mother's psychological focus is directed toward relaxation, thus distracting her mind from the contractions; whereas the Lamaze method teaches meaningful behavior in response to the stimulus (contractions) thereby conditioning the perception of and reaction to the pain. The Lamaze method assigns a very active role to the father also. These methods reduce the force of the stressor—pain—and enhance the ability of the homeodynamic system to adapt to the labor process. Emphasizing the normality of the pregnancy process, these two methods concentrate on providing a safe delivery and minimizing the dangers inherent in the overutilization of anesthetics by using these chemical agents in small amounts and only for the purpose of ensuring maternal comfort.

A lessening of fear and anxiety about the labor process is accomplished by _____ .

providing information

In the Read method of childbirth education, the psychological focus is on _____ .

relaxation

The Lamaze method of childbirth education teaches meaningful behavior in response to contractions, decreasing pain perception through

_____ .

conditioning

The use of either of the two methods provides for the mother's comfort while the need for and use of medications is _____ .

decreased

Most formalized programs for childbirth education not only serve to eradicate some of the fears and fantasies surrounding childbirth but also provide a setting in which positive attitudes toward the processes of labor and delivery can emerge. An effective program for childbirth education should be geared toward meeting the specific needs presented by the expectant family and should develop *positive attitudes* toward the promotion of health by having the couple and/or their children, when possible, participate in sessions that provide information about the processes of pregnancy, labor, and delivery.

Generally, the information imparted during such sessions may include teaching of: anatomy and physiology, growth and development of the fetus, nutrition, clothing, types of exercises in which the mother may engage, the experiences that may be expected during labor and delivery, and care of the neonate. These sessions may further serve to facilitate a smooth transition between the home and the hospital by having the expectant family become familiar with the hospital environment through tours of available labor, delivery, postpartum, and nursery facilities; also, they will meet those members of the staff who will be in attendance during and after the baby is born.

Sessions may be individual and/or group. Often in group sessions, the couples and families share feelings and ideas, thus assisting each other to gain confidence and support.

Effective childbirth education provides _____ _____ and _____ .

The classes give instruction in_____ , _____ ,

_____

_____ , _____ ,

_____ , and _____ .

In group classes, couples often share _____ and

_____ .

positive attitudes;

promotion of health

anatomy; physiology;

growth and development of fetus;

health care;

labor and delivery; child care

experiences;

feelings

POST-TEST   Indicate whether each statement is true or false by circling the appropriate letter. Then turn to page 189 and see how well you have done.

1. A purpose of childbirth education is to reduce the fears and anxieties about labor and delivery.   T   F

2. The perception of pain is increased by fear.   T   F

3. The pain stimulus is modified by the sensory discrimination system.   T   F

4. An altered focus can change the perception of a painful stimulus.   T   F

5. Social expectations do not affect the reactions to and perceptions of pain.   T   F

6. Isolation can be a factor in increasing the perception of pain.   T   F

7. The Read method of childbirth education teaches the mother to relax.   T   F

8. The Lamaze method teaches the mother specific techniques to use in response to contractions.   T   F

9. Childbirth education's focus is to eliminate the use of drugs during labor and delivery.   T   F

10. To be effective, childbirth education must meet the individual couple's needs.   T   F

In the specific areas with which you had difficulty return to the material and review.

BIBLIOGRAPHY

Buxton, Charles L.: *A Study of Psychophysical Methods for Relief of Childbirth Pain,* W. B. Saunders Co., Philadelphia, 1962.

Chabon, Irwin: *Awake and Aware,* Dell Publishing Co., New York, 1972.

Durocher, Mary Ann, "Parent Educator in the Outpatient Department," *American Journal of Nursing,* Vol. 65, pp. 99-101, 1965.

Karmel, Marjorie: *Thank Your Dr. Lamaze,* J. B. Lippincott Co., Philadelphia, 1959.

Mann, David, et al.: *Educating Expectant Parents,* Visiting Nurses Service of New York, New York, 1961, Chap. 9 (p. 142 especially).

Maternity Center Association: *Meeting the Childbearing Needs of Families in a Changing World,* Maternity Center Association, New York, 1962.

McCaffery, Margo: *Nursing Management of the Patient with Pain,* J. B. Lippincott Co., Philadelphia, 1972.

Nicholson, J. Eastman: *Expectant Motherhood,* 4th ed., Little, Brown, Boston, 1963.

Read, Grantly-Dick: *Childbirth Without Fear,* Harper and Bros., New York, 1944.

PRETEST ANSWERS

1. The provision of information to the public and anxiety, social expectations, and isolation   2. Conditioning, altered focus of attention, fear   3. Information and emotional support; promote health   4. Develop positive attitudes and promote health   5. Anatomy and physiology, growth and development of the fetus, nutrition, clothing, exercises, the experiences of labor and delivery, and care of the neonate

POST-TEST ANSWERS

1. T   2. T   3. F   4. T   5. F   6. T   7. T   8. T
9. F   10. T

UNIT III EXAMINATION The following multiple-choice examination will test your comprehension of the material covered in the third unit of this program. Do not guess at the answers; if you need to do this then you have not learned the content. Return to the program and review areas that give you difficulty, before going on with the examination.

Circle the letter of the best response to each question. After completing the unit examination, check your answers on page 332 and review those areas of difficulty before proceeding to the next unit.

Maria and Jose Rivera have been married for one and a half years. Maria stopped taking oral contraceptives several months ago and now suspects that she is pregnant.

1. Which one of these common signs and symptoms associated with pregnancy is a probable sign of pregnancy?
   a. Amenorrhea
   b. Frequent micturition
   c. Enlarged and tender breasts
   d. Goodell's sign

2. When instructing Maria regarding the collection of the specimen for a biological pregnancy test, you would tell her to:
   a. Save the first voided specimen in the morning
   b. Withhold fluid intake during the night and collect the first voided specimen in the morning
   c. Report to the laboratory in the morning for a blood specimen
   d. Take a warm voided specimen to the laboratory

3. A positive reaction to the pregnancy test depends on the presence of:
   a. Pregnanediol in the blood
   b. Chorionic gonadotrophin in the blood
   c. Pregnanediol in the urine
   d. Chorionic gonadotrophin in the urine

4. A positive sign of pregnancy is:
   a. Hegar's sign
   b. Nausea and vomiting
   c. Fetal heart sounds
   d. The mask of pregnancy

5. As the care provided for the pregnant woman has improved, what has been the most significant factor in improving maternal well-being and decreasing mortality?
   a. Antepartum care
   b. Management of labor
   c. Nursing care during delivery
   d. Care of the physician during delivery

6. The parents' attitudes towards pregnancy and childbearing are most significantly influenced by:
   a. The support of the doctors and nurses
   b. Childbirth education courses
   c. Their own parent-child relationships
   d. Peer pressures

7. The pregnant woman during the first trimester often feels that the baby is:
   a. An independent being, with definite features and characteristics
   b. A welcome, wanted responsibility with no threat to her own personal identity or freedom
   c. A true being with a direct communication and relationship with her
   d. A vague concept without reality, but with many implications for the future

8. The father can be most supportive to the mother during pregnancy by:
   a. Insisting that she get proper exercise and diet
   b. Protecting her from all responsibility of outside pressures and those of the family
   c. Accepting her moods and introversion
   d. Keeping her so busy that her mind is occupied with household affairs

9. The primary source of the hormones estrogen and progesterone during the first six to eight weeks of pregnancy is the:
   a. Corpus luteum
   b. Pituitary gland
   c. Adrenal cortex
   d. Embryonic chorion

10. When explaining about health care to the pregnant mother, you stress the importance of good dental care and visits to the dentist early in pregnancy since:
    a. Even with adequate nutrition, the number of dental caries increases in proportion to growth of the fetal skeleton
    b. Dental health is directly related to the welfare of the mother and developing fetus
    c. The incidence of pathological change is related to the increase of the maternal hormones
    d. Destruction of the tooth structure is directly related to a marked increase in the maternal basal metabolic rate

11. The sign that makes the pregnancy a reality to mother is:
    a. Cessation of menses
    b. Breast changes
    c. A positive pregnancy test
    d. Quickening

12. Back pain experienced during the fourth and fifth months may be due to:
    a. The larger size of the fetus, tiring the mother more easily
    b. Increased mobility of the joints which causes more of the weight to be supported by the surrounding muscles
    c. Contractures of the pelvis
    d. Descent of the presenting part into the lower pelvic cavity

13. Episodes of cystitis are common in pregnancy due to:
    a. Dilatation and softening of the ureters
    b. Frequency
    c. Increased retention of fluid
    d. Alterations in the hormones producing bladder dysfunction

14. In the first trimester, the enlargement of the uterus is due to:
    a. Alterations of the basal metabolic rate
    b. Increased size of the fetus
    c. Hormonal action causing the cells to increase in size and number
    d. Shortening of the round ligaments

15. While in the antepartum clinic, you are talking with a pregnant mother who is in her second trimester. She has heard from the family that sexual intercourse causes abortions, and she is concerned because she is experiencing an increase in sexual desire. She shyly asks you if this is really true. Your best response would be:
    a. "You would like to limit your sexual activity."
    b. "You must be uncomfortable during sexual intercourse."
    c. "Sexual desires often increase during pregnancy and unless the doctor told you otherwise, intercourse is not harmful to the baby."
    d. "You should discuss this with your doctor and husband."

16. Heartburn is a common discomfort of pregnancy which results from:
    a. A high level of hydrochloric acid to speed up digestion
    b. Pressure on the stomach pushing the contents upwards, producing acid rebound
    c. A diet high in acidic foods
    d. Chemical interaction with the fetus causing more acid to be produced by the mother's stomach

17. Which suggestion is most helpful in remedying heartburn?
    a. Avoid fruits and vegetables high in acid content
    b. Drink a glass of carbonated beverage before meals
    c. Rest after each meal and refrain from snacking
    d. Eat smaller and more frequent meals

18. Another mother in the second month of pregnancy asks you about douching and when is the best time. Which response is most appropriate?
    a. "You must not douche during pregnancy since it may cause an abortion."
    b. "It is not necessary to douche during pregnancy; if you develop secretions during this time the doctor will advise treatment."
    c. "Douching may continue during pregnancy if you use a hand bulb syringe and mild solution."
    d. "You need to douche more frequently because of the increased vaginal secretions."

19. In the 36th to 40th weeks of gestation, a healthy mother should have a medical evaluation every:
    a. Week
    b. Two weeks
    c. Three weeks
    d. Four weeks

20. The reason why childbirth education is important is that it:
    a. Serves to have the father take over the nurse's role
    b. Eliminates the need of any anesthesia and analgesia
    c. Provides understanding of the labor process and delivery
    d. Eliminates the need for teaching during the labor period

21. The theory of pain establishes the fact that:
    a. The perception of pain is the same for all
    b. The perception of pain is related to stimulus only
    c. The perception of pain is related to many factors, physical and psychological
    d. The perception of pain is dependent on psychic factors

22. The Read method is the technique that attempts to lessen which of the following:
    a. The fear-pain interaction by providing information
    b. The actual pain by focusing on each contraction
    c. The force of the contraction by concentration
    d. The length of the contraction by focusing directly on it

23. The Lamaze method of childbirth education utilizes breathing techniques to produce:
    a. A heightened level of anxiety in response to contractions
    b. A conditioned response to the contractions
    c. A loss of consciousness during the contraction
    d. An elimination of all stimuli

24. Effective childbirth education should be:
    a. General, since all couples have similar needs
    b. On an individual basis so that other couples will not talk about bad experiences
    c. Conducted outside the hospital to decrease anxiety levels
    d. Geared to the needs of the group or individual and provide pertinent information about pregnancy, labor, and delivery

UNIT IV

THE INTRAPARTUM PERIOD

INTRODUCTION The labor process proceeding to delivery of the baby brings to an end the pregnancy state. The labor and delivery period is one of vast changes that occur very rapidly. During this period, physiological and psychological stressors are present which are of sufficient strength to produce a crisis state. Also, there is a very real element of danger for both the mother and the baby. Consequently, the adaptive responses of the mother, baby, and father are mobilized.

The adaptations that have occurred in the family members during the antepartum period provide a basis for those that will take place during the labor and delivery period. The couple's perceptions of their roles and of the behavior expected are the foundation of their approach to the labor and delivery process. Their perceptions, as well as their individual self-concepts, often determine the behavior they consider acceptable; these perceptions can, in themselves, cause much emotional stress. For example, if the father is the most important figure in the mother's life, she often reacts to the way in which she perceives that he feels about labor and delivery.

Labor may be viewed by the couple with excitement and anticipation, for it is the bringing to an end of the long waiting period, and the meeting of the new offspring, yet there is fear also as they enter this unknown from which they cannot turn back. As the time of delivery approaches, the father often practices a dry run to the hospital, attempting to ensure that he will be able to play his part well. Also at this time, the woman is often afraid that she will be unable to cope with the ominous "happening" of labor. The fear of being overwhelmed and of being unable to cope is related to the mother's self-concept. Some women wish to block the whole process and ask the physician to make sure that they will be asleep.

Other factors influencing the couple's perceptions about labor and delivery are: the mother's state of health, the couple's relationship with each other, their relationship with the medical and hospital staff, and whether or not they participated in childbirth education classes. Many cultural influences also affect the couple's view of parturition.

CHAPTER ONE
PREMONITORY SIGNS OF LABOR

OBJECTIVES *Identify the seven premonitory signs of labor.*

Identify nursing intervention measures that should be instituted when premonitory signs of labor appear.

GLOSSARY *Bloody show:* A blood-tinged vaginal mucoid discharge
Premonitory signs: Physiological changes that occur during the last several weeks of pregnancy and herald the onset of true labor
Nitrazine paper: A chemically treated paper that reacts to indicate the pH of substances
Litmus paper: A chemically treated paper that reacts to indicate the pH of substances
Braxton-Hicks contractions: Tightening and relaxing of the uterine muscle, irregular in rhythm

PRETEST   In the spaces provided, fill in the word or words that best complete(s) the statements. Then turn to page 203 and check your answers.

1. In most primigravidas, lightening occurs on or about _____ _____ weeks before term.

2. Several weeks before term, there is a loss of body fluids producing a weight loss of about _____ pounds.

3. Shortly before the onset of labor, the contractions known as Braxton-Hicks become _____ in intensity and are felt more _____ .

4. Bloody show occurs as a result of _____ and the expulsion of the _____ .

5. Pressure on the bladder by the uterus is responsible for the sign of urinary _____ that occurs at this time.

6. Another premonitory sign of labor is rupture of the _____ .

7. Testing of the amniotic fluid leaking from the vagina can be done by using _____ or _____ paper.

Premonitory signs of labor signify the culmination of the pregnancy experience. Becoming apparent during the last several weeks of pregnancy, these signs usually herald the onset of actual labor, and information regarding their nature and characteristics should be given to the mother during the last four weeks of gestation.

1. *Lightening:* This is _____   the moving of the fetus into

_____   the true pelvis;

_____

which usually occurs about two to four weeks previous to the onset of labor in most primigravidas, that is, during the

_____ trimester. This is commonly referred to   third

as "dropping."

     Consequently, the fundus is lower in the pelvis. In multigravidas this often does not occur until labor is well established.

2. *Decreased weight:* Because of hormonal changes, there is a decrease in the amount of water retention and of amniotic fluid volume; as a result, there may be a significant loss of 2 to 3 pounds in the mother's weight at term.

3. *Braxton-Hicks contractions:* Up to now they may have been

_____ and appeared at _____   mild; intermittent

intervals.

     These contractions may become more pronounced and more frequent in their occurrence. However, they do not result in cervical dilatation, and they are commonly referred to as *false labor.* At times, these contractions are so difficult to distinguish from those contractions of actual or true labor that the mother proceeds to the hospital whereupon a vaginal exam is done to assess whether dilatation and effacement is occurring. Nursing assessment of the mother's feelings of disappointment as well as possible loss of self-esteem as a result of response to a "false alarm" is important.

4. *Bloody show:* Appearance of blood-tinged mucus from the vagina. Is generally due to the partial dislodging of the mucus

plug, which up to now has served to _____   seal off cervix;

_____ and thus _____   prevent

_____ from invading the uterus. Bloody show   infection

indicates the onset of cervical changes.

5. *Rupture of membranes:* The rupture of the amniotic sac may result in a sudden gush of amniotic fluid from the vagina or in a constant leakage of this fluid. At times when the leakage of amniotic fluid is small, it may be confused with incontinence of urine; if rupture of membranes is suspected, a definitive diagnosis can be made by checking the fluid with nitrazine or litmus paper. An alkaline reaction will be a positive sign that membranes have ruptured, since the pH of the amniotic fluid is alkaline in character. Once the rupture of the membranes is suspected, the mother should notify her physician or call the hospital immediately and proceed there as directed.

6. *Frequency:* Usually due to _____ exerted by | pressure;

the _____ on the _____ ; is | uterus; bladder;

usually present after _____ occurs. | lightening

7. *Increased physical activity:* At this time, there is a typical urge to become involved in household chores (several days before actual labor begins) requiring a great deal of physical energy. It is important that the mother be informed that rest is essential, since conservation of strength and energy for the actual processes of labor and delivery is important at this time.

During a clinic visit late in the third trimester, a mother tells you that a friend has told her that she "looks like she has dropped" and asks you what this means. You would tell her that this is called _____ and | lightening;

that it means that the _____ has _____ | fetus; moved;

into the _____ . | true pelvis

Since the fetus is in the lower pelvis, you would expect pressure to be

placed on the _____ and therefore _____ | bladder; frequency

to occur.

The loss of weight of about _____ | 2 to 3;

pounds is primarily due to _____ that | hormonal changes;

cause a decrease of _____ and _____ | water retention; amniotic

_____ . | fluid volume

In providing a mother with guidance related to premonitory signs of labor, you may tell her that the irregular contractions she has been feeling

throughout the third trimester known as _____ | Braxton-Hicks contractions;

_____ will now become _____ and more | pronounced;

_____ in their occurrence. | frequent

She should also know, however, that these contractions will not result in _____ .

These contractions are commonly referred to as _____ _____ . Because these contractions are difficult to differentiate from the contractions of _____ , the mother often may proceed to the hospital.

Another premonitory sign of true labor is the appearance of blood-tinged mucus known as _____ . This results from the dislodging of the _____ which up to now has served to _____ . This usually is an indication of _____ .

A sudden gush of fluid from the vagina is an indication of _____ _____ . Rather than in a rush, the amniotic fluid may _____ . This often is confused with _____ .

If there is an uncertainty, a test with _____ or _____ paper will be a positive diagnostic measure. When this results in an _____ pH reaction, it is an indication that the _____ have indeed ruptured. If the mother suspects ruptured membranes, she should immediately _____ _____ and _____ .

The mother may tell you also that she feels like cleaning the house and completing all chores that up to now have remained undone. You will tell her that _____ activity is another premonitory sign of labor and that she needs to _____ since conservation of _____ and _____ for the actual processes of labor and delivery is essential.

cervical dilatation
false labor;

true labor

bloody show;
mucus plug;
prevent infection;
cervical changes
ruptured membranes;

leak slowly;
urinary incontinence
nitrazine;
litmus;
alkaline;
membranes;
call the physician;
go to the hospital

increased physical;
rest;
energy; strength

POST-TEST   Indicate whether each statement is true or false by circling the appropriate letter. Then turn to page 203 and check how well you have done.

1. Bloody show results from cervical dilatation.   T   F

2. The mucus plug often becomes dislodged as a result of cervical changes.   T   F

3. The rupture of the membranes is always signaled by a sudden gush of fluid from the vagina.   T   F

4. Lightening may occur in multiparas during the actual labor process.   T   F

5. "Dropping" is a word often utilized by lay people to signify the descent of the fetus into the true pelvis.   T   F

6. To differentiate whether false or true labor is in progress, a vaginal examination may have to be done.   T   F

7. Braxton-Hicks contractions always signal the onset of true labor.   T   F

8. Increased physical activity evidenced by mothers during the later part of their pregnancies is of no significance and concern to nurses when instituting nursing intervention measures.   T   F

9. When membranes rupture, the mother should wait until other signs of labor appear before calling her physician.   T   F

10. A premonitory sign of labor is an increase in weight of about 5 to 6 pounds.   T   F

11. The decrease in weight is due to hormonal activity and alterations at this time.   T   F

In the specific areas with which you have difficulty, return to the material and review.

BIBLIOGRAPHY Davis, Edward M. and Reva Rubin: *Delee's Obstetrics for Nurses,* 18th ed., W. B. Saunders Co., Philadelphia, 1966.

Fitzpatrick, Elise, Sharon Reeder, and Luigi Mastroianni: *Maternity Nursing,* 12th ed., J. B. Lippincott Co., Philadelphia, 1971.

Hellman, Louis and Jack Pritchard: *Williams' Obstetrics,* 14th ed., Appleton-Century-Crofts, New York, 1971.

PRETEST ANSWERS　1. Two to four　2. Two to three　3. Stronger; frequently　4. Cervical dilatation; mucus plug　5. Frequency　6. Membranes　7. Nitrazine; litmus

POST-TEST ANSWERS　1. T　2. T　3. F　4. T　5. T　6. T　7. F　8. F　9. F　10. F　11. T

CHAPTER TWO

ADAPTIVE PROCESSES DURING LABOR AND DELIVERY

OBJECTIVES *Identify the four steps in Leopold's maneuver.*

Identify the landmarks of the fetal skull.

Identify the four types of presentation.

Identify fetal position according to the four quadrants of the mother's pelvis.

Define lie and attitude or habitus.

GLOSSARY *Attitude* or *habitus:* The relationship of the fetal parts to one another
Lie: The relationship of the long axis of the baby in utero to the long axis of the mother
Presenting part: The fetal part closest to the internal os
Presentation: Refers to the part of the fetus closest to the cervix
Station: The relationship of the presenting part to the ischial spines
Fontanel: Found at an intersection of several sutures; an irregular membraneous space
Suture: Membraneous interspace separating the bones of the fetal skull
Vertex: Portion of the fetal skull located between the anterior and posterior fontanels
Bregma: Portion of the fetal skull over the anterior fontanel
Sinciput: Portion of the fetal skull known as the "brow"
Occiput: Portion of the fetal skull behind the posterior fontanel
Position: Relationship of the presenting part to the four quadrants of the mother's pelvis

PRETEST   In the spaces provided, fill in the word or words that best complete(s) the statements. Then turn to page 217 and check your answers.

1. Fetal attitude or habitus refers to _____

   _____

   _____ .

2. Fetal lie is the _____

   _____

   _____ .

3. The presenting part is the _____

   _____

   _____ .

4. Station refers to _____

   _____

   _____

   _____ .

5. The fetal skull is made up of _____ bones.

6. The fetal skull bones can overlap and mould to allow for adaptation to the bony pelvis because of the _____ and _____ .

7. The fetal skull is divided into four areas; these are the _____ , _____ , _____ , and _____ .

8. Leopold's maneuver is a method of palpating a pregnant woman's abdomen in order to _____

   _____

   _____ .

The reciprocal adaptations taking place between the mother and the baby are clearly illustrated by the anatomical positions adopted by the growing and developing fetus within the confines of the maternal uterus. In accommodating itself to the uterine cavity, the fetus assumes a typical *attitude* or *habitus,* defined as the relationship of fetal parts to one another. This typical attitude is usually characterized by marked flexion of the head, with the chin against the chest, the spinal column bowed forward, the arms flexed and folded against the chest, and the thighs usually flexed against the abdomen. By assuming this habitus, the fetus is then able to occupy the small space provided within the uterus, since it has decreased its length by half.

The fetus is able to adapt to the maternal uterus by assuming an attitude known as _____. This typical attitude may be defined as the _____ _____ .

habitus;

relationship of fetal parts to one another

Habitus, also called _____ , is usually characterized by marked _____ of the head, with the chin against the _____ . The fetal spinal column is _____ _____ , and the arms are _____ and _____ over the chest, with the thighs usually flexed against the _____ .

attitude;

flexion;

chest; bowed

forward; flexed;

folded;

abdomen

In this habitus the fetus occupies the _____ space within the _____ cavity, since its length has been _____ by about _____ its normal size.

smallest;

uterine;

decreased; one-half

Another term describing the relationship between the mother and the baby is *lie. Lie* is the relationship of the long axis of the baby in utero to the long axis of the mother. At term, most babies are found with the head down toward the birth canal (a cephalic presentation). This is referred to as a *longitudinal lie,* since the long axis of the fetus is in a longitudinal relationship to the long axis of the mother. Other lies may be assumed by the fetus; however, they are usually considered to be high-risk situations requiring special measures and interventions. These lies will be examined in the second volume of this book.

The relationship between the mother and the baby is also described by the anatomical lie of the baby. This is defined as the _____ _____ to the _____ of the _____ .

relationship of the long axis of baby;

long axis; mother

At term, when the baby's lie in utero is one in which the head is pointing toward the birth canal, he is said to have assumed a _____ lie in relation to the mother.

longitudinal

We have made reference to the term *presentation,* which describes the part of the fetus lying nearest to the cervical opening, that is, to the *internal os.*

The internal os is the upper part of the _____, opening into the _____ cavity.

cervix;

uterine

Presentation, therefore, refers to the part of the fetus lying _____ to the _____ .

nearest;

internal os

By now, you have probably deduced that when the presenting part is identified, the lie of the baby is also determined. For example, it follows that if the head is the part lying nearest to the cervical opening, the baby is in a _____ lie.

longitudinal

The degree to which the presenting part has descended into the maternal bony pelvis is defined as the *station of the presenting part.* Station is stated in numerical terms representing the distance, expressed in centimeters, between the presenting part and the ischial spines.

The term *station* is related to the presentation of the fetus since it identifies the _____ to which the _____ _____ has descended into the _____ _____ .

degree; presenting part;

maternal bony pelvis

This numerical determination of degree of descent identifies the distance between the _____ and the _____ and is usually expressed in _____ .

presenting part;

ischial spines;

centimeters

When the station of the baby is 0, this means that the presenting part is *at the level of the ischial spines.* If the presenting part is found *above* the ischial spines, the station is indicated by using a (−) sign next to the number indicating the distance of the presenting part above the ischial spines. Thus, for example, −1 or −2 would mean that the presenting part is located either 1 or 2 centimeters above the ischial spines.

If the presenting part is at −4 station or _____ **4 centimeters above;**
_____ the _____ **ischial**
spines, it is not yet in the pelvic inlet and it is often said to be *floating*.

As the presenting part descends into the birth canal and is past the ischial spines, the (+) sign is placed next to the number identifying the degree of descent past the spines, so that each centimeter marking the station below the ischial spines would be written as +1, +2, etc. This would mean that the presenting part is _____ or **1 centimeter;**
_____ , etc., below the ischial spines. **2 centimeters**

If the presenting part is at +4 station or 4 centimeters below the _____ , it is on the perineum. **ischial spines**

The descent of the fetus into the true pelvis is measured in relation to the _____ . **ischial spines**

Station is a measurement in centimeters of the distance between the _____ and the _____ **presenting part; ischial spines**
_____ .

A minus sign next to the number representing the degree of descent indicates that the presenting part is _____ the ischial spines, **above;**
whereas a plus sign indicates that the presenting part is located _____ **below**
the ischial spines.

0 station means that the presenting part is at the _____ **level of the ischial spines**
_____ .

When the presenting part is at −4, it is said to be _____ . **floating;**
If, on the other hand, the presenting part is at +4, it is said to be on the
_____ . **perineum**

The fetal head is the largest anatomical structure that must pass through the birth canal during the process of delivery. From an obstetrical point of view, knowledge related to the size, shape, and general characteristics of the fetal skull is essential in the identification of the critical adaptations taking place between the baby's head and the maternal bony pelvis, since if the baby's head can pass through the bony pelvis, there usually will be no difficulty with the rest of the delivery.

The fetal skull is made up of *seven bones: two frontal bones, two parietal bones, two temporal bones,* and *one occipital bone.* These bones are separated by membraneous interspaces called *sutures.* The *sagittal suture* is found between the two parietal bones; the *frontal suture* is found between the two frontal bones; the *coronal suture* is located between the frontal and parietal bones; and the *lambdoidal suture* is found between the posterior margin of the parietal bones and the occipital bone. The accompanying diagram (see below) will assist you in locating these important anatomical structures.

The largest anatomical structure passing through the birth canal is the

_____ ; therefore, if the baby's _____   fetal head (skull); head;

can pass through the _____ there   bony pelvis;

usual   be no difficulty with the rest of the delivery. The fetal skull is

composed of _____ bones. These are the _____   seven; two frontal;

_____ bones, _____ bones,   two parietal;

_____ bones, and _____   two temporal; one occipital;

_____ bone. The membraneous spaces between the bones of the fetal

skull are called _____ . Separating the two parietal bones is   sutures;

the _____ suture, whereas the suture found between the   sagittal;

two frontal bones is the _____ suture. Between the frontal   frontal;

and the parietal bones the _____ suture is located, whereas   coronal;

the suture that lies between the parietal and occipital bones is the_____   lambdoidal

suture.

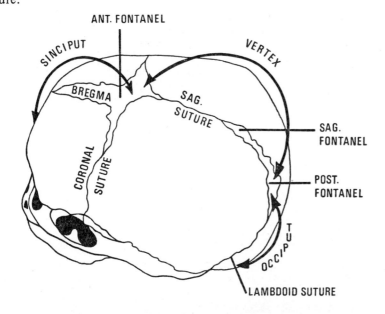

Fetal skull.

At the point at which several sutures intersect, an irregular space closed by a membrane may be found. This is a *fontanel*. There are four fontanels present in the fetal skull. The anterior fontanel, which is a diamond-shaped structure, is found at the junction of the sagittal and coronal sutures. The posterior fontanel, a smaller, also diamond-shaped anatomical landmark, may be found at the junction of the coronal and lambdoidal sutures. In addition, there are two temporal fontanels.

The sutures and fontanels of the fetal skull are important anatomical structures since, because of their mobility, they make it possible for the fetal skull bones to override and mould as it adapts to the space provided by the maternal bony pelvis.

The posterior fontanel and the sutures ossify by the end of the second month after birth, whereas the anterior fontanel—also known as the "soft spot"—may not be completely ossified until some time after the first year of life.

At the point at which several sutures intersect, a _____ may be found.   fontanel

The irregularly shaped structure covered by a membrane and located at the point at which the lambdoidal and sagittal sutures intersect is the

_____ .   anterior fontanel

The smaller, diamond-shaped structure that may be found at the junction of the frontal, coronal, and sagittal sutures is called the _____   posterior fontanel

_____ .

The fontanels and sutures are significant structures since, because of their mobility, they allow the bones of the skull to _____ or   override;
_____ , thus making possible the passage of the fetal head   mould;
through the maternal _____ .   bony pelvis

Ossification of the posterior fontanel and sutures takes place by the
_____ after birth, whereas the anterior fontanel   second month;
usually ossifies sometime after the _____ of   first year
life.

The type of labor a mother will have is often determined by the part of the baby's head that is presenting. The areas of the fetal skull are assigned names that identify the part of the baby's skull that is presenting. The *occiput* is the portion found behind the posterior fontanel. The *vertex* is the area between the two fontanels and extends on both sides of the head to the parietal protuberances. The *bregma* is the area of the large or anterior fontanel, and the *sinciput* is the area of the fetal skull commonly called the "brow."

The incidence of vertex presentation is about 95 percent of the cases at or near term; this is, therefore, the most commonly found and most desired type of fetal presentation from an obstetrical point of view. In this position, the head of the fetus is completely flexed, with the chin almost touching the thorax.

The fetal skull is divided into four regions. The region below the posterior fontanel is the _____ ; the area between the anterior and posterior fontanels is the _____ .

occiput;

vertex

The area of the fetal head where the anterior fontanel is found is the _____ , and the region of the fetal head extending from the anterior fontanel to the nose is the _____ or _____ .

bregma;

sinciput;

brow

The most commonly found fetal head presentation is the _____ .

vertex

Although another part of the fetal head, such as the mentum (chin) or sinciput (brow), may be the presenting part, these are usually thought of as being high-risk situations and as such will be discussed in the second volume of this text.

The determination of the baby's *position* in utero is another factor that will yield valuable information regarding the type of delivery. The term *position* describes the *relationship of the fetal presenting part to the maternal bony pelvis.*

The fetal position is determined by locating the presenting part in relation to the maternal bony pelvis. The mother's pelvis is divided into four imaginary quadrants (see drawing, page 212): right anterior, right posterior, left anterior, and left posterior.

In describing the baby's position, the presenting part is determined by either Leopold's maneuver (a method of palpating the maternal abdomen) or vaginal or rectal examinations. The presenting part is located in relation to the quadrant of the mother's pelvis towards which it is directed. Thus, if the occiput of the fetus is presenting to the right anterior portion of the maternal pelvis, the position is described as being a Right Occiput Anterior or ROA. The right or left anterior positions are considered to be the most favorable positions for a labor and delivery of normal duration and ease.

Position is the relationship of the _____ _____ to the _____ _____ .

fetal presenting part;

maternal bony pelvis

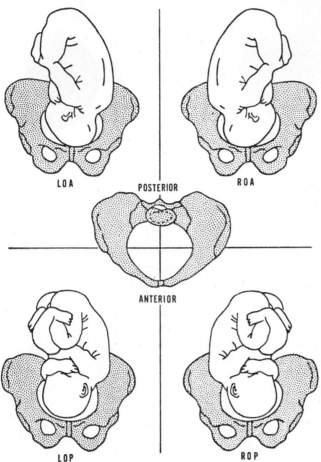

LOA   POSTERIOR   ROA

ANTERIOR

LOP   ROP

Fetal positions.

Fetal position is determined by dividing the maternal bony pelvis into four imaginary quadrants; these are the _____ , _____ , _____ , and _____ quadrants.

right anterior; right posterior; left anterior; left posterior

Determination of fetal position may be done by _____ , _____ , or _____ .

Leopold's maneuver; vaginal examination; rectal examination

If the occiput of the fetus is palpated to be on the left side of the maternal pelvis and facing toward the front, this is called a _____ position and is generally written _____ .

left occiput anterior;

LOA

The assessment of fetal presentation and position yields invaluable information that assists in predicting and determining whether the type of delivery will be normal spontaneous, whether it will be a multiple delivery, where the fetal heart may be located, and whether engagement has taken place; also it is a means of assessing the possible emergence of stressors that may give rise to high-risk situations for either the mother or the baby.

One of the methods commonly utilized by nurses in assessing and identifying the dynamic physiological adaptation processes taking place between the mother and the fetus is *Leopold's maneuver.*

This maneuver refers to the method by which the maternal abdomen is palpated to determine the fetal presentation, that is, the _____ _____ _____ and position, or the _____ _____ to the _____ _____ .

part of the fetus closest to the internal os;

relationship of the fetal presenting part; maternal body pelvis

Leopold's maneuver is done in four consecutive steps, which should be carried out as follows:

> *Step one:* With the mother in a supine position, place yourself so that you are directly facing her head. You will maintain this position through steps two and three. Using both hands, palpate the fundus with the tips of your fingers; in this way you will be able to determine which part of the fetus is in the fundus, differentiating between the fetal head and buttocks. The fetal head will feel like a small, round, hard structure and may be freely moved back and forth between the hands; the buttocks, on the other hand, will feel like a large, round mass.

The first step of this maneuver serves to determine _____ _____ _____ and to differentiate between the _____ and the _____ .

which part of the fetus is in the fundus;

head;
buttocks

If the part being palpated can be easily moved back and forth between the hands, this is the _____ and can be felt as a _____ , _____ , _____ structure.

head;
small; round; hard

Step two: While still maintaining the same position for the mother, that is, having her in the _____ position, with you located directly _____

_____, place the palms of your hands on either side of the abdomen over the uterus and exert gentle, yet deep, pressure. This will enable you to determine where the fetal back and the small anatomical parts, such as the arms and legs, may be found. The back of the fetus will be felt as a smooth, firm, continuous plane whereas the small parts may be felt as several irregularities.

This step requires you to place the palms of your hands on either side of the abdomen over the _____ and

_____ pressure.

The purpose of this step is to locate _____ and the _____ .

Step three: This step serves to determine the presenting part and degree of descent, that is, whether the presenting part is floating or engaged. Placing your thumb and forefinger directly above the symphysis pubis, apply gentle pressure down and toward the mother's back. If the presenting part is not low into the true pelvis, it will be freely movable, therefore indicating that engagement has not taken place.

The third step of Leopold's maneuver is done in order to determine _____ and whether it is _____ or _____ . This procedure requires you to place your _____ and _____ above the _____

_____. If the presenting part has not descended into the

_____ , the presenting part will be

_____ indicating that

_____ has not occurred.

Step four: This fourth and final step requires you to change position: this time you will locate yourself so that you face the feet of the mother. Place the tips of your first three fingers of both hands on both sides of the mother's lower abdomen (i.e., over the lower uterine portion), then press down and slide your fingers toward the symphysis pubis or in the direction of

---

supine;

facing her head

uterus;

exert gentle, deep

the back;

small parts

the presenting part;

floating; engaged;

thumb;

forefinger; symphysis pubis;

true pelvis;

easily movable;

engagement;

the birth canal. In a vertex presentation, the fingers of one hand will meet no resistance, indicating that the fetal back is being palpated, while the other hand will be arrested by a rounded protuberance representing the brow of the fetus or the *cephalic prominence*. This maneuver will provide important information regarding flexion of the head; if the maneuver yields the previously described findings, the head is said to be well flexed. It further confirms the location of the fetus's back and provides information as to the degree of descent into the pelvic inlet. This final and fourth step is of particular importance when the head of the baby is engaged; however, it will yield no information when the head is still floating.

The position that you will assume for this step will require you to face the mother's _____ .

feet

To begin the examination, you will place the _____ of

tips;

the _____

first three fingers;

of both your hands on _____ of the

both sides;

_____ , that is over the _____

lower abdomen; **lower uterine**

_____ segment.

You will exert a _____ pressure, while at the same

downward;

time _____ your fingers in the direction of the _____

sliding; birth canal

_____ . If the fingers of one hand meet no

(symphysis pubis);

resistance, this indicates that the _____ is being palpated;

back;

the other hand will be arrested by a _____

rounded protuberance;

_____ . This structure represents the _____

fetal brow;

_____ , otherwise known as the _____

cephalic prominence (sinciput)

_____ .

If the findings determined by this maneuver are as described herein, the fetal head is said to be _____ .

well flexed

This step also provides information as to the _____

degree of

_____ into the pelvic inlet.

descent

The information obtained by this maneuver is of importance when the

_____ is _____ ; however, it will provide

head; engaged;

no information as to the fetus's position when the _____

head;

is _____ .

floating

POST-TEST   Indicate whether each statement is true or false by circling the appropriate letter. Then turn to page 217 and check how well you have done.

1. The fetal attitude refers to the psychological reaction of the fetus to the mother.   T   F

2. The fetal lie is the direction of the baby's axis in relation to the long axis of the mother.   T   F

3. The presenting part is measured in relation to the tuberosities.   T   F

4. Station is an indication of the descent of the fetus.   T   F

5. The fetal skull is normally able to mould.   T   F

6. The vertex is the area of the fetal head between the two fontanels.   T   F

7. Leopold's maneuver is done when the mother is sitting up.   T   F

In the specific areas with which you had difficulty, return to the material and review.

BIBLIOGRAPHY

Fitzpatrick, Elise, Sharon Reeder, and Luigi Mastroianni; *Maternity Nursing,* 12th ed., J. B. Lippincott Co., Philadelphia, 1971.

Hellman, Louis and Jack Pritchard: *Williams' Obstetrics,* 14th ed., Appleton-Century-Crofts, New York, 1971.

Ziegel, Erna and Carolyn C. Van Blarcom: *Obstetric Nursing,* 6th ed., The Macmillan Co., New York, 1972.

PRETEST ANSWERS

1. The relationship of the fetal parts to one another   2. Relationship of the long axis of the baby to the long axis of the mother   3. Part of the fetus closest to the internal os   4. The level of descent of the fetus into the bony pelvis in relationship to the ischial spines   5. Seven   6. Sutures; fontanels   7. Occiput, vertex, sinciput, bregma   8. Identify the position, presentation, and descent of the fetus

POST-TEST ANSWERS

1. F   2. T   3. F   4. T   5. T   6. T   7. F

CHAPTER THREE

THE BEGINNINGS OF TRUE LABOR

OBJECTIVES   *Differentiate between true labor and false labor.*

Identify the major characteristics of true labor contractions.

Identify physiological changes of the cervix as labor begins.

Identify the arrangement of the uterine musculature.

GLOSSARY   *True labor:* Characterized by contractions effecting progressive dilatation of the cervix
False labor: Characterized by Braxton-Hicks contractions with no progressive dilatation of the cervix
Contraction: A tightening and relaxing of the uterine muscles
Effacement: Process whereby the cervical canal is progressively shortened to a point where it is obliterated and is pulled up into the lower uterine segment
Dilatation: Process in which the external os opens to 10 centimeters

PRETEST   In the spaces provided, fill in the word or words that best complete(s) the statements. Then turn to page 225 and check your answers.

1. The process of effacement is _____

_____

_____

_____

_____ .

2. The process of dilatation is _____

_____ .

3. The outer muscular layer of the uterus is shaped like_____ .

4. The middle muscular layer of the uterus is shaped like _____

_____ .

5. The middle muscular layer acts as a ligature after the placental separation and in this way _____ .

6. The rhythm of the uterine contraction is produced by _____ found within the muscle fibers.

7. The contraction is divided into three segments: _____ , _____ , and_____ .

8. The most contractile portion of the uterus is the _____ .

9. The time from the beginning of one contraction to the beginning of the next is the

_____ .

10. The time from the beginning of the increment of the contraction to the beginning of the decrement of that contraction is the_____ .

The actual processes of labor are said to begin with the presence of **uterine contractions** that, with the passage of time, increase in frequency and duration, become more intense, and result in the progressive dilatation of the cervix. When all of these things have occurred, true labor is said to have begun.

Although there are many hypotheses that seek to explain the mechanisms triggering the onset of labor, the facts remain unknown. Many factors have been suggested as causing the events leading up to delivery. Some authorities have advanced the idea that alterations in hormonal balance of **progesterone and estrogen** serve to initiate labor by increasing uterine irritability; others address themselves to the possibility that, at term, the placenta no longer functions to provide the fetus with the necessary life-supporting elements; still others feel that the overdistended uterus creates enough stimulus to bring about the release of oxytocin and thus initiate contractions. Recently, research has identified high levels of prostaglandins present in the amniotic fluid, giving rise to the hypothesis that perhaps the presence of this hormone may be the long-sought-after solution to the mysteries of labor.

Generally, it is felt that the interaction of several of these physiological occurrences produces the progressive, stronger, rhythmic, longer-lasting uterine contractions that result in the expulsion of the products of conception. Whatever the causative elements, we do know that somewhere between the thirty-eighth and forty-second weeks of gestation, most women will begin true labor.

The preparation of the uterus and cervix for labor and delivery begins several weeks before the actual onset of labor. The uterus becomes more irritable; and any abdominal manipulation may elicit Braxton-Hicks contractions, which now become more frequent and at times are confused with those characterizing true labor. It is generally thought that these contractions serve to begin to prepare the cervix for effacement and dilatation, since it is at this time that the cervix begins to soften and the internal os may begin to open.

Effacement is the progressive shortening of the cervical canal to the point at which it is obliterated as the cervix is pulled into the lower uterine segment. *Dilatation* takes place as the external os begins to stretch and open as a result of the pressure created by the presenting part, the amniotic sac, and the action of the uterine contractions; cervical dilatation is completed when the opening of the external os is 10 centimeters.

Braxton-Hicks contractions are at times confused with those contractions that characterize _____.   true labor

Braxton-Hicks contractions prepare the cervix for _____   dilatation;

and _____ . It is at this time that the cervix may begin to   effacement;

_____ and the _____ may   soften; internal os

begin to open.

Effacement is defined as the progressive _____ of the

_____ . It becomes completely

_____ as it is pulled up into the lower _____

of the _____ .

It was stated earlier that uterine contractions are generated by the action of pacemakers found within muscle fibers of the uterus. As you recall, the uterus is a _____ shaped, muscular organ that is divided anatomically into four segments, the _____ , the _____ , the _____ , and the _____ .

pear;

corpus;

fundus; cervix; isthmus

This highly vascular organ is composed of three muscle layers that, because of their arrangement, lend the uterus its elastic and contractile quality. During parturition, this anatomical arrangement of muscle fibers functions in (1) propelling the presenting part toward the birth canal and (2) preventing profuse bleeding after placental separation.

The *outer or hoodlike* layer of muscle fibers is arranged *over* the *fundus* and extends out into the various ligaments. These fibers exert a *downward pressure* on the fetus during uterine contractions. The *innermost layer* consists of *sphincterlike* fibers around the *internal os, orifices* of the *tubes,* and *body of the uterus.* This layer presses on each side of the baby to straighten the fetal spine so that the downward thrust of the uterine contractions are effective. The *middle layer* of muscle fibers consists of *interlaced* or *figure-eight* fibers that *contract down* on the *uterine blood vessels after the placenta separates,* thus acting as natural ligatures. It is also the middle layer that provides *additional force* during labor contractions.

The uterus has differentiated muscles that aid in parturition in different ways; these layers number _____ .

three

The uterine muscles serve two major functions during parturition: _____ and _____ .

propulsion; ligation

The outer uterine muscles are found over the _____ ; these also extend out over the _____ .

fundus;

ligaments

The outer layer exerts pressure on the fetus during contractions in a _____ direction.

downward

The innermost layer of muscle fibers is located around the _____

_____ , _____ , and uterine _____ .

internal os;

tubal orifices;

body

This inner layer acts by contracting on each _____ of the fetus.

side

The muscle fibers of the middle layer are arranged in a _____ pattern.

figure-eight

During the first and second stages of labor, this middle layer acts to provide additional _____ .

force

After placental separation, the middle layer helps to control bleeding by acting as natural _____ .

ligatures

The contractions initiating true labor propel the presenting part toward the birth canal. These uterine contractions are *involuntary, produce discomfort,* and are *rhythmic* due to *pacemakers* found within the muscle fibers of the uterus. They are usually felt starting low in the back and radiating around to the front in a girdlelike fashion. They can be monitored by placing a hand on the abdomen and feeling the tightening up of the uterus. These contractions *increase in discomfort, intensity, frequency,* and *duration* during true labor and lead to *effacement* and *dilatation* of the cervix. The contraction is divided into *three segments: an increment* (building up), *acme* (peak), and *decrement* (relaxation). Between each contraction there must be a period of complete *uterine relaxation* to allow for *reoxygenation* of the fetus.

The *frequency* of a contraction is the time lapse from the beginning of one contraction to the beginning of the next. The *duration* of a contraction is measured from the *onset* of the *increment* to the *onset* of the *decrement*.

When timing contractions, you must clarify how the institution in which you are working keeps their records. The *intensity* of a contraction refers to how *hard* the fundus gets during the *acme* of the contraction. A commonly used practice for determining the relative intensity of the acme of the contraction is the following: Touch, in this order, your lips, nose, chin and forehead. The firmness encountered as you do this is comparable to the intensity you feel as the uterine contractions reach their acme and is labeled 1+ (lips), 2+ (nose), 3+ (chin), and 4+ (forehead).

Contractions are timed in one of three ways. In a prepared mother, in order not to break her concentration, they are usually timed from the time

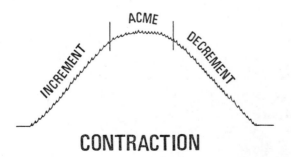

CONTRACTION

Contractions.

she commences her special breathing until she relaxes. If you are the one monitoring contractions, you will place your fingers lightly on the *fundus,* the most *contractile* portion of the uterus, and record the contractions by what your fingers feel in relation to the seconds and minutes on your watch. A measurement of the exact duration and true intensity of the contraction and base level of relaxation of the uterine muscles can be obtained only by the use of an internal monitoring device. The electric monitor is connected to a catheter that has been inserted into the uterine cavity through the cervix, and it measures internal pressures, relaying the information onto a graph.

Uterine contractions cannot be controlled by the mother and are termed _____ .

involuntary

In true labor, the uterine pacemakers control the _____ of the contraction.

rhythm

As labor progresses, the contractions increase in _____ , _____ , and _____ .

duration; frequency; intensity

Frequency of contractions is timed from the onset of one contraction to the _____ .

onset of the next

The duration of a contraction is timed from the onset of the increment of the contraction to the beginning of the _____ .

decrement

The intensity of the contraction is measured by how hard the contraction becomes at the _____ .

acme

When you are monitoring a contraction, your fingers are placed on the fundus because it is the most _____ portion.

contractile

POST-TEST   Indicate whether each statement is true or false by circling the appropriate letter. Then turn to page 225 and check how well you have done.

1. The mechanism that actually initiates labor is not clearly understood.   T   F

2. Braxton-Hicks contractions are thought to begin the process of effacement and dilatation.   T   F

3. Effacement is the progressive shortening of the cervical canal.   T   F

4. The muscles of the uterus propel the fetus through the birth canal.   T   F

5. The uterine contractions are under voluntary control.   T   F

6. As labor progresses, the contractions become less frequent.   T   F

7. The acme of the contraction occurs as it reaches a peak.   T   F

8. The most contractile part of the uterus is the body.   T   F

9. An *exact* measurement of the intensity of the contraction is obtained by placing a hand on the mother's abdomen.   T   F

In the specific areas with which you had difficulty, return to the material and review.

BIBLIOGRAPHY   Fitzpatrick, Erna, J. Eastman Nicholson, and Sharon Reeder: *Maternity Nursing,* 11th ed., J. B. Lippincott Co., Philadelphia, 1966.

Hellman, Louis and Jack Pritchard: *Williams' Obstetrics,* 14th ed., Appleton-Century-Crofts, New York, 1971.

PRETEST ANSWERS   1. The progressive shortening of the cervical canal to a point at which it is obliterated and is pulled into the lower uterine segment   2. The opening of the external os to 10 centimeters   3. A hood   4. A figure-eight   5. Helps to control the bleeding   6. Pacemakers   7. Increment; acme; decrement   8. Fundus   9. Frequency   10. Duration

POST-TEST ANSWERS   1. T   2. T   3. T   4. T   5. F   6. F   7. T   8. F   9. F

CHAPTER FOUR

STAGES AND PHASES OF LABOR

OBJECTIVES   *Identify the four stages of labor.*

Identify the three phases of Stage One.

Identify the psychological and physiological symptoms and alterations that take place during labor and delivery.

Identify nursing intervention measures to be applied during each of the stages and phases of labor.

GLOSSARY   *Stage One:* A division of the labor process extending from the beginning of true labor to full cervical dilatation

Stage Two: A division of the labor process extending from full cervical dilatation to the birth of the baby

Stage Three: A division of the labor process extending from the birth of the baby to the delivery of the placenta

Stage Four: A division of the labor process; the first hour after the delivery of the placenta

Fetal distress: Relating to the anoxia of the fetus in utero

Phases of labor:

    Effacement phase: Period from 0 to 3 centimeters of dilatation

    Dilatation phase: Period from 4 to 7 centimeters of dilatation

    Transition phase: Period from 8 to 10 centimeters of dilatation

PRETEST In the spaces provided, fill in the word or words that best complete(s) the statements. Then turn to page 254 and check your answers.

1. The first stage of labor is divided into _____ .

2. The first stage ends at _____ _____ .

3. The second stage ends with _____ _____ .

4. The third stage ends with _____ _____ .

5. The fourth stage extends until _____ _____ .

6. During the first stage of labor, the fetal heart is monitored every _____ _____ and after _____ _____ .

7. The normal fetal heart rate is _____ _____ .

8. The breathing that is most effective during the first phase of labor is _____ _____ .

9. It is important to encourage the mother to empty her bladder frequently during labor because _____ _____ _____ .

10. Some of the physical signs indicating that the mother is in the transition phase are _____ , _____ , _____ , _____ , and _____ .

11. The mother can effectively bear down with the contractions during _____ _____ .

12. Amniotic fluid should appear _____ colored.

13. During the second stage, the fetal heart rate is monitored _____ _____ .

14. The seven cardinal fetal movements are: _____ , _____ ,

_____ , _____ ,

_____ , _____ , and

_____ .

15. The signs of separation of the placenta are: _____

_____ , _____

_____ , and the _____

_____ .

16. During the fourth stage of labor, it is important to check consistency of the uterus

since the uterus _____

_____

_____ .

The duration of the processes of labor is dependent upon the influence and interaction of many variables. Physiological variables affecting the duration of labor are: the position of the fetus in utero and the anatomical configuration of the presenting part, the size and diameter of the maternal bony pelvis, the effectiveness and force of uterine contractions. Psychological variables, such as fears and anxieties related to the safety of the baby or to the actual events of giving birth, also affect the duration of labor. These psychological variables are influenced by the mother's knowledge of what she is to expect during labor and delivery—her degree of preparedness and whether or not she has had previous deliveries. Mothers who have had childbirth education and multigravid women are known to have shorter labors that those mothers who have not had any previous antepartal classes or who are primigravidas.

The processes of labor have been divided into four stages, according to the changes in the maternal anatomical structures brought about as the baby progresses through the birth canal. *Stage One* begins with the contractions of true labor and is terminated at full cervical dilatation, 10 centimeters. This stage is divided into three *phases:* effacement, dilatation, and transition; these are demarcated by the degree of cervical dilatation occurring. Effacement is the phase of from 0 to 3 centimeters of cervical dilatation; dilatation is the phase of from 4 to 7 centimeters of cervical dilatation; transition is the phase of from 8 to 10 centimeters of cervical dilatation.

The character, intensity, and duration of contractions, as well as maternal behavior and physical signs, change according to the phase of dilatation. It is important to remember that the time it will take the cervix to become fully dilated is dependent upon the interaction of the aforementioned physiological and psychological variables.

Stage Two begins with full cervical dilatation and ends with the birth of the baby. *Stage Three* begins after the delivery of the baby and ends with the expulsion of the placenta. *Stage Four* is the first critical hour following the delivery of the placenta.

Usually, the processes of labor are shorter for the _____ mother and the _____ than for the _____ mother and the _____ .

These processes are divided into _____ stages as follows: Stage One lasts from _____ to _____ dilatation. Stage Two begins with _____ dilatation and ends with the _____ of the _____ . Stage Three ends with the _____ . Stage Four is the _____ hour after the delivery of the placenta.

prepared;

multigravida; unprepared;

primigravida

four;

the onset of true labor;

10 centimeters, full cervical;

full cervical;

birth;

baby; delivery of the placenta;

first

Generally, the expectant mother is admitted into the hospital at the beginning of Stage One, that is, when contractions are signaling that true labor has begun. The admission procedure usually includes a sterile vaginal examination that identifies the amount of dilatation and other important factors such as the position and the presentation of the fetus, the station of the presenting part, and the degree of cervical effacement. In addition, a soap solution enema may be ordered by the physician to empty the lower intestinal tract and stimulate uterine contractions. A perineal shave may also be done routinely in anticipation of easier surgical repair of any perineal body incisions that may be needed as means of facilitating delivery processes.

The mother's vital signs should be taken immediately upon admission, and the fetal heart rate should be monitored. The strength, duration, and frequency of uterine contractions should be carefully noted and recorded. Usually, the contractions are mild in intensity and last about 30 seconds during this first phase. Their frequency is between five and ten minutes.

At this time, the nurse who is coming into contact with the family should bear in mind that the sudden environmental change from home to hospital and the at times impersonal technical aspects of the admission procedures may become additional sources of stress. When not explained, these technical procedures usually increase any fears and anxieties that the mother and the father may be experiencing related to the unknown events of labor and delivery.

The admission procedure usually includes taking the maternal
_____ signs, monitoring the fetal _____

_____, and doing a perineal _____ . The mother is

examined vaginally to determine the degree of cervical_____

and _____ and to assess the fetal _____

and _____ and the station of the presenting part.

| vital; heart rate; |
| shave; |
| dilatation; |
| effacement; presentation; |
| position |

To empty the lower intestinal tract, a _____

_____ may be ordered; this procedure also aids in

_____ contractions.

| soap solution enema; |
| stimulating uterine |

To monitor a fetal heart rate (FHR), a *fetascope* and/or ultrasound monitor may be used. Before beginning this procedure, however, it is necessary for you to locate the head and the back of the fetus. The method that will assist you in determining the position of these anatomical parts is

_____ .

| Leopold's maneuver |

In a *vertex* presentation, the fetal heart rate is best heard by placing the fetascope over the lower abdomen on the side on which you palpate the fetal spine. Normally, the fetal heart rate is between 120-160 beats per minute and is regular in rhythm. Should there be a sudden drop or rise of 20 beats per minute or should there be any noticeable change in rhythm, the physician should be notified immediately.

It is important to remember that uterine contractions tend to slow the fetal heart rate; therefore, it should be assessed 30 seconds after the end of each contraction.

When listening for the fetal heart rate, you may hear a synchronous whistling sound. This is called the *souffle*. If the beat is between 120-160 per minute, you are more likely hearing the funic souffle, or the pulsation of blood through the umbilical arteries, corresponding to the fetal heart rate. If the beat is 80 to 90, what you are probably hearing is the pulsation of the uterine blood vessels, which corresponds to the mother's heart rate. To validate this, count the rate of beats you are hearing and at the same time take the mother's pulse. If they are the same, this will verify the fact that you have not located the fetal heart rate.

During Stage One, the fetal heart rate should be monitored and recorded *every 15 minutes.* In addition, it must be checked *following procedures* such as sterile vaginal examinations and enema administration and after artificial or spontaneous *rupture of the membranes.* All of these situations may produce fetal distress, and thus checking the fetal heart rate will assess the baby's health status. While this method of fetal health assessment is being carried out, the activity of the baby should be noted. Any objective observations related to increased fetal movement, as well as subjective maternal statements regarding this, may be an additional indication of fetal distress which should be reported to the physician.

One of the ways in which fetal health status is assessed is through monitoring the _____ .

fetal heart rate

The normal heart rate of the fetus is usually between _____ and _____ beats per minute, and its normal rhythm is _____ .

120;

160;

regular

Fetal distress may be indicated by a change of_____ in fetal heart rate, or by an alteration in _____ .

20 beats;

rhythm

During Stage One, the FHR should be monitored every _____ minutes. Should there be an increase in fetal activity observed by either the nurse or the mother, this may be an indication of _____ _____ .

15;

fetal distress

Since contractions tend to _____ the FHR, assessment of this should be instituted after the contraction is over. Other situa-

slow

tions and procedures warranting the checking of the fetal heart rate are
_____ , the administration of an
_____ , and artificial or spontaneous_____
_____ .

    When a sterile vaginal examination is to be done, the mother is carefully draped and strict aseptic technique is employed. This type of examination aids in determining fetal _____ and _____ and the relationship of the presenting part to the ischial spines known as the _____ . In addition, this examination will yield information related to changes in the cervix such as _____ and _____ .

    During this procedure, all of those present in the room should wear surgical masks, the examiner should use sterile gloves, and the vulva and entroitus should be sprayed with an antiseptic solution such as Betadine immediately prior to the examination to reduce the hazards of contamination. This examination requires that the mother be placed in a lithotomy position, that she keep her buttocks flat against the surface upon which she is lying, and that she attempt to relax perineal and abdominal muscles by breathing through her mouth.

    A sterile vaginal examination requires that strict aseptic technique be employed. This can be ensured by the examiner wearing _____ gloves, all those present in the room wearing _____ masks, and the maternal _____ and entroitus being sprayed with an_____ solution.

    During this procedure, the mother is placed in a _____ position and should be instructed to keep her buttocks flat against the examining table.

    To ensure relaxation of the _____ and _____ muscles, the mother should be instructed to _____ through her_____ .

    The generally "tranquil" period of time of the *effacement* phase of labor provides nurses with an opportunity to review and reinforce any teachings with the parents or to provide them with essential information

---

vaginal examination;
enema; rupture of membranes

presentation; position

station;

effacement;

dilatation

sterile;
surgical;
vulva;
antiseptic
lithotomy

abdominal; perineal;
breathe;
mouth

relating to the processes of labor. Essential content to be reinforced or discussed should be that relating to the mother's breathing and other activity during contractions. During this first phase of labor, breathing patterns are generally *normal* and effortless. However, as the processes leading to parturition progress, particularly during the dilatation phase, normal, effortless breathing becomes difficult. At that time, breathing patterns can be assisted by combining periods of *slow chest breathing* as the increment begins, altering to *more rapid, shallow chest* breathing at the acme, then returning to the slower breathing during the decrement.

In reinforcing teaching related to breathing patterns and techniques, you will tell the mother that during the effacement phase, she should breathe _____. During the dilatation phase, her breathing pattern may become more _____ to maintain. Breathing patterns may be assisted by telling the mother to use _____ breathing at the beginning of the _____ of the contraction. As the contraction reaches the acme, the mother uses _____ chest breathing. When the contraction begins to diminish in intensity, that is, during the _____ , the mother may return to the slower chest breathing patterns.

normally;

difficult;

slow chest;

increment;

more rapid, shallow;

decrement

The *dilatation* phase of Stage One occurs when the cervix dilates from 4 to 7 centimeters. During the dilatation phase, the interval between contractions is about three to five minutes, and the contractions last 40 to 50 seconds and become stronger in intensity. During this phase, the mother seems to be concentrating more on the contractions, although she is still cooperative and is listening for encouragement and reassurance in dealing with the discomfort generated by the contractions.

The dilatation phase is part of the _____ stage of labor. This phase is marked by _____ dilatation ranging from _____ to _____ centimeters. The contractions during this phase are characterized by an increase in _____ . The interval between the contractions is usually _____ to _____ minutes and their duration is usually from _____ to _____ seconds.

first;

cervical;

4; 7;

intensity;

three;

five;

40; 50

During the dilatation phase, the mother may complain of lower back pain. This discomfort may be relieved by applying the counterpressure of a firm, steady force exerted on the area by a hand or fist.

The duration and strength of contractions and the time between them usually signal the progress of labor. Thus, constant assessment is important. The fetal heart rate should be monitored every 15 minutes and after treatments.

During labor, it is undesirable for the mother to have any intake of solid foods; however, she should be watched for signs of dehydration. Some physicians may permit clear fluids at this time; others prefer to administer the necessary fluids parenterally, generally in the form of 5 percent dextrose in water. The oral route of administration may be contraindicated should anesthetics need to be administered during delivery.

Since rupture of the membranes increases the hazards of infection, the mother's temperature should be taken more frequently once this has occurred. Oral temperature, pulse, and respirations are taken every two hours.

Analgesics, such as Demerol alone or in combination with Vistaril or Sparine (potentiators), or scopolamine (an amnesic) may be given during the dilatation phase to relieve the discomforts produced by the contractions. However, since any sedative will quickly pass through the placental barrier and to the fetus, sedation should be considered carefully so as to decrease the chances of causing *respiratory depression* of the baby.

Urine output must be carefully watched at this time, and the mother should be encouraged to void at least every two hours; this will help prevent any impediment to the descent of the fetus through pressure created by a full bladder. The urinary output should be measured and recorded and the urine should be tested for albumin, sugar, and acetone.

Back pain that the mother may experience during labor can be helped by providing _____ .   counterpressure

Either clear fluids or intravenous solutions are given in order to keep the mother _____ .   hydrated

A complication of ruptured membranes is _____ .   infection

With ruptured membranes, it is important to monitor the mother's _____ more frequently.   temperature

During this time, it is also important to continue to monitor the uterine _____ and the fetal _____ .   contractions; heart rate

The mood of the mother is still one of _____ during the dilatation phase.   cooperation

In order to allow the uterus freedom for effective contractions, the mother should be encouraged to keep her _____ empty.   bladder

The *transition* phase of Stage One is marked by cervical dilatation of between 8 and 10 centimeters. During this phase, many maternal physiological and behavioral changes can be observed. The mother becomes more irritable, appears angry and hostile, and objects to any directions given or procedures that need to be carried out.

The dynamics of these mood changes have been described by some physicians as the mother's psychological need to reject the fetus in order to facilitate her acceptance and participation in its expulsion.

The uterine contractions are now closely spaced—one to two minutes apart, are of great intensity, and last as long as 60 seconds. The mother appears tired and seems to fall asleep when not in the grips of uterine activity.

During this phase diaphoresis increases, nausea with or without vomiting may occur, and there is uncontrolled shaking of the legs.

Checking of the perineum may reveal an increase in bloody show and bulging as the presenting part descends onto the pelvic floor; the labia may begin to separate and, because of the pressure of the presenting part, involuntary micturition may occur. It is not unusual to hear the mother say at this time that she is also experiencing the need to defecate. As labor continues, dilatation of the rectum can be observed.

The prepared mother may understand these events as heralding the processes of delivery. However, continuous support and reinforcement is needed.

The transition phase of Stage One occurs when the cervix is _____ to _____ centimeters _____ .

8; 10; dilated

During this time, observable mood and affect changes are _____ , _____ , and _____ . Any directions or procedures that will tend to disturb the mother may be strenuously objected to by her.

anger; irritability; hostility

Uterine contractions at this time are spaced closely, about _____ to _____ minutes apart; they are more _____ and may last as long as _____ seconds.

one; two; intense 60

Physiological reactions that may appear at this time are increased _____ and _____ , and uncontrolled _____ of the _____ is often present.

diaphoresis; nausea; shaking; legs

When the perineum is checked, _____ show, _____ of the perineum and separation of the _____ may be observed.

bloody; bulging; labia

The transition phase usually is an indication that the _____ of the baby is close.

birth (delivery)

During the transition phase, the mother's breathing techniques may become difficult to maintain, and constant support is necessary. Thus, the mother should be instructed to respond to the initiation of the contraction by taking several deep breaths, then using *accelerated* shallow breathing as the contraction increases in intensity, and slowing at the decrement. The mother may feel the urge to bear down with the contraction. If the degree of cervical dilatation does not warrant this activity at this time, instruct the mother to expire air by blowing through her mouth or *panting,* thus preventing her from bearing down.

The transition phase of labor may make breathing patterns _____ to maintain. At this time, you should tell the mother to use accelerated _____ breathing as the contraction increases in intensity. The mother may feel the urge to _____ _____ with the contraction. If cervical dilatation is not completed, she should be instructed to _____ . This will aid in relaxing her and will prevent her from pushing down.

difficult;

shallow chest;

bear down;

pant

During this transition phase, instructions given to the mother should be very short, specific commands. Primarily, she should be made to understand that she is *not* to bear down with the contractions until she is commanded to do so even though she may experience this urge. Bearing down before the cervix is ready will cause the cervix to become edematous, a situation that may impede the progress of labor.

During this time, any directions given to the mother should be in the form of short _____ . It is important that she does not _____ even though she may experience the urge to do so, since doing this before the _____ is _____ may produce _____ and thus _____ labor.

commands;

bear down;

cervix; ready;

edema; impede

If the mother is a primigravida, she may be instructed to push at the completion of Stage One, once the cervix is dilated to 10 centimeters. A multigravida may begin pushing earlier than a primigravida: late in Stage One, since the cervix is softer and can respond at this time.

Pushing is encouraged by giving short specific verbal directions at the beginning of each contraction. During the increment of the contraction, the mother should be told to breathe in and out twice, then to breathe in and hold the air in the lungs. She should then be told to place her chin against her chest, hold on to her thighs keeping her elbows out, and push down for about 10 to 15 seconds, then blow out, take in more air, hold it, and push again.

Once Stage Two is in progress, that is, when the cervix is _____ centimeters _____ , the primigravida is instructed to push. During the increment of the _____ , the mother is told to _____ twice. She should then take in a breath and _____ . She should position herself by placing her chin against her _____ holding on to her _____ .

At this point, she is told to _____ for a period of about _____ seconds. Then she should blow out and take in more air, hold it, and push again.

10;

dilated;

contraction;

breathe in and out;

hold it;

chest;

thighs

push;

10 to 15

This pattern should be repeated for as long as the contraction lasts. At the end of the decrement, the mother is told to take several deep breaths to restore normal respiratory functioning. It is important that the instructions given to the mother at this time be short, specific, and in the form of commands since this is one of the most difficult periods of the labor process for the mother.

Let us check to see whether you are able to identify important nursing assessment and intervention measures that should be instituted while the mother is in the first stage of labor.

Nursing intervention and assessment measures begin with the admission of the mother into the labor and delivery suite as the rhythmic, intense contractions that differentiate _____ labor from the less intense contractions of false labor known as _____ contractions become evident.

These true labor contractions may be expected to last about _____ seconds and are usually present during the *efface-ment* phase of labor. This phase is said to be occurring when the cervix is known to be dilated between _____ and _____ centimeters.

Because contractions during this phase are of _____ intensity, coming between _____ and _____ minutes apart, not much discomfort is experienced by the mother.

As part of the admission procedure, the nurse will be expected to monitor these contractions and the _____

true;

Braxton-Hicks

30;

0; 3

mild;

five; ten

fetal heart;

rate, which can be easily obtained once she is able to locate the position of the fetus through palpation of the maternal abdomen by means of _____ maneuver. A fetal heart rate between _____ and _____ beats per minute is considered to be normal. Any departure from this rate, either drop or raise, should be _____ to the _____ immediately.

Leopold's; 120;

160;

reported;

physician

Since contractions are known to slow the fetal heart rate, the nurse should assess fetal cardiac activity _____ seconds _____ _____ .

30; after the contraction

In assessing the physiological condition of the mother, the nurse should take and record vital signs as follows: blood pressure every two hours and temperature, pulse, and respiration every four hours. If the membranes have ruptured, these last three vital signs should be taken every two hours. There should be no significant variance in maternal blood pressure during labor.

Additional assessment of the mother requires that the _____ _____ be taken. If the membranes are intact, the temperature, pulse, and respiration should be monitored every _____ hours. However, if the membranes have ruptured, these signs should be obtained every _____ hours. The blood pressure should be taken every _____ hours.

vital signs;

four;

two;

two

If you recall, soap solution enemas may be ordered by the physician. These are done to empty the colon and thus decrease the chances of contamination during labor and delivery, while at the same time allowing for an easy descent of the fetus through the birth canal. Administration of enemas is known to stimulate contractions and speed up the processes of labor; this in turn may affect the fetus, so the _____ _____ should be monitored immediately following this procedure.

fetal heart rate

Maternal behavior should be closely observed after a soap solution enema to determine whether contractions have increased in rate and frequency and whether their rhythm has altered.

After a soap solution enema, maternal contractions should be monitored and their _____ , _____ , and

rate; duration;

_____ should be noted. In addition, the health status of the

⬇

frequency;

fetus is assessed by monitoring the _____

fetal heart rate

_____ .

An enema is given in order to _____ the

empty;

_____ ; this is done to prevent _____

colon; pressure;

on the contracting_____ , decrease the dangers of

uterus;

_____ , and allow an easier_____

contamination; descent;

of the_____ .

fetus

An additional nursing responsibility is the preparation of the maternal perineum and rectal area prior to delivery. Shaving this area facilitates cleansing and repair of the *episiotomy* (cutting of the perineal body), a procedure that is done to enlarge the vaginal orifice to allow for an easier delivery and to prevent lacerations of the perineum which may occur during the birth of the baby.

Further preparation of the mother for delivery at the time of admission

includes shaving the _____ and _____

perineal; anal;

areas. This procedure serves to facilitate repair of the _____ ,

episiotomy;

which is done during the actual birth of the baby. This cutting of the

_____ serves to _____

perineal body; prevent lacera-

_____ and allow for an_____ delivery by

tions; easier;

enlarging the_____ orifice.

vaginal

While these procedures are being carried out, aseptic techniques must

be maintained. Also the nurse should observe the perineum for the presence

of bloody show, the_____

blood-tinged mucus;

that is one of the_____ signs of labor.

premonitory

As labor progresses, the amount of bloody show increases in proportion to the amount of cervical dilatation, so that this sign becomes an indication of the progress of labor.

Also, if the membranes have ruptured, there may be amniotic fluid leaking from the vagina. Its amount and color (normally clear) should be carefully noted, and comfort measures such as personal hygiene in the form of sponge baths and dry linen should be given since the presence of these amniotic secretions can be a source of discomfort to the mother.

Careful observation of the perineum is indicated in order to note the

presence of the blood-tinged mucus known as_____ .

bloody show;

The presence of this sign serves as an indicator to the progress of
_____ , since an increased amount of this secretion occurs in
direct proportion with the degree of _____

_____ .

  Leakage of _____ from the vagina should
be noted; this fluid should be observed for _____ and

_____ .

  To ensure maternal comfort, _____

and _____ should be given at this time.

  Complete cervical dilatation signals the beginning of Stage
_____ , which culminates in the delivery of the baby.

During this stage, uterine contractions decrease in frequency to about
three to four minutes apart and do not seem to create as much discomfort. It
is at this point that the mother is allowed to push with each contraction, an
activity that seems to provide her with much relief. After each contraction,
the fetal heart rate is monitored and the perineum should be checked for the
presence of *caput* (the presence of the fetal head at the vaginal opening).
Throughout this time, the mother remains in the labor room. Once caput is
seen, the mother is then moved to the delivery room.

  Full cervical dilatation is an indication that the _____
stage of labor has begun. This stage ends with the _____ of
the _____ . Contractions at this time decrease in
_____ , occurring about _____ to
_____ minutes apart.

  When the fetal head or _____ can be seen at the
vaginal opening, the mother is then _____

_____ .

Once in the delivery room, the mother is placed upon the delivery table
in a lithotomy position with both legs placed into the stirrups attached to
the table. It is important to remember that when both the legs are placed into
the stirrups, they be lifted at the same time so as to prevent placing strain
on the muscles of the thighs and perineum. Once the mother is so positioned,
she is draped with sterile materials and the vulva is cleansed with antiseptic
solution. Hand grips are usually provided for the mother to grasp as she bears
down with each contraction.

Answer column (right margin):

labor;

cervical dilatation

amniotic fluid;

amount;

color

sponge baths;

clean linen

Two

second;

birth;

baby;

frequency; three;

four

caput;

moved to the delivery room

On the delivery table, the mother is placed in a _____ | lithotomy;

position, and when her legs are placed on the stirrups, both of them should be

_____ at the _____ . This is | lifted; same time;

done in order to prevent undue _____ on the _____ | strain; perineal muscles

_____ and thighs.

After each contraction, the fetal _____ | heart rate

continues to be monitored.

After the sterile drapes are put in place, the woman's_____ | vulva

is cleansed with an antiseptic solution.

Understanding of the delivery processes requires knowledge of the *seven cardinal fetal movements* that take place as the baby adapts to the maternal bony pelvis and as it responds to the force of uterine contractions. These movements are described below:

1. *Engagement* has occurred when the widest diameter of the presenting part reaches the ischial spines.

2. *Descent* is the propulsion of the fetus through the true pelvis, beginning with engagement and ending with delivery.

3. *Flexion* occurs when the descending presenting part bends as the fetus accommodates to the resistance of the cervix, the pelvic wall, and the pelvic floor.

4. *Internal rotation* occurs when the presenting part rotates 90 degrees. Remember from our sections on diameters and measurements of the maternal bony pelvis that the widest diameter of the inlet is the _____ diameter, whereas | transverse;

   the widest diameter of the outlet is the _____ | anterior-posterior

   _____ diameter.

In a vertex presentation, the fetal head will adapt to these pelvic measurements and will enter the inlet in the transverse position such as LOT; then, during labor, it will rotate 90 degrees to an LOA position in order to emerge from the outlet. To reach the pelvic floor, the fetal head has rotated on the shoulders so that the occiput can come under the pubic arch. This movement is essential for delivery and cannot be felt by the mother.

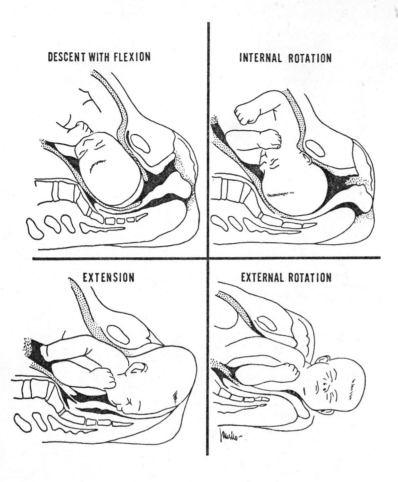

DESCENT WITH FLEXION   INTERNAL ROTATION

EXTENSION   EXTERNAL ROTATION

Fetal cardinal movements.

Let us check your knowledge so far:

The fetal movements that take place as the baby adapts to the maternal bony pelvis are known as the _____ movements.

cardinal fetal

When the widest diameter of the presenting part reaches the level of the ischial spines, _____ has taken place.

engagement

Descent means that the _____ is being _____ through the _____ pelvis.

fetus; propelled;

true

Flexion, another cardinal fetal movement, describes the _____ of the presenting part as it accommodates to the resistance presented by the_____ and the _____ _____ and _____ .

bending;

cervix; pelvic walls;

floor

1. WHAT ♀ Brings to labor
2. Stage I
   phases –
   feelings
   + Nsg care
   ≃ SOME REPEAT of
   Physio

Call Hutch -
    def. of ~~Premie~~ -
when is Abortion
    20 wks ?

In adapting to the widest measurement of the pelvic inlet, that is, the _____ diameter, and to the widest diameter of the outlet, or the_____ diameter, the fetal head will enter in the _____ position and will rotate_____ degrees to an LOA position.

transverse;

anterior-posterior;

transverse; 90

Now let us go on with the rest of the cardinal fetal mechanisms.

5. *Extension* begins upon completion of internal rotation. The vertex passes under the pubic arch as labor continues, and as the mother bears down, the fetal head deflexes. As the labia separate, the occiput, then the vertex, and finally the brow and face appear.

6. *External rotation* or *restitution* occurs shortly after the birth of the head. This means that the fetal head rotates back to a transverse position. The shoulders at this time rotate to an anterior-posterior position as they come through the pubic arch.

7. *Expulsion* is the final mechanism taking place as the anterior shoulder appears under the pubic arch; and through the propelling force of the uterine muscles, the rest of the fetal body is spontaneously delivered.

The completion of internal rotation marks the beginning of a fifth mechanism of labor called _____ . This comes about as a result of the fact that the mother's _____ down _____ the fetal head.

extension;

bearing; deflexes

External rotation or _____ occurs after the _____ of the_____ . This means that the fetal head has _____ back to the_____ position.

restitution;

birth; head;

rotated; transverse

When the anterior shoulder appears under the pubic arch, the fetal mechanism known as_____ begins, and the rest of the baby's body is born.

expulsion

Since the processes of delivery may cause some degree of maternal discomfort or even pain, the physician may choose to do a pudendal block (injecting a local anesthetic agent at the junction of the pudendal nerves) or a local infiltration with an anesthetic agent injected into the perineum. This will enable him to perform the episiotomy if needed and later on make the necessary surgical repairs of the incision.

As the mother pushes with each contraction, more and more caput becomes visible, and the final mechanisms of internal rotation and extension of the fetal head may be seen. As the largest diameter of the baby's head appears surrounded by the perineum, this is called *crowning*. It is just before this time that the episiotomy is usually done. The type of episiotomy to be done is dependent upon the physician's preference. Some physicians may choose to cut the perineal body at a slant to either the right or left (mediolateral episiotomy); others may choose to make a medial incision (midline episiotomy). It is felt that a mediolateral episiotomy causes more maternal discomfort postpartally and may produce complications such as infections and hematomas.

To relieve the pain generated by the processes of delivery and/or an episiotomy, a local anesthetic may be administered at the junction of the pudendal nerves; this is known as a _____ .

Also, the perineum may be anesthetized by means of a _____

_____ .

pudendal block;

local infiltration

Once the baby's head is born, the physician grasps the baby's chin with a sterile towel while holding the perineum in order to keep the chin from sliding back after the next contraction. This is called Ritgen's maneuver. At this time, the physician instructs the mother not to push but to pant while he controls the delivery of the head. He checks to be sure that the umbilical cord is not wrapped around the baby's neck before applying even, upward traction to deliver the posterior shoulder. Then the anterior shoulder is delivered by downward traction. Following this, expulsion of the rest of the body takes place.

Once the baby is born, the physician proceeds to aspirate any mucus from the baby's nose and mouth using a rubber bulb syringe; this will help to ensure a patent airway and will aid in establishing respirations; the onset of respirations will be signaled by the cries of the baby. The umbilical cord is clamped with two hemostats and is cut between the two hemostats. The baby is then transferred to a warm bassinet where a special umbilical clamp is applied to the cord about 1½ inches from the neonate's umbilicus, and a total assessment of its health status is carried out. The activities related to the assessment and care of the newborn are outlined more clearly in chapter 5 of this unit.

Once the head of the baby is born, the physician checks the umbilical cord to ensure that it is not _____

the baby's neck.

wrapped around

Immediately following the birth of the baby, the physician uses a rubber bulb syringe to _____ from the _____ and _____ . This will establish a patent _____ and will help in initiating _____ . The umbilical cord is _____ and _____ and an _____ is applied.

aspirate mucus;

nose; mouth;

airway; respirations;

clamped; cut;

umbilical clamp

Stage Three of labor and delivery begins after the birth of the baby and ends with delivery of the placenta. Placental separation usually occurs between five and 20 minutes after the birth of the baby. Signs of this event are: (1) elongation of the section of umbilical cord extending from the vagina; (2) a sudden small gush of blood from the vagina; (3) the uterus becoming firm and globular in shape, rising into the abdomen.

Placental separation begins _____ to _____ minutes following the delivery of the baby. Signs of placental separation are _____ _____ , sudden _____ _____ from the vagina, and the _____ becoming _____ and _____ in shape and rising into the _____ .

five; 20;

elongation of **umbilical cord** from vagina; **small gush of** blood; uterus; firm; globular; abdomen

The expulsion of the placenta takes place by either of two mechanisms: In the Schultz mechanism, the fetal surface, which is shiny, comes through the vagina first. In the Duncan mechanism, the maternal side of the placenta is delivered first.

With the delivery of the placenta, the third stage of labor has been completed. At this point, the physician carefully examines the secundines (the membranes and the placenta) to ascertain that it is complete and that no fragments have remained in the uterus. Retained placental tissue can prevent the uterus from contracting completely and may cause postpartal complications such as hemorrhage. To ensure that uterine contraction takes place, oxytocics may be administered at this time.

Placental expulsion occurs by means of one of two mechanisms: one is the _____ mechanism; in this mechanism, the fetal surface of the placenta is _____ first. The other mechanism, known as the _____ mechanism, is when the _____ side of the placenta is delivered first.

Schultz;

delivered;

Duncan; maternal

Careful examination of the membranes and the placenta, which together are called the _____ , ensures that no fragments have remained in the _____ . Retention of _____ tissue will prevent the uterus from _____ and may cause _____ hemorrhage.

       Drugs such as _____ may be given at this time to aid in _____ of the uterus.

secundines;

uterus; placental;

contracting;

postpartal

oxytocics;

contraction

Stage Four immediately follows the delivery of the placenta. Although the processes of labor have been completed, this is a most critical hour for both the mother and the baby.

For the mother, hemorrhage may be a danger; bleeding of more than 500 cubic centimeters indicates that this complication is present.

A bleeding uterus is usually indicated by a soft, boggy consistency when you palpate it abdominally. During this stage, it is important that the uterus be checked periodically and that the fundus be carefully palpated to make sure that it is firm; if signs of uterine relaxation are present, the fundus should be carefully massaged until it regains its firmness. It is important at this time to assess the amount of bleeding and presence of any clots. If massage is needed repeatedly to maintain firmness, or if there is excessive bleeding, the physician should be notified immediately.

The first hour following the delivery of the placenta is the _____ stage of labor. At this time, it is important that the uterus be carefully observed and palpated to ensure that it has remained _____ and to prevent postpartal _____ .

       If the uterus appears soft and boggy, the _____ should be carefully _____ until this organ regains firmness.

fourth;

firm; hemorrhage

fundus;

massaged

Immediately after delivery, the uterus can be located in the lower abdomen; however, after several hours, it will rise up to about the level of the umbilicus.

During this first critical hour of the fourth stage of labor, the mother may experience a shaking chill. This reaction does not commonly result in an elevation of body temperature nor is it associated with any type of infection. The mother should be covered with a warmed blanket and, if alert, can at this time be given warm tea to drink. Some institutions adhere to the policy that the mother be kept in a recovery room where she is bathed and carefully observed for signs of complications during this first critical hour. Vital signs are monitored frequently and a total assessment is done of maternal reactions brought about by the sudden return to a nonpregnant state.

Immediately after delivery the uterus may be found to be in the
_____ ; several hours after delivery,
however, the uterus _____ up to the _____
of the _____ . During the first hour after delivery, the
mother may experience a _____ ;
therefore, she should be _____ with a _____
blanket. If so indicated, she may be given _____
by mouth. Monitoring the _____ at this time is
very important.

lower abdomen;

rises; level;

umbilicus;

shaking chill;

covered; warmed;

warm tea;

vital signs

As the mother is transferred to the postpartum unit, she should be
instructed to check and feel her fundus and should be shown how to massage
it should it become soft; she should also be told to report this event to a staff
member since recurrence of uterine softness and bogginess will be an indication that clots or placental fragments remaining within the uterus are preventing this organ from remaining contracted.

The completion of the fourth stage of labor marks the beginning of new
interactions and relationships within the family system. The reality of the
baby is now a concrete event that will add a new dimension to the types of
ongoing adaptations that began when conception took place.

These adaptive processes and the changes brought about within the
family structure are explored in the fifth unit of this programmed text.
Before going on to that, however, let us see how you can apply your
knowledge of the processes of labor and delivery to interactions with one of
the families you met earlier in this book.

During a very busy morning in the labor room, Bill and Jean Garry
anxiously present themselves at the door. Bill is carrying Jean's suitcase and
holding Jean protectively around the shoulders. They have just come from
Dr. Franklin's office where he verified that Jean's membranes are ruptured
and that her cervix is 4 centimeters dilated. They tell you that contractions
started three hours ago and that they are now five minutes apart.

During the admission procedure you would:

A. Assess the couple's anxiety level and ask them if they have seen
the delivery suite. You find out what they remember from the
antepartal classes about the admission procedure before you
start to explain what you will do during the admission.

Go to page 249 bottom.

B. Recognize the danger of ruptured membranes; tell Bill to go to
the waiting room and tell Jean that she must get into bed and
stay there. Explain to her that as soon as you are able, you will
return with the necessary equipment for admission, since right
now the labor room is really busy.

Go to page 250 bottom.

C. Greet Bill and Jean, take them to the labor room, and, recognizing that they may be anxious about Jean's impending delivery,

reassure them that they have nothing to worry about. Then proceed to explain to them all of the procedures that are to be done throughout Jean's stay in the labor room.

Go to page 251 top.

Four hours after admission, Jean suddenly complains of nausea and vomits a small amount of clear liquid. Her legs seem to tremble involuntarily, and, as you check the perineum, you note an increase in bloody show. Uterine contractions are now closer together, almost continuous, and quite intense. Jean's demeanor seems to have undergone quite a radical change; she is no longer cooperative, complains that "she can't do this any longer," snaps at Bill when he tries to comfort her, and, when you attempt to feel her abdomen or check the fetal heart rate, won't allow you to touch her. Your response to Jean at this time should be:

A. "It must be very difficult for you to be so uncomfortable and so tired. I'll wait until you feel better before bothering you again."

Go to page 251 middle.

B. "Would you like me to ask Bill to wait outside so that I can give you a bath? You'll feel more comfortable if there are fewer people around to bother you."

Go to page 250 top.

C. "This is a very difficult time for you, but labor is almost over and I am going to listen to the baby's heart rate and continue to observe your progress."

Go to page 249 top.

Jean has delivered a 7-pound baby girl. The baby has been transferred to the newborn nursery while Jean has been moved to the recovery area following the completion of the third stage of labor. During your interaction with her, she tells you that she feels quite tired; in spite of this, however, she appears to want to talk, as she asks you where they took the baby and when she will be able to see her again. In addition to giving her a bath and taking the vital signs, which of the following statements includes appropriate nursing measures that will aid in meeting Jean's physical and psychological needs at this time?

A. Check the fundus for firmness, explaining to Jean what you are doing. Encourage her to try to sleep and not worry about the baby, since the baby will be kept in the nursery until everyone is sure that she is all right.

Go to page 250 middle.

B. Explain the reasons for your frequent examination of the fundus and teach Jean how to massage it if it becomes relaxed. Tell her that the baby was taken to the newborn nursery and that you will find out how soon after delivery babies are brought to the mother.

Go to page 251 bottom.

C. Keep careful watch of the fundus and perineum and take this opportunity to tell Jean about hospital routines and infants' feeding schedules; teach her about the positive aspects of breast-feeding such as its psychological importance in fostering the baby's feelings of security. Tell her that she will be able to see her baby very soon.

Go to page 249 middle.

In selecting statement *C,* you have recognized the fact that in spite of Jean's behavior and discomfort, she needs to be closely observed since she is in the transition phase. Your response indicates your ability to differentiate between situations requiring supporting statements and those requiring definitive commands; the transition phase is one of the latter situations.

Return to page 248 middle and continue with the program.

Your choice of statement *C* is incorrect. True, the fundus and the perineum should be watched at this time as part of appropriate nursing assessment measures, but is it appropriate to tell Jean about hospital routines and feeding schedules at this time? Not only that, but by stressing the importance of breast-feeding, you are imposing your own value judgment regarding the type of method that is best. Suppose Jean does not wish to breast-feed? What if Deladumone had been administered to her to suppress lactation? What feelings would this information elicit in Jean at this time? Finally, are you *sure* Jean will be able to see her baby *very soon*?

Return to page 248 and choose another response.

Your choice of statement *A,* "Assess the couple's anxiety . . .," indicates that you have remembered that at this time the upcoming unknown events of labor are sources of stress and emotional tension. In addition, you have been able to integrate excellent teaching principles by asking the couple to give you "feedback" relating to their knowledge of the admission procedure. In doing so, you will be able to establish priorities regarding the type of information that you will proceed to give them.

Turn to page 248 and continue with the program.

The Intrapartum Period

In choosing statement *B,* you evidence your lack of understanding as to how to deal with Jean at this time. Are you sure that giving her a bath or removing Bill will serve to increase her comfort during this phase of labor? Also, aren't you overlooking the need to maintain assessment measures during this time?

Return to page 235. Review the material and choose another response from page 248.

Your choice of statement *A,* is wrong. Although it is true that checking her fundus for firmness is an important assessment measure to be carried out at this time, the rest of the statement does not meet Jean's psychological needs. Even though it is true that she is tired, nevertheless she seems to have some concerns regarding her baby. Do you really think she will be able to rest without having an answer to her question? Besides, what about your response, "the baby will be kept in the nursery until everyone is sure she is all right." Doesn't this imply that there may be something wrong with Jean's baby girl? What kind of reaction do you think this information might evoke in Jean?

Return to page 248 and choose another response.

Your choice of statement *B* indicates that you have been unable to identify the fact that at this time the couple may be anxious; rather than allaying this condition, your actions and statement might have served to increase it: you have separated Bill from Jean and have left her quite isolated in her room not knowing if and when anyone will return to care for her. You have told her to get into bed and stay there without explaining the reasons why, and finally, you have used words such as "equipment" which generally have an impersonal and ominous ring to them.

Return to page 247 and choose another response.

In selecting statement *C*, you have provided the couple with false reassurances as you told them not to worry; at the same time, you have prevented any further expression of feelings. By proceeding to explain *all* of the procedures that will be carried out, you have overlooked the fact that usually anxiety is heightened by the pressures created in having to deal with too much information all at once. Although you did recognize the presence of anxiety, you were unable to identify that, in its presence, there usually is a short attention span, particularly to details, which serves to prevent the assimilation of large amounts of information.

Return to page 247 and choose another response.

Your response in choosing statement *A*, "It must be difficult for you . . .," fails to meet Jean's needs at this time. You seem to have forgotten that nursing intervention measures are to be instituted during the transition phase of Stage One, and why they are important. By the time Jean feels better, she will no longer need you to feel her abdomen or check the fetal heart rate!

Return to page 235. Review the material and choose another response from page 248.

Your selection of statement *B* is quite correct. Not only are you meeting Jean's physiological needs at this time by assessing the condition of the fundus, but also you are teaching her how to do this herself. In addition, you have provided her with important information about her baby, that is, the fact that she has been moved to the nursery; this information may allay any anxieties she may have, and your telling her that you will find out how soon she will be seeing her shows your interest in her.

Advance to page 252 and take the post-test.

POST-TEST   Indicate whether each statement is true or false by circling the appropriate letter. Then turn to page 254 and check how well you have done.

1. The first stage of labor is from 0 to 3 centimeters of cervical dilatation.   T   F

2. The transition phase of labor is from 8 to 10 centimeters of cervical dilatation.   T   F

3. The second stage of labor begins with the birth of the baby.   T   F

4. The delivery of the placenta ends the third stage of labor.   T   F

5. The first hour after delivery of the placenta is a critical hour for the mother.   T   F

6. During the first stage of labor, it is important to monitor the fetal heart rate every 15 minutes.   T   F

7. After the membranes have ruptured, the mother's vital signs are checked every two hours.   T   F

8. The mother's blood pressure normally rises during labor.   T   F

9. The color of the amniotic fluid is normally clear.   T   F

10. As soon as the mother feels the urge to push, she should bear down.   T   F

11. Panting makes it difficult for the mother to push down.   T   F

12. The mood of the mother during the dilatation phase is one of anger and hostility.   T   F

13. An increased amount of bloody show passed will indicate that cervical dilatation is occurring.   T   F

14. Caput refers to the baby's head once it is delivered.   T   F

15. Flexion is the movement that occurs as the baby's head bends when it meets the resistance of the cervix and pelvic walls.   T   F

16. Separation of the placenta is indicated by a gush of blood, lengthening of the cord, and upward movement of the uterus in the abdomen.   T   F

17. It is important that the uterus stay contracted during the fourth stage of labor.   T   F

In the specific areas with which you had difficulty, return to the material and review.

BIBLIOGRAPHY   Allen, Shelly, "Nurse Attendance During Labor," *American Journal of Nursing,* Vol. 64, p. 70ff., July 1964.

Bell, David Scarborough: *Textbook of Physiology and Biochemistry,* 5th ed., Livingstone, Edinburgh, 1963.

Brotanek, V. et al., "Changes in Uterine Blood Flow During Uterine Contractions," *American Journal of Obstetrics and Gynecology,* Vol. 103, pp. 1108-1116, April 15, 1969.

Case, Lynda, "Ultrasound Monitoring of Mother and Fetus," *American Journal of Nursing,* Vol. 72, pp. 725-727, April 1972.

Copher, David E. and Morris M. White, "Evaluating Fetal Well-Being Under Clinical Conditions by Continuous Electronic Monitoring," *Measuring for Medicine and the Life Sciences,* Vol. 5, Nos. 1-2, pp. 1-8, May-Aug. 1970.

Danforth, D. N. and C. A. Baldwin, "Pain Relief in the Parturient," *Medical Clinics of North America,* Vol. 52, No. 137, pp. 137-146, Jan. 1968.

Effer, S. B., et al., "Quantitative Study of the Regularity of Uterine Contractile Rhythm in Labor," *American Journal of Obstetrics and Gynecology,* Vol. 105, pp. 909-915, November 15, 1969.

Farell, Monique S., "Adolescent in Labor," *American Journal of Nursing,* Vol. 68, pp. 1952-1954, Sept. 1968.

Fitzpatrick, Erna, J. Eastman Nicholson, and Sharon Reeder: *Maternity Nursing,* 11th ed., J. B. Lippincott Co., Philadelphia, 1966.

Hellman, Louis and Jack Pritchard: *Williams' Obstetrics,* 14th ed., Appleton-Century-Crofts, New York, 1971.

Hoff, F. E., "Maternal Childbirth, How Any Nurse Can Help," *American Journal of Nursing,* Vol. 69, p. 1451, July 1969.

Kitzinger, Sheila: *The Experience of Childbirth,* rev. ed., Penguin Books, Harmondsworth, Great Britain, 1967.

Kopp, Lois M., "Ordeal or Ideal—The Second Stage of Labor," *American Journal of Nursing,* Vol. 71, p. 1141, June 1971.

Lasayer, Carol, "Electronic Monitoring of Mother and Fetus," *American Journal of Nursing,* Vol. 72, pp. 728-730, April 1972.

Masouch, I., "Fetal Nursing During Labor," *Nursing Clinics of North America,* Vol. 3, pp. 307-314, June 1968.

Shainess, Natalie, "The Psychological Experience of Labor," *New York State Journal of Medicine,* Vol. 63, pp. 2923-2932, Oct. 15, 1963.

Tryon, F. A., "Assessing the Progress of Labor Through Observation of the Patient's Behavior," *Nursing Clinics of North America,* Vol. 3, p. 315, June 1968.

Ulin, Priscilla, "Changing Techniques in Psycho-prophylactic Preparation for Childbirth," *American Journal of Nursing,* Vol. 68, pp. 2587-2591, Dec. 1968.

Young, E. W., "Prepared Childbirth: Its Impact on Nursing," *Canadian Nurse,* Vol. 64, pp. 39-43, Jan. 1968.

PRETEST ANSWERS   1. Three phases   2. A cervical dilatation of 10 centimeters   3. The delivery of the baby   4. The delivery of the placenta   5. One hour after the delivery of the placenta   6. 15 minutes; treatments and examination and rupture of the membranes   7. 120-160 beats per minute   8. Normal, regular breathing   9. A full bladder slows descent and interferes with the effectiveness of contractions   10. Strong, frequent contractions; sleeping between contractions; diaphoresis; nausea and vomiting; shaking of legs; increased bloody show   11. The second stage   12. Clear   13. After every contraction   14. Engagement; descent; flexion; internal rotation; extension; external rotation; expulsion   15. Lengthening of the cord; a sudden gush of blood; rising up of uterus into the abdomen   16. Should be firm or contracted to decrease the bleeding or hemorrhage

POST-TEST ANSWERS

1. F	2. T	3. F	4. T	5. T	6. T	7. T	8. F
9. T	10. F	11. T	12. F	13. T	14. F	15. T	16. T
17. T							

CHAPTER FIVE

IMMEDIATE ASSESSMENT AND CARE OF THE NEONATE

OBJECTIVES *Identify three immediate major physiological changes occurring in the neonate.*

Identify the five scoring categories and the method used in assessment of the neonate using Apgar scoring.

Identify two ways used to identify the neonate and the mother.

Identify the immediate needs of the neonate.

GLOSSARY *Mucus trap:* A mechanical device used to suction the nasopharynx of the newborn, consisting of a glass bulb with a catheter for insertion on one end and a mouthpiece on the other end

Pulmonary surfactant: A substance made up of phospholipoids which is necessary for adequate surface tension of the alveoli

Apgar scoring: A numerical method of rating the respiratory effect, heart rate, muscle tone, reflex irritability, and color of the newborn

Ophthalmia neonatorum: A gonococcal infection of the eyes of the newborn

PRETEST   In the spaces provided, fill in the word or words that best complete(s) the statements. Then turn to page 262 and check your answers.

1. There are three physiological systems that undergo change immediately at the time of birth; these are the _____ , _____ , and _____ .

2. In order for the neonate to establish effective respirations, it is important to remove _____ .

3. Effective surface tension in the lungs is provided by the _____ _____ .

4. As the umbilical cord is clamped, there is a major change in the _____ .

5. Body heat is produced by _____ and _____ .

6. The neonate immediately after birth is placed in a _____ .

7. The five areas that are scored on the Apgar assessment are _____ _____ , _____ , _____ , _____ , and _____ .

8. Before the infant leaves the delivery room, prophylactic medication usually is applied to _____ to eliminate _____ .

9. Proper identification of the infant is ensured by _____ and _____ .

10. An evaluation of the infant is done quickly to check _____ .

As the birth process is completed, immediate major physiological changes take place. A drastic change occurs in the *respiratory system*; the newborn is no longer able to obtain oxygen from the maternal system but now must establish his own *ventilation* immediately. It is felt that during a vertex delivery the thorax is compressed after the delivery of the head, and this assists in eliminating much of the amniotic fluid that is still present within the pulmonary system. As the head of the baby is born, the *mucus and fluid secretions* are removed from the *oral and nasal passages* by the doctor, using a rubber bulb syringe. Since effective ventilation is dependent upon *clear air passages,* further suctioning of the nose and pharynx is often done using a mucus trap. This mucus trap allows for gentle suctioning, lessening the trauma to the mucus membranes. During this time, the *infant's head* is kept *low,* to allow for the drainage of fluid and to prevent aspiration.

As the infant is born and is no longer able to obtain oxygen from the maternal blood, change takes place in the _____   respiratory system;

and establishment of _____ occurs.   ventilation

As the thorax is compressed during delivery, this _____   aids in the elimination of

_____ .   amniotic fluid

The head of the neonate is kept low to _____   aid in the drainage of fluid

_____   and mucus;

and to _____ .   prevent aspiration

The pulmonary system of the neonate must have sufficient *surface tension* in the lungs for the effective exchange of gases to take place. This surface tension is provided by a combination of phospholipoids called *pulmonary surfactant.* There must be sufficient amounts or the alveoli will collapse or overexpand.

Delay in the establishment of adequate respiratory function for over a minute is indicative of a problem. As respirations are established normally by the neonate, a major transitional task has been accomplished.

Surface tension in the lungs is provided by _____   pulmonary surfactant

_____ .

This must be present in sufficient amounts to provide for _____   adequate ventilation

_____ .

As the neonate is born, an immediate change takes place in the *circulatory system* also: when the umbilical cord is clamped and cut, circulation through the placenta ceases. Other circulatory changes are in a *tran-*

sitional state, taking several days, weeks, or even months until the change is permanent.

Thus the blood no longer flows directly between the two atria because the _____ closes.

foramen ovale

Since the blood must now circulate through the pulmonary system, the _____ constricts.

patent ductus

Also, the blood is directed through the liver instead of bypassing it as the _____ constricts.

ductus venosus

The third major change that takes place after the infant is born is the alteration of the *metabolic system.* The infant's system is now independent of the maternal system and must maintain *body heat.* This requires the use of body stores of glucose and nutrients as well as muscular movements. The *kidney* now assumes the total responsibility for the elimination of nitrogenous wastes, and the *digestive tract* must break down and assimilate nutrients.

The neonate can no longer depend on the maternal system to provide and maintain _____ .

body heat

The kidneys now function to _____
_____ .

eliminate nitrogenous waste

The digestive tract must now _____
and _____ .

break down;
assimilate nutrients

Apgar scoring[1] is a means of *immediate assessment* of the newborn to determine the need for resuscitation (the assistance and establishment of respiration) and to determine the health status of the baby. The evaluation is done in *five categories.* The neonate is rated from 0 to 2 in each category; thus there is a maximum total score of 10. This scoring is usually done at one minute and at five minutes after the baby is delivered and is scored as follows:

1. *Heart rate:* 2 if over 100 beats per minute; 1 if below; 0 if absent

2. *Respiratory effort:* 2 if good with crying; 1 if slow and irregular; 0 if absent

3. *Muscle tone:* 2 if active motion; 1 if some flexion of extremities; 0 if absent

4. *Reflex irritability:* 2 for vigorous cry; 1 for cry; 0 for no response

5. *Color:* 2 for pink including extremities; 1 for pink body and blue extremities; 0 for pale or blue color

How would you evaluate a newborn at one minute who was: pink with bluish extremities, crying vigorously, moving both arms and legs, had good respirations, and had a heart rate of 95? The score would be _____ .   8

That would mean that each category except color and heart rate received a score of 2 and these received a score of 1.

It is important to note whether the infant experiences any respiratory distress between the first and fifth minute, since this will not be indicated by the Apgar score. Often, if the infant receives a low score, the rating is repeated again at ten minutes to reassess the baby's status.

After the cutting of the cord, the immediate care of the newborn is to place him in a *heated crib* or Kreiselman because he is experiencing a sudden *environmental drop* in temperature. During this time, the head is kept *low* to enable the remaining mucus and amniotic fluid to drain out.

At this time, *prophylactic medication* is applied to the baby's eyes to prevent *ophthalmia neonatorum*, which may be contracted during the passage through the birth canal because of the presence of gonococcus organisms. This medication usually is *silver nitrate*, which after its application is flushed with sterile normal saline to prevent conjunctivitis.

The infant is immediately placed in a _____ crib   heated;

because of the _____ .   sudden drop in temperature

Medication is applied to the infant's eyes because of the possibility of

infection due to _____ .   gonococcus

This medication is _____ .   silver nitrate

It is also necessary to *identify* the *baby* and the *mother* as a unit. This is done by placing matching *arm bands* on both the mother and baby. Usually, an extra band is placed around the baby's ankle to provide identification should the other one slip off. Also, *footprints* are taken of the baby, and on the same sheet the *mother's right index finger print* is taken. These are checked at the time of discharge.

It is important to identify the mother and baby as a _____ .   unit;

This is done using _____ and   arm bands;

_____

_____ .

An initial physical examination is carried out in the delivery room. The general appearance is noted, then the baby is checked for cleft palate, patent anus, congenital hip malformation, continuous spinal column, and the presence of three vessels in the cord. The examiner checks the head by feeling the sutures and fontanels. This brief examination will determine gross abnormalities.

A physical examination is done to _____

_____ .

At this time the mother and father are given an opportunity to hold the baby, if they have not already done so. The nursing responsibility is to be supportive as the parents meet this new member of the family. They need assistance in holding, examining, and adjusting to the reality of their newborn.

When the parents hold the infant for the first time, the nurse's role is to be _____ .

Most hospitals have the policy that the baby then proceeds to the nursery for a period of observation in a warm environment. Once the neonate's temperature stabilizes, an admission bath is given and he is bundled for sleep.

Right margin answers:

footprints of baby and finger print of mother

check gross physical characteristics

supportive

POST-TEST Indicate whether each statement is true or false by circling the appropriate letter. Then turn to page 262 and see how well you have done.

1. Effective ventilation for the neonate is assisted by removing the fluid and secretions from the mouth and pharynx.　　　　T　F

2. In order for adequate exchange of gases to occur in the lungs, the surface tension must be sufficient.　　　　T　F

3. An immediate change in the neonate's circulatory system is the permanent closing of the foramen ovale.　　　　T　F

4. There is no immediate change of the neonate's metabolism at birth.　　　　T　F

5. If the heart rate is over 100, the neonate receives an Apgar score of 1.　　　　T　F

6. If the neonate's extremities are partially flexed, you would assign the score of 1.　　　　T　F

7. Respiratory distress will always show up in the one-minute and five-minute scoring.　　　　T　F

8. Silver nitrate is used in the delivery room to prevent infection from developing around the umbilical cord.　　　　T　F

9. It is important to identify the infant before he leaves the delivery room.　　　　T　F

10. The parents often meet and hold the new offspring in the delivery room and at this time need no nursing support.　　　　T　F

In the specific areas in which you had difficulty, return to the material and review.

REFERENCES   1. Virginia Apgar, "The Newborn (Apgar) Scoring System, Reflections and Advice," *Pediatric Clinics of North America*, Vol. 13, pp. 645-650, Aug. 1966.

BIBLIOGRAPHY   Apgar, Virginia, "The Newborn (Apgar) Scoring System, Reflections and Advice," *Pediatric Clinics of North America,* Vol. 13, pp. 645-650, Aug. 1966.

——, "Resuscitation of the Newborn, When and How to Do It." *Hospital Topics,* Vol. 44, p. 105 ff., Nov. 1966.

Arnold, Helen, Nancy Putnam, Betty Lou Barnard, Murdina Desmond, and Arnold Rudolph, "The Newborn—Transition to Extra-Uterine Life," *American Journal of Nursing,* Vol. 65, pp. 77-80, Oct. 1965.

Hervada, Arturo, "Nursing Evaluation of the Newborn," *American Journal of Nursing,* Vol. 67, pp. 1669-1671, Aug. 1967.

Hodgman, Joan, "Clinical Evaluation of the Newborn Infant," *Hospital Practice,* May 1969, pp. 70-86.

PRETEST ANSWERS   1. Respiratory; circulatory; metabolic   2. Fluid and secretions   3. Pulmonary surfactant   4. Circulation   5. Muscular movement; metabolism   6. Warm crib   7. Heart rate; respiratory effort; muscle tone; reflex irritability; color   8. The eyes; gonococcal infection   9. An arm band; footprints   10. Gross physical characteristics

POST-TEST ANSWERS   1. T   2. T   3. T   4. F   5. F   6. T   7. F   8. F   9. T   10. F

The following multiple-choice examination will test your comprehension of the material covered in the fourth unit of this program. Do not guess at the answers; if you need to do this then you have not learned the content. Return to the program and review areas that give you difficulty, before going on with the examination.

Circle the letter of the best response to each question. After completing the unit examination, check your answers on page 332 and review those areas of difficulty before proceeding to the next unit.

1. Upon examination of the fetal head, you will find the posterior fontanel as the junction of the:
    a. Sagittal and lambdoidal sutures
    b. Lambdoidal and coronal sutures
    c. Sagittal and coronal sutures
    d. Coronal and temporal sutures

2. Palpation of the maternal abdomen utilizing Leopold's maneuver will:
    a. Determine the degree of cervical dilatation
    b. Determine the position of the fetus
    c. Determine whether the membranes are ruptured or intact
    d. Determine the presence or absence of fetal distress

3. Upon the mother's admission to the labor and delivery suite, the doctor examined the mother and found that the fetus was well flexed. This describes the fetal:
    a. Attitude
    b. Position
    c. Presentation
    d. Station

4. After a vaginal examination was done by the doctor, the fetal position was charted as ROA. You would explain to the mother that this means:
    a. The back of the baby's head is turned so it is on the left side of the mother and towards the front
    b. The back of the baby's head is turned so that it is on the right side of the mother and towards the front
    c. The back of the baby's head is directly posterior
    d. The baby's head is turned to the right side of the mother and towards the back

5. When the fetal presentation has been determined as vertex, the fetal heart will be found:
    a. In the upper quadrant of the mother's abdomen and through the fetal back
    b. In the upper quadrant of the mother's abdomen and through the fetal thorax
    c. In the lower quadrant of the mother's abdomen and through the fetal back
    d. In the lower quadrant of the mother's abdomen and through the fetal thorax

6. While listening to the fetal heart rate with the fetascope, you hear a soft blowing at 82 beats a minute; this is probably:
    a. The funic souffle
    b. The uterine souffle
    c. The fetal heart
    d. The amniotic fluid moving

7. A fetal heart rate is taken when the mother is admitted in early labor. The rate is 120 beats per minute; this is:
   a. Within the upper limits of normal
   b. Within the lower limits of normal
   c. Above the normal range
   d. Below the normal range

8. As the fetus passes through the birth canal, certain adaptations are possible since:
   a. The fontanels are very large
   b. The long bones are not ossified
   c. The cephalic bones are able to override
   d. The frontal bone is ossified

9. The order of the cardinal fetal movement is:
   a. Descent, internal rotation, flexion, engagement, restitution, extension, expulsion
   b. Flexion, restitution, engagement, internal rotation, descent, extension, expulsion
   c. Engagement, descent, flexion, internal rotation, extension, restitution, expulsion
   d. Extension, descent, flexion, internal rotation, engagement, restitution, expulsion

10. Effective timing of contractions is done by the nurse by placing the fingers lightly on the fundus of the uterus. This is because the fundus is:
    a. The most accessible area
    b. The portion where the least discomfort is perceived by the mother
    c. The most contractile part of the uterus
    d. The area that never fully relaxes

11. The duration of the contraction is the time from:
    a. The beginning of the acme to the end of the decrement
    b. The beginning of the increment to the start of the acme
    c. The beginning of the decrement to the end of the decrement
    d. The beginning of the increment to the beginning of the decrement

12. A mother admitted to the labor and delivery suite had a vaginal examination and was found to be 70 percent effaced and 4 centimeters dilated. This indicates that she is in:
    a. The first stage, effacement phase
    b. The first stage, dilatation phase
    c. The second stage, transition phase
    d. The second stage, effacement phase

13. A mother in labor who is in the effacement phase should be instructed during the contractions to:
    a. Bear down
    b. Hold her breath as long as possible
    c. Do accelerated and decelerated breathing
    d. Breathe normally

14. When the mother becomes 6 centimeters dilated, station +1, you would expect the contractions to be:
    a. Irregular and mild
    b. Regular every five minutes and mild
    c. Regular every three minutes and of moderate intensity
    d. Regular every one minute and severe in intensity

15. Several minutes after the doctor has evaluated the cervical dilatation as 6 centimeters, the mother begins to cry out, saying, "The baby is coming; the baby is coming." The most appropriate nursing action would be to:
    a. Reassure her that everything is all right and explain what 6 centimeters means
    b. Tell her that she is mistaken and that the doctor should know
    c. Examine her perineum
    d. Get the analgesic that the doctor ordered p.r.n.

16. Upon transferring the mother to the delivery room table, you observe that she begins grunting and bearing down with contractions; upon examining the perineum, you are aware that crowning has occurred. Your most appropriate action would be to:
    a. Tell the mother to pant as you open a pack of sterile towels
    b. Tell the mother to stop pushing since the doctor is not yet ready
    c. Run out and get a doctor
    d. Stay with the mother and explain that the doctor is scrubbing and will be ready in a minute

17. After the cord is clamped and the baby placed in the Kreiselman crib, your first action would be to:
    a. Wrap the baby in a warm sterile blanket
    b. Do the identifying procedure
    c. Clear the nasopharynx
    d. Do the Credé procedure

18. The most critical time for the mother occurs during:
    a. The first postpartal hour
    b. The first 24 hours postpartum
    c. The stage of placental separation
    d. The delivery of the head of the neonate

19. After the delivery of the placenta, the doctor tells you to add 10 cubic centimeters of Pitocin into the mother's intravenous infusion. This is done to:
    a. Shorten the third stage of labor
    b. Help the mother to void
    c. Raise the mother's blood pressure after the blood loss due to parturition
    d. Control postpartal bleeding

UNIT V

THE FAMILY DURING THE POSTPARTUM PERIOD

CHAPTER ONE

CHANGES DURING THE PUERPERIUM

OBJECTIVES   *Identify the physiological processes of uterine involution.*

Identify physiological adaptations of major anatomical and physiological systems, such as urinary, gastrointestinal, endocrine, and circulatory.

Identify the three classifications of lochia.

Identify the physiology of lactation.

Identify the two psychological phases of the puerperium.

Identify nursing intervention measures.

GLOSSARY   *Puerperium:* The period lasting for six weeks after delivery
Autolysis: The breaking down of protein into smaller compounds
Atrophy: The shrinking of the size of the cell
Lochia: Vaginal discharge occurring after delivery
Engorgement: Increased vascularity and milk accumulation in the breast occurring around the third day of the postpartum period

PRETEST   In the spaces provided, fill in the word or words that best complete(s) the statements. Then turn to page 287 and check your answers.

1. The puerperium is the _____
    _____
    _____ .

2. Involution is defined as _____
    _____ .

3. The mother feels physically _____
    _____ after the delivery.

4. Emotionally, she may feel _____ after the delivery.

5. Two maternal emotional needs that must be met by the father postpartally are
    _____ and
    _____ .

6. Reva Rubin describes two postpartal phases; these are the _____
    and the _____ phases.

7. During the first phase, the father's role becomes_____ and
    _____ .

8. The father also needs _____ , _____ , and
    _____ from the staff.

9. During the second of Ms. Rubin's phases, the mother vacillates between a need for
    _____ and a need for _____ .

10. The nurse should be aware of the postpartal, anticlimactic letdown experienced by
    many mothers, called _____ .

11. Involution of the uterus is accomplished by the processes of _____
    and _____ .

12. The new endometrium is regenerated from the _____
    _____ .

13. Most of the endometrium is formed by the _____ day.

14. The area over the placental site heals by the _____ **week.**

15. Involution can be assessed by nursing observations concerning the _____ and the _____ _____ .

16. Lochia rubra consists of _____ , _____ , and _____ and lasts for _____ .

17. Lochia serosa consists of _____ and lasts for _____ .

18. Lochia alba consists of _____ and lasts for _____ .

19. The uterus descends into the pelvis at the rate of _____ _____ .

20. After delivery, the urinary bladder becomes _____ sensitive.

21. The mother's perineum should be checked each postpartal **day for signs of** _____ , _____ , _____ , and _____ .

22. The return to normal water metabolism is accomplished through _____ and _____ .

23. The intestinal tract may be _____ during the postpartal **period.**

24. The principle of perineal care during the postpartal period is _____ .

25. Lactation is initiated by the release of _____ .

26. The sucking of the neonate stimulates the release of the pituitary hormone _____ .

27. After-pains are _____ .

28. Good circulation, decreasing the possibility of phlebitis, is **aided by early** _____ and graduated _____ .

29. The definition of postpartal morbidity is _____

_____

_____

_____ .

30. In a nonlactating mother, menstruation resumes in _____ to

_____ weeks postpartum.

31. A breast-feeding mother may not menstruate for up to _____

months.

The *puerperium* is the period of maternal physiological and psychological changes and adaptations beginning immediately following the delivery of the baby and lasting from five to six weeks. It has been said that the vast and rapid changes occurring during the puerperium closely border nonhealth states, for in no other situation do such severe physiological and psychic alterations occur without their signaling the emergence of a nonhealth state. During this time, because of the sudden return to a nonpregnant state, the mother is subjected to severe stresses brought about by the need to achieve a homeodynamic balance. The markedly rapid, progressive, and sudden physiological and psychological alterations and adaptations that occur during the puerperium seem quite marvelous.

During the period of the puerperium, as the maternal organism strives to maintain a delicate balance among all of the systems, nursing interventions are geared to ensuring that this balance is maintained and to preventing the emergence or intrusion of stressors that may disrupt the continuation of homeodynamic processes.

The puerperium is a period beginning _____ _____ and lasting for about _____ to _____ .

immediately after delivery;

five;

six weeks

This is a period marked by sudden, rapid, and progressive _____ and _____ changes.

physiological; psychological

Nursing interventions at this time are geared to ensuring the maintenance of _____ and the prevention of _____ .

homeodynamic balance;

emergent stressors

Immediately following delivery, the mother experiences a feeling of exhaustion due to the tremendous physiological exertions to which she has been subjected during labor. Nevertheless, the feelings of exhilaration and relief brought about by the experience often prevent her from becoming aware of her exhaustion. In the days and weeks to come, during the puerperium, she undergoes physiological adaptations relating to the restoration of hormonal balance, tissue healing, decrease in blood volume, weight loss, and repositioning of various anatomical organs. Concomitantly, psychological and social adaptations are necessary. There is an adjustment of roles and family patterns in the expanded family. New feelings, interactions, and repositioning of various anatomical organs. Concomitantly, psychological

The feeling experienced by the mother immediately following delivery is _____ . This is generally due to the _____ _____ she has been subjected to during _____ .

exhaustion; physiological

exertion; labor

These feelings may be masked by other feelings such as
_____ and _____ .

⮟ exhilaration; relief

The many physiological adaptations taking place relate to restoration of

_____ , _____ ,

decrease in _____ , _____

_____ , and repositioning of _____

_____ .

hormonal balance; tissue healing;

blood volume; weight loss;

various organs

The social and psychological adaptations that take place parallel to the physiological changes are adjustment of _____ , reorganization of _____ , and the experiencing of new _____ and _____ while assuming new responsibilities.

roles;

family patterns;

feelings; interactions

Throughout this time, the mother is in need of assurance of her husband's love and of his interest in the baby. The first two to three days of the puerperium are marked by her need to be passive and wholly dependent on others. As described by Reva Rubin, this is the "taking-in" phase of the postpartum period.[1] As the first few hours following delivery pass, the mother may experience increasing emotional tension, a state heightened by pervading feelings of anticlimax and emptiness. She has the realization of the baby's separation from her and its existence as an individual independent of her. It is this awareness of the baby's reality that begins to trigger the many changes in attitudes that are to take place as her maternal role is redefined.

During this taking-in period, the mother's passivity and dependence often become identifiable as she for a time relinquishes her right to make the most insignificant decisions, willingly follows suggestions and directions given by others, and gratefully accepts anything that may be done for her.

Characteristic of this stage is the mother's need to relive the experiences of labor and delivery; it is as though, by talking about it, she repeats the process and thus obtains confirmation of the end results and validates the adequacy of her own performance.

The first few days of the puerperium, particularly from the _____ to _____ days, maternal needs are those of _____ and _____ . This is generally referred to as the _____ of the puerperium. This period is characterized by the need to relive the experiences of _____ and _____ . The

first; third;

dependency; passivity

taking-in phase;

labor; delivery;

mother's passive behavior is demonstrated by the fact that, for a time, she may relinquish her right to make _____ . She tends to follow _____ and _____ and accepts anything that others may choose to do for her.

decisions;

directions; suggestions

The mother's taking-in period places the father in the position of having to assume the companionship and supportive roles totally in spite of the fact that he too may be experiencing conflicting feelings and may feel exhausted by the emotional strain of the baby's delivery.

In the first two to three days, during the taking-in phase, the father must assume the _____ and _____ roles.

companionship; supportive

The excitement he shares with the mother related to the advent of the baby can be surpassed only by his concern over the mother's welfare. He may be confused and worried by her reaction to the birth of the baby, her passivity and dependence, which may lead him to believe that there may be something wrong. As he realizes that this is a generally expected reaction on the part of the mother, he begins to assume responsibilities for decision making which, up to now, might have been shared. Although the mother is in the hospital, there is the reality of having to maintain a semblance of order within the household; daily routines must be adhered to, particularly if there are other children at home, for they must be fed, clothed, and cared for while the mother is away. In addition, it is a major responsibility of the father to prepare other family members for the many changes that are to take place once the new infant is brought into the family structure. Although the mother's need for dependence at this time may be fully placed on him, the father, too, is in need of support and reassurance, for he may also have doubts as to his ability to cope in caring for the baby and may question whether he will be capable of meeting the needs presented by the new family member.

Nursing intervention at this time requires recognition of these difficulties and assessment of the father's strengths and weaknesses in coping with the stresses placed on him as he assumes these responsibilities. Intervention measures are geared toward maintaining adequate communication between the father and the nurse, providing support and assistance, and supplying information related to what to expect in dealing with maternal and neonate changes.

Nursing intervention requires _____ and _____ of maternal and paternal needs.

recognition;

assessment

The mother's struggle for reestablishment of her autonomy and independence marks the onset of the second phase of the puerperium, or the "taking-hold" phase, which generally lasts for a period of about ten days.

During this time, the mother's concerns range from the need to obtain control of bodily functions to the anxieties that emerge as she begins to question her ability to care for the baby and to nurture and handle him. At times, some of the problems presented by this aspect of her maternal role are overwhelming; she may question her ability to be a good mother, and she may interpret small, apparently insignificant difficulties in providing physical care for the baby as a confirmation of her doubts. Often, conflicts emerge between her newly found responsibilities and her previous personal experiences. At times these conflicts elicit feelings of despair and inadequacy. These conflicts seem to gain further reinforcement from the fact that the special prerogatives with which her pregnant state endowed her are no longer solely hers, for these must now be be shared with the baby.

The second significant period of the puerperium is the _____   **taking-hold phase;**

_____ , a period generally lasting for about

_____ days.   **ten**

Main maternal concerns at this time are obtaining control of

_____ and coping with the _____   **bodily functions; anxieties;**

created by her questioning of her _____ as a mother.   **abilities**

The intensity of these conflicts may be increased if the father becomes totally involved with the baby and does not evaluate and respond to the mother's feelings and reactions. There may be a tendency on his part, for example, to want to direct his attention toward the infant as he seeks to validate that the baby is normal and that he is able to participate in its care. Proud and elated over the prospect of parenthood, he may not be sufficiently in tune with the unspoken doubts and questions the mother may have. Successful nursing intervention and assessment should include guidance to the father so that he is made aware of the mother's difficulties at this time. Skillful nurse-father interactions at this time should foster a sharing of ideas and feelings between the parents which, in turn, will lead to a strengthening of family bonds.

Nurse-father interactions should foster situations in which there can be

_____   **sharing of ideas and feelings**

between the parents.

Guidance for the father by the nurse should include information and

reassurance about both the _____ and the _____ .   **mother; baby**

Careful assessment of these psychological factors becomes an essential component of the nursing care given to the mother at this time. Nursing interventions may serve to reinforce the mother's feelings of inadequacy, for she may compare the nurse's skill in handling the baby with her own clumsy ways, thus further reinforcing her feeling of lack of effectiveness as a mother. Because of this, constant reassurance and explanation related to the management of the infant are important. Doing this time, the mother should be allowed to perform all of the necessary maternal tasks as means of demonstrating to her that, in time, she will be able to assume all of the responsibilities implied in caring for the infant.

Effective nursing intervention at this time includes allowing the mother

to perform necessary _____ . **maternal tasks**

Additional components of the nurse's intervention are _____ **reassurance;**

and _____ related to the management of the infant. **information**

Most women experience emotional upsets commonly referred to as the postpartum "blues," which may occur any time after the birth of the baby. This condition is a period of mild depression during which the mother may find herself crying for unknown reasons, and may become irritable, lose her appetite, and be unable to sleep. Generally, it is thought to be due to the many hormonal changes taking place at this time. This process, however, is not to be confused with the severe emotional imbalances characteristic of postpartum psychosis, a pathological condition often requiring intensive therapy.

There may be maternal mood changes that the mother cannot explain.

These are generally known as _____ . **postpartum blues**

Typical symptoms and behavior at this time are _____ , **irritability;**

_____ , _____ , **crying; inability to sleep;**

and _____ . **loss of appetite**

Encouragement and praise coupled with constant reinforcement and careful teaching are essential components of the nursing care of the mother and the baby during the first few days of the puerperium. Skillful handling of the mother at this time will assist successful adaptation after the family is discharged from the hospital.

The puerperium is the period of time in which the maternal physiological systems undergo vast alterations as their homeodynamics readapt to the nonpregnant state and lactation becomes established. The adaptation to the nonpregnant state takes about six weeks to complete, although many dramatic changes occur during the first five days.

    The nurse must be knowledgeable concerning the expected changes in the various systems and the signs of normal progress, in order to assess accurately the maternal health status related to these adaptations. Providing information to the family about the normal changes helps to alleviate undue anxiety as these changes occur.

During the puerperium, the maternal systems _____   readjust to the nonpregnant state
_____ .

The period of the puerperium lasts about _____   six weeks
_____ .

During the first five days, the maternal systems _____   undergo vast dramatic changes
_____ .

    One important change that occurs during the puerperium is that the uterus, which grew greatly in size during pregnancy and which contained the fetus, adjusts to the nonpregnant state by the process of *involution.* Through the process of involution, the size and weight of the uterus is greatly and rapidly reduced. From an organ weighing about 2 pounds at the time of delivery, it becomes one that weighs a mere 2 ounces ten days later. Involution takes place by *autolysis* and *atrophy*. Autolysis is the breaking down of the cellular proteins of the inner layers of the uterus into less complex components; these are absorbed by the circulatory system and later are excreted by the urinary system. Atrophy is the shrinking of the previously hypertrophied cells. At this time, the outer layer of the decidua is shed and cast off as part of the vaginal discharge called *lochia.* The inner decidual layer is the new endometrial uterine lining. The endometrium, except over the placental site, is regenerated within the first ten days after delivery. The placental site takes about three weeks to regenerate and does so without scarring.

Involution of the uterus is the process whereby the uterus _____   returns to the nonpregnant state
_____ .

    The two mechanisms responsible for involution are_____   autolysis;
and _____ .   atrophy

    Immediately after delivery the uterus weighs _____ ,   2 pounds;
whereas ten days later it weighs _____ .   2 ounces

    It is extremely important to assess the progress of involution so that any deviations can be recognized and remedied immediately. There are two ways of assessing this: (1) by abdominal palpation of the fundus of the uterus; (2) by observing the type and amount of lochia.

When the uterus is palpated, the fundus should be felt in the midline. The height of the fundus is usually at the level of the umbilicus shortly after delivery, and it descends by one fingerbreadth each day until, by the tenth day, it is no longer an abdominal organ. It is important to have the mother void before you palpate the uterus, since a full bladder can displace the uterus upward and to the side. The *consistency* of the uterus should be observed for firmness; a soft, spongy uterus may indicate a poorly contracted uterus and may be due to retained clots or placental tissue, in which case hemorrhage is likely to occur. So that this severe complication may be prevented, a relaxed uterus should be massaged immediately and clots expressed. If the uterus continues to relax, the doctor should be notified. The routine postpartal medical orders often include the administration of an oxytocic such as Methergine to aid in keeping the uterus firmly contracted.

Two nursing observations that assess the progress of involution are
_____ and _____
_____ .

palpating the fundus; observing type and amount of lochia

Shortly after delivery, the fundus can be palpated _____
_____ .

at the level of the umbilicus

The uterus descends about _____ daily.

one fingerbreadth

A full bladder may displace the uterus to _____ and
_____ .

the side; upward

The uterus should be located in the abdominal _____ .

midline

The consistency of the uterus should be _____ .

firm

If the nurse palpates a soft, boggy uterus, her first action would be to
_____ .

massage it

Another postpartal change concerns vaginal discharge. In assessing the amount and type of *lochia,* the nurse must be aware of the changes that occur as the puerperium progresses. During the first three days after delivery, the lochia is moderate in amount and bright red in color and is termed *lochia rubra.* This discharge consists of blood, cells from the outer layer of the decidua, and cells remaining from the amniotic fluid. After about the third day postpartum and until approximately the tenth day, the lochia becomes lighter in color and lesser in amount. It is now more serous, contains less blood, and is pinkish in color; this lochia is known as *lochia serosa.* The postpartal vaginal discharge may last three to six weeks after delivery. After the tenth day, however, the discharge is whitish to yellow in color and scanty in amount. This lochia is known as *lochia alba.* The odor of lochia is normally fleshy; therefore, any foul odor should be reported immediately as should the passing of any placental tissue or large clots. It is also important when observing the amount of discharge to report an increase or decrease.

It is important for the mother to know that there may be a sudden gush of lochia when she gets out of bed during the first several days after delivery. She should be informed also that the flow may be heavier for a short time upon going home and resuming normal activities.

The lochia during the first three postpartal days is _____ _____ to _____ in color, is   bright red;
_____ in amount, and is called _____   brownish;
_____ .   moderate; lochia rubra

After the third day, the lochia is called serosa and the color changes to
_____ ; this type of lochia lasts until the   light pinkish;
_____ day. Lochia alba continues until the _____   tenth; third;
to _____ week and is _____   sixth; whitish-yellow
in color.

The normal odor of lochia is _____ .   fleshy

If the mother excitedly tells you that she had a sudden gush of lochia when she got out of bed, you would tell her that _____   this is a normal occurrence
_____ .

During this period, the vagina and cervix are regaining their muscle tone and lacerations are in the process of healing. The cervix, although it attains a nonpregnant state, never closes as tightly as it did in the prepregnant state. The recovering vagina again develops rugae.

During this period, it is important also to check the mother's *perineum* at least once daily. The nurse should be observing the healing of the episiotomy, if one has been done, and should be checking the perineum for signs of edema, inflammation, or hematomas. Most of the discomfort the mother experiences during the early puerperium as she sits and/or walks is due to the episiotomy. Some of the measures that may help to relieve this discomfort are: sitz baths, heat lamps, anesthetic ointments or sprays, ice bags (during the first 24 hours), or astringent pads such as witch hazel. The nurse might also suggest that the mother tighten her gluteal muscles before sitting, and the doctor might also prescribe analgesics for the pain.

During the puerperium, the cervix and vagina regain _____   muscle tone
_____ .

As you check the perineum, you observe for signs of episiotomy
_____ and for reportable occurrences such as _____ ,
_____ , and _____ .

> healing; edema;
> inflammation; hematomas

Some measures that may alleviate discomfort from the episiotomy are

_____ , _____ ,
_____ , or _____ .

> sitz baths; heat lamps;
> ointments; sprays

During the first 48 hours of the puerperium, it is important that careful assessment of the maternal *intake and output* be maintained. Following delivery, the mother may experience difficulty in voiding; usually, this is the result of bladder insensitivity to the stimulus created by overdistention. The causative factors creating this condition are many: it may be the result of trauma to the bladder during parturition, due to pressure created by the fetus; or it may be caused by urethral edema. In addition, factors such as changes in intra-abdominal pressure and the use of anesthetic agents might have served to decrease the bladder's muscle tone. Thus, it is a nursing responsibility to encourage the mother to void; also the nurse should measure the output, since at times the mother may void small amounts with a large residual remaining in the bladder, which predisposes to urinary tract infection. It may be necessary to obtain an order for and proceed with a catheterization at this time.

From the second to the fifth day of the puerperium, there is a great shift of body fluid and an elimination of about 2 liters of fluid by diuresis and diaphoresis. This restoration of the prepregnant body fluid level accounts for much of the 5-pound weight loss during this time.

The decreased sensitivity and overdistention of the bladder may be a result of _____ , _____
_____ , _____
_____ , and _____ .

> trauma to bladder; urethral
> edema; decreased abdominal
> pressure; anesthetics

It is important for the nurse to encourage the mother to void early after delivery since she may not _____
_____

> feel the urge to void

The maternal body eliminates large quantities of fluid through
_____ and _____ .

> diuresis; diaphoresis

The great shift in body fluids occurs from the _____
to the _____ day.

> second;
> fifth

The bowel pattern is another part of the nursing assessment. During labor the mother often receives an enema and then has her intake of solid food reduced, so that normally it is the second or third day after delivery before she has a bowel movement. Other factors that influence this pattern are the poor tone of the stretched abdominal muscles and pain experienced from the episiotomy and often also from hemorrhoids. A mild laxative is often ordered, and if necessary an enema may follow.

The mother usually has an irregular bowel pattern due to the enema at delivery as well as _____ ,

_____ , and

_____ , and

_____ .

reduced solid intake;

stretched abdominal muscles;

pain from episiotomy;

hemorrhoids

Hygienic care of the perineal area, or "peri care," is taught to the mother at the time of first voiding after delivery. The perineum is rinsed with clean water and patted dry with special wipes. This prevents contamination of the episiotomy and the urinary meatus which may occur if the area is wiped with toilet paper, and also increases the mother's comfort. Peri care should be carried out after each voiding or bowel movement.

Peri care serves several functions: _____

_____ and _____ .

prevention of contamination;

provision of comfort

Lactation is initiated by the pituitary lactogenic hormone, prolactin. The first two days after delivery, colostrum is secreted by the breast; on the third day the milk comes in. During the first milk let-down, the breasts are very engorged and painful because of the increased blood flow and the accumulation of milk. Often, warm compresses to the breasts are soothing. When the baby is put to the breast, the sucking action stimulates oxytocin to be released by the pituitary gland; this hormone then causes the milk to let down.

If the mother does not wish to breast-feed, she is given an anti-lactogenic agent, such as Deladumone, late in the first stage of labor to suppress the production of milk. If the mother complains of breast discomfort, ice packs and a tight bra or breast binder may alleviate some of this; analgesics may also be ordered.

Breast care involves cleansing with clean water without soap and wearing a good supporting bra. Creams such as Masse and ointments such as A & D may be ordered for sore nipples.

Lactation is initiated by _____ .

In the first two days postpartum, the breast secretes _____ .

prolactin

colostrum

On the third day the breasts become _____ .   engorged

The release of oxytocin is stimulated by_____   the baby's sucking

_____ .

The mother who wishes to bottle-feed the infant receives an
_____ at the time of delivery.   antilactogenic agent

"After-pains" result from the intermittent contractions of the uterus
due to the release of oxytocin and are often experienced by the mother more
intensely while she is breast-feeding. The multiparous mother also experiences
more after-pains because the uterine muscles are more flaccid.

The maintenance of good circulation is ensured by early ambulation.
The mother can get out of bed as soon as she feels able but, the first time,
assistance is necessary so that she has support if she feels dizzy or weak.

Postpartum exercises assist in the maintenance of good circulatory
function and at the same time speed the recovery of the muscle tone of the
abdomen and perineum. These are graduated exercises and are specific to the
need. Vigorous exercises are contraindicated at this time.

Early ambulation helps to ensure _____ .   good circulation

The routine assessment of the maternal status includes laboratory
studies of hemoglobin, hematocrit, and white blood count. By the third day
postpartum, hemoglobin and hematocrit should be at the predelivery levels.
There is an elevated number of leukocytes. This is in response to the labor
and delivery process and is not indicative of infection.

As the maternal systems adapt, some of the normal findings of the
postpartum period tend to obscure the signs and symptoms of infection. It
has been established that a rise in the mother's temperature after the first 24
hours is indicative of infection. Therefore, postpartal morbidity has been
defined as a maternal elevation of temperature to 100.4°F or over for a
period of 48 hours excluding the first 24 hours after delivery.

Hemoglobin and hematocrit should return to their predelivery levels by
the_____ postpartal day.   third

During the first postpartal week, a marked leukocytosis is considered to
be_____ .   normal

The postpartal mother is considered to have an infection if after the
_____ hours her temperature remains at   first 24;
_____ or over for a period of _____ days.   100.4°F; two

Within six to eight weeks after delivery, menstruation usually resumes in the nonlactating mother. If the mother is breast-feeding, resumption of the menses takes place anywhere between the second and the eighteenth month after delivery. Generally, however, most women do not menstruate for as long as they continue to nurse their infants. This period of amenorrhea was thought to be an effective safeguard against subsequent pregnancies. The falsity of this belief is demonstrated by the fact that a large number of women do ovulate during the breast-feeding period and have, in fact, become pregnant.

During the postpartum stay in the hospital, the mother may ask the nurse for information related to the advisability of resuming sexual intercourse. It is usually recommended that the couple abstain from sexual contact for a period of about four to six weeks or until after the first postpartal visit has established that total healing and regeneration of reproductive organs and tissues has taken place. Often, however, this advice is not followed by the parents, so it becomes important that they be made to understand that a pregnancy may occur even though menstruation has not been reestablished.

If contraceptive methods are to be recommended upon the first postpartal visit, it is important that oral contraceptive measures not be utilized by the lactating mother. These are contraindicated.

POST-TEST   Indicate whether each statement is true or false by circling the appropriate letter. **Then** turn to page 287 and check how well you have done.

1. The puerperium begins with the second stage of labor and lasts for **six** weeks.   **T   F**

2. The mother often is not aware of the exhaustion that arises as a result **of** parturition.   **T   F**

3. Both the mother and the father experience role changes as a result of **the** birth of their child.   **T   F**

4. When the mother is in the "taking-in" phase, the nurse should be **aware** that she needs to be allowed dependency.   **T   F**

5. During the taking-in phase, the father assumes the supportive role.   **T   F**

6. The "taking-hold" phase of the puerperium usually lasts for about **a period** of ten days.   **T   F**

7. Main maternal concerns during the taking-hold phase are control **over** bodily functions and the anxieties created by her questions relating to **her** maternal role.   **T   F**

8. An effective way of handling the mother's anxieties at this time is to **allow** the mother to handle the baby.   **T   F**

9. "Postpartum blues" means that the mother wants to dress the baby only **in** blue.   **T   F**

10. Typical symptoms and behavior of the postpartum blues are crying, irritability, and loss of sleep and appetite.   **T   F**

11. The process of involution takes place by autolysis.   **T   F**

12. If the mother tells you that she has had no lochial discharge on the **first** postpartum day, she should be told this is normal.   **T   F**

13. To assess uterine involution, the nurse should palpate the fundus.   **T   F**

14. Usually episiotomies should not cause any discomfort to the mother.   **T   F**

15. Following delivery, there may be a loss of bladder tone.   **T   F**

16. A shift of body fluids occurs within the first day postpartum.   **T   F**

In the specific areas with which you had difficulty, return to the material and review.

REFERENCES   1. Reva Rubin, "Puerperal Change," *Nursing Outlook,* Vol. 9, pp. 753-755, Dec. 1961.

BIBLIOGRAPHY   "Babies Have Fathers Too,"*American Journal of Nursing,* Vol. 71, p. 198, Oct. 1971.

Carner, Charles, "After Baby Blues," *Today's Health,* Dec. 1967, pp. 32-35.

Carriers, "Third Day Blues," *Briefs,* p. 1, Sept. 30, 1966.

Clausen, Joy Princeton, et al.: *Maternity Nursing Today,* McGraw-Hill Book Co., New York, 1973.

Edwards, J., "Needed: Patient-Oriented Nursing in the Maternity Unit," *Hospital Topics,* Vol. 48, pp. 83-86, March 1970.

Hogan, A. I., "The Role of the Nurse in Meeting the Needs of the New Mother," *Nursing Clinics of North America,* Vol. 3, p. 337, June 1968.

Jeffcoate, T. N. O., "Emotional and Physical Stress After the Baby Comes," *Briefs,* pp. 38-39, March 1966.

Mayer, "Family Centered Care Helps New Parents," *Modern Hospital,* March 1966, pp. 106-130.

Moore, M. L., "The Mother's Changing Needs," *Briefs,* No. 32, p. 79, May 1968.

Moore, Mary Lou: *The Newborn and the Nurse,* W. B. Saunders Co., Philadelphia, London, Toronto, 1972.

Morley, A. W., "The Important Ten B's of Postpartum Hospital Care," *Hospital Topics,* Vol. 44, pp. 107-111, Feb. 1966.

Newton, A. and M. Newton, "The Mothers' Reactions to Their Newborn Babies," *Journal of the American Medical Association,* p. 206, July 2, 1962.

Ribble, Margaret A.: *The Rights of Infants,* rev. ed., Columbia University Press, New York, 1966.

Rubin, Reva, "Attainment of the Maternal Role, 1. Processes," *Nursing Research,* Vol. 16, pp. 237-245, Summer 1967.

———, "Attainment of the Maternal Role, 2. Models and Referrants," *Nursing Research,* Vol. 16, pp. 342-346, Fall 1967.

———, "Basic Maternal Behavior," *Nursing Outlook,* Vol. 9, p. 683, Nov. 1961.

———, "Maternal Touch," *Nursing Outlook,* Vol. 11, p. 828. Nov. 1963.

———, "Puerperal Change," *Nursing Outlook,* Vol. 9, p. 753, Dec. 1961.

Stella, Sr. Mary, "Family Centered Maternity Care: How It Works," *Hospital Progress,* Vol. 41, p. 92, March 1960 and p. 70, April 1960.

Yunek, Marilyn Jo, "Postpartum Care is More Than a Routine," *Nursing Outlook,* Vol. 17, p. 50, Jan. 1969.

PRETEST ANSWERS

1. Period lasting from five to six weeks after delivery 2. The return of the uterus to the nonpregnant state 3. Exhausted or tired or fatigued 4. Exhilarated 5. Evidence of his love; acceptance of the baby 6. "Taking-in"; "taking hold" 7. Supportive; companionship 8. Support; reassurance; information 9. Independence; reassurance 10. Postpartal blues 11. Autolysis; atrophy 12. Inner decidual layer 13. Tenth 14. Third 15. Height of the fundus; color and amount of the lochia 16. Blood; tissue; amniotic cells; three days 17. Serosanguinous discharge; four to ten days 18. Yellowish, white discharge; ten to 15 days 19. One fingerbreadth per day 20. Less 21. Episiotomy healing; edema; infection; hematoma 22. Diuresis; diaphoresis 23. Sluggish 24. Asepsis 25. Prolactin 26. Oxytocin 27. Uterine contractions 28. Ambulation; exercises 29. A temperature of 100.4° for 48 hours after the first 24 postpartal hours 30. Six; eight 31. 18

POST-TEST ANSWERS

1. F   2. T   3. T   4. T   5. T   6. T   7. T   8. T
9. F   10. T   11. T   12. F   13. T   14. F   15. T   16. F

CHAPTER TWO

CHARACTERISTICS OF THE NEONATE

OBJECTIVES *Identify the normal characteristics of the respiratory system.*

Identify the four transitory conditions that may be found within the circulatory system.

Identify six normal reflexes of the neonate which are gradually lost.

Identify the types of nutrients that the neonate is able to assimilate.

Identify the characteristics and patterns of elimination.

Identify the important factors in the evaluation of the newborn.

GLOSSARY *Acrocyanosis:* A condition characterized by bluish hands and feet due to poorly integrated circulation

Erythropoiesis: The production of red blood cells

Physiological jaundice: A condition in the newborn in which there is a transitory rise of bilirubin due to a deficiency of transferase

Meconium: First stool of the newborn, having a tarry green color.

PRETEST   In the spaces provided, fill in the word or words that best complete(s) the statements. Then turn to page 297 and check your answers.

1. The normal respirations of the neonate range between _____ _____ .

2. The rhythm of the neonate's respirations is characteristically _____ .

3. The blood coagulation shortly after birth is _____ .

4. Physiological jaundice occurs because of_____ _____ .

5. The grasp reflex is demonstrated by_____ _____ _____ _____ .

6. The response of the newborn to a sudden jarring stimulus is the _____ _____ .

7. The stepping reflex occurs when the infant is_____ _____ _____ .

8. The neonate can easily digest _____ and _____ .

9. At the third to the fifth day, the characteristic color of the stool is_____ _____ .

10. Infants have more frequent stool when they are fed by_____ .

11. Moulding of the neonate's head is considered _____ .

12. The hips should abduct to each side _____ .

The neonate is capable of making certain physiological and psychological adaptations in response to the stressors of a new environment. Of course, however, in order for him to survive, many of his needs must be provided for by the family. The caring and looking after—the supportive role—is often shared or supplemented by professionals during the first several days in hospital. As the nurse becomes involved with the family, especially if this is the first child, the roles supplemented are the supportive and companionship ones, as the new mother and father learn these roles and establish new skills and begin to interact with their new offspring. Your understanding of the characteristics of the newborn is the basis of your nursing intervention.

The newborn's systems are in various stages of maturity, and their level of functioning is dependent on this factor. The *respiratory system* manifests characteristic respirations as its functioning alters towards the adult state. The newborn's *respirations* are *irregular* in *rate* and *rhythm,* averaging between *30 and 40* per minute. The *diaphragm* and the *abdominal* muscles create the respiratory movements. The neonate breathes normally through the *nose* only. If this passage is blocked, the neonate will not be able to breathe; he will not open his mouth for the passage of air. Care must be taken to maintain a clear nasopharynx.

The systems of the newborn are at different levels of _____ .

    maturity

The neonate cannot survive in isolation but only when _____

    others provide care

_____ .

The respiratory system adapts to the new environment and establishes respirations that are _____ in rate.

    irregular

The muscles that are used during respiration are the _____

    diaphragm;

and the _____ .

    abdominal muscles

The newborn breathes only through the _____ .

    nose

It is important to check the nasopharynx to ensure that it is

_____ .

    patent (clear)

With the new family, nursing intervention is geared toward supplementing the _____ and _____ roles.

    supportive; companionship

The circulatory system adapts quickly to provide oxygenation to all systems. The heart beats at between 120 and 140 beats per minute. The heartbeat alters according to activity. Occasionally, the circulation to the extremities is poorly integrated at the periphery and the newborn has bluish hands and feet. This condition is called *acrocyanosis.* It normally lasts for a short period after birth, but 12 hours or longer in a cold environment.

There is transitory *deficiency* in the *coagulation* of *blood* after birth lasting for several days until the flora of the gastrointestinal tract can produce vitamin K. A standard procedure in many hospitals is to administer vitamin K$_1$, thereby establishing a satisfactory prothrombin time.

Erythropoiesis is not well established during the first six to eight weeks; thus a decreasing hematocrit is produced.

During the first several days of life, the liver is not able to convert adequately all the bilirubin to a water-soluble form that can be excreted. The enzyme transferase, which is necessary in the conversion of the bilirubin, is inadequate in amount at this time. This buildup of indirect bilirubin causes a temporary *physiological jaundice*, which begins between 48 and 72 hours after birth, peaks at around six days, and lasts until 14 days after birth, at which time the liver becomes able to convert this bilirubin. Total bilirubin levels above 13 milligrams per 100 milliliters are considered *abnormal* and are higher than those often seen with physiological jaundice.

Acrocyanosis occurs when there is cyanosis present of the _____ and _____ .

hands; feet

The newborn relies on the circulatory system to provide _____ .

oxygenation

Blood coagulation of the newborn is _____ _____ .

lower than normal (deficient)

Medication that may be given to the newborn routinely to prevent coagulation problems is _____ .

vitamin K$_1$

The hematocrit of the newborn is high, but it gradually decreases because _____ is not well established at birth.

erythropoiesis

Physiological jaundice occurs because of the immaturity of the _____ . This phenomenon can occur normally between _____ and _____ after birth.

liver; 48; 72 hours

The level of total bilirubin is abnormal when above _____ _____ .

13 milligrams per 100 milliliters

The *neurological system* of the newborn is only *partly matured*. The *temperature control* (hypothalamus) is relatively *unstable* during the first several days. Thus, the environmental temperature must be controlled. The newborn does not tolerate extremes of hot or cold. The newborn's temperature normally stabilizes at about 98.0°F. Heat is produced by the newborn by an increased metabolic rate and also by neonatal movements. It is not until later that the newborn's sweating mechanism is functioning.

There are six reflexes that the newborn displays and gradually loses: the grasp, Moro, tonic neck, rooting, placing and stepping, and crawling.

The *grasp reflex* can be demonstrated by placing a finger or an object in the palm of the newborn, who will grasp the object. This same grasping reflex can be shown by the infant curling his toes around an object that touches the sole of the foot. Both of these reflexes normally last only three to four months.

The *Moro reflex,* also termed the "startle reflex" occurs after a sudden loud noise or sudden jarring of the bed. This reflex is characterized by the *sudden upward* and *outward movement* of the *arms* followed by an embrace with the thumbs and forefinger in a "C" position, while the *knees* are drawn *upward* so that the *feet* are *touching* each other. At this time, a cry is often elicited from the newborn. This reflex lasts about eight weeks.

The *tonic neck reflex* is demonstrated as the newborn's *head turns to one side* and *arm and leg of that side extend* while the *other arm* and *leg* on the *opposite side flex.* This is often termed the "fencing" position. The mother should be shown this reflex since it is very useful to her when she is washing and dressing the baby. This reflex continues for a few months, but at times it is incomplete and difficult to elicit.

The newborn's temperature is unstable due to the immature

_____ .   nervous system (hypothalmus)

Heat is produced by the neonate by _____   increased metabolism;

_____ and_____ .   muscular movement

The reflex that is seen as the newborn holds onto a pencil is the

_____ .   grasp reflex

The Moro reflex is called the _____ .   startle reflex;

The Moro reflex can be elicited by_____   a sudden jarring or noise

_____ .

When the newborn's head turns to one side and the arm and the leg on

that side _____ , this reflex is termed the_____   extend; tonic neck reflex

_____ .

The *rooting response* occurs when there is pressure on the cheek of the newborn and the newborn reacts by turning his head towards the stimulus and opening his mouth. This is especially important for the mother to understand so that she can help the infant find the nipple and so that she is aware that excess stimuli can confuse the baby.

The *crawling reflex,* also called the "swimming reflex," occurs when the newborn is on his abdomen and supported by the examiner's hand; the baby moves his arms and legs in a swimming or crawling motion. This reflex is lost before the infant learns to crawl.

The *stepping reflex* is seen when the newborn exhibits walking movements as he is held in an upright position, leaning forward, with his feet on a flat surface. This reflex, too, is lost before the infant learns to walk. The *placing reflex* is shown when the baby is held erect and the dorsal surface of the foot is under the flat surface. The baby will lift his foot and place it on top of the table.

The other reflexes that the infant exhibits are present throughout life: *sneezing, blinking, yawning, hiccupping, shivering, and crying* in response to pain are all present and serve as protective devices. The *sucking, swallowing, and gag reflexes* must be operating effectively to enable the neonate to take food.

There are four reflexes that ensure that the newborn can find and take food. These are the _____ , _____ , _____ , and _____ reflexes.

rooting; sucking; swallowing; gag

There are three reflexes that are lost before the infant learns the motor skills. These are the _____ , _____ , and _____ reflexes.

crawling; stepping; placing

In the immediate newborn period, the *gastrointestinal tract* adapts from the handling of amniotic fluid to the breakdown and absorption of proteins and carbohydrates. The digestion of fats and starches at this time is poor. The amount of fluid intake during the first several days is often very limited, varying from 3 to 11 ounces per day; it gradually increases so that the infant is taking about 12 to 18 ounces by the third day.

The first passage of stool may occur normally shortly after birth or within the first 24 hours. This thick, greenish, tarry material is termed *meconium.* Within three to five days, the stools are greenish yellow and are known as *transitional stools.* Then the characteristic stools are established depending on whether the baby is breast-fed, having frequent (four to eight) stools daily which are soft golden yellow with a sour odor, or bottle-fed, with less frequent stools, often once a day, firm and brownish yellow in color. The mother should be aware of the typical pattern and should report to the physician any watery stools.

The newborn's gastrointestinal tract can digest _____ and _____ .

protein; carbohydrates

The first stool, called _____ , appears _____ .

meconium; within 24 hours

At three to five days, the stools appear _____ and are called _____ .

greenish yellow; transitional

Breast-fed infants have stools that are _____ , _____ , and _____ colored.

soft; frequent; golden yellow

The sour odor of the stool is normal when the baby is fed by _____. The stools are less frequent when the infant is fed by _____.

breast;

bottle

The urinary system is now responsible for the maintenance of the electrolyte balance and the excretion of waste. Shortly after birth the neonate usually voids, emptying the bladder. It is considered normal if voiding is delayed up to 24 hours. During the first four days, the amount of urine passed is small, and it increases in amount and frequency during the first week, so that the newborn voids up to ten to 15 times a day.

The kidneys are responsible for _____ and _____.

During a 24-hour period, the infant voids _____ times.

electrolyte balance;

excretion of waste

ten to 15

In many institutions, the nurse is the person responsible for admitting the newborn to the nursery and doing the initial systems evaluation. The early identification of problems and difficulties is essential for the life of the newborn and the maintenance of his homeodynamics.

The first information the nurse must evaluate is the family history of health problems such as maternal diabetes. Then, information about the prenatal history and the labor and delivery is taken. The nurse must note any fetal distress, medications received by the mother which affect the baby, and the duration of the labor and delivery. The blood types of both parents, and the Apgar score, are important. It is extremely important to be aware if the neonate has received resuscitative measures.

The nurse's observations of the neonate should include the following: The size (normally around 7 to 7½ pounds) and the color (normal according to racial pigmentation) should be checked. Any cyanosis of the lips or ears should be reported. The head should be examined for shape, degree of moulding (often egg-shaped), and closing of the fontanels and sutures. The ears are checked for level: the upper pina should be at eye level. The eyes are examined for normal shape and clarity of lens. Occasionally conjunctival hemorrhage is present if labor was difficult; there are no sequelae. If the infant is held upright, the eyes usually open. The nasal passages are checked for patency and the mouth is checked to make sure that the hard palate is fused and has a normal arch. There may be Epstein's pearls (these are small white dots of epithelial cells on the center line on the hard palate). There may be milia on the baby's face; this condition is normal since sebaceous glands are not functioning at this time. The skin color should have no jaundice or cyanosis. Black, Oriental, and Southern European children often have bluish patches, called Mongolian spots, over their buttocks and lower backs. These are normal and disappear. The nose and chin appear small and poorly developed—this is necessary for ease of feeding but often causes worry to new parents.

The initial assessment of the neonate in the nursery must take into consideration the_____ ,

_____ , _____ ,

_____ ,

_____ , _____ ,

and _____ .

family history;
history of pregnancy; **type and**
duration of labor **and drugs used;**
Apgar score; resuscitation;
blood type

The head should be examined for_____ , _____ ,

and _____ .

size; shape;

The ears should be_____

_____ .

fontanels and sutures

at the level of the eyes

The baby is held upright and away from the bright light to check the eyes for _____ .

opacity

The examiner checks the infant's mouth for _____

and _____ .

cleft;

arch of the palate

The color of the neonate should have no _____ or

_____ .

cyanosis;

jaundice

The *extremities* should move *equally* as the reflexes are tested, and the knees, when flexed on the abdomen, should be the same height and should abduct equally to a frog position to rule out congenital hip problems.

The *spine* should be checked to note that the vertebrae are continuous. The *anus* is checked for patency. The *genitalia* should be of normal size and color, and the testes are normally in the scrotum.

The *abdomen* should be soft and rounded. The *umbilical cord* is examined to locate the *three vessels*.

The infant's cry should be a normal pitch and strength, and the respiratory and cardiac rates should be within normal limits.

As the spine is felt, it is normally _____ .

continuous

The abdomen is _____ and _____ .

soft; rounded

The three vessels in the umbilical cord are the _____

and the _____ .

vein;

two arteries

The infant's cry should be assessed for _____ and

_____ .

pitch;

strength

POST-TEST   Indicate whether each statement is true or false by circling the appropriate letter. Then turn to page 297 and see how well you have done.

1. Observations of the neonate's respirations will indicate that they are thoracic and diaphragmatic.   T   F

2. The neonate's respirations are regular in rate and rhythm.   T   F

3. There is a normal coagulation of the blood of the neonate immediately after birth.   T   F

4. Erythropoiesis in the immediate newborn period is occurring at a normal rate.   T   F

5. Physiological jaundice is often dangerous for the infant.   T   F

6. The tonic neck reflex is also known as the startle reflex.   T   F

7. The infant never loses the stepping reflex.   T   F

8. The gag reflex is necessary for the infant to be able to feed satisfactorily.   T   F

9. The infant has difficulty in breaking down fats in order to digest them.   T   F

10. The stools of the bottle-fed infant are firmer and less frequent than those of the infant who is breast-fed.   T   F

11. If the amount of urine during the first two days of life is scanty, this is an indication of a problem.   T   F

12. The extremities of the newborn should move equally on both sides.   T   F

13. The spine should have continuous vertebrae.   T   F

14. The normal cry of the newborn is often a high-pitched squeal or low grunt. T   F

In the specific areas with which you had difficulty, return to the material and review.

BIBLIOGRAPHY
Arnold, Helen, "The Newborn, Transition to Extra-Uterine Life," *American Journal of Nursing,* Vol. 65, pp. 77-80, Oct. 1965.

Burnes, C. A., "Patricia," *American Journal of Nursing,* Vol. 67, p. 2576, Dec. 1967.

Cominos, Helen, "Teaching Newborn Care to Adopting Parents," *Nursing Outlook,* Vol. 19, p. 4215, June 1971.

Desmond, M. M., et al., "The Clinical Behavior of the Newly Born," *Journal of Pediatrics,* Vol. 62, p. 307, March 1963.

Hervada, Arturo R., "Nursery Evaluation of the Newborn," *American Journal of Nursing,* Vol. 67, pp. 1669-1671, Aug. 1967.

Marlow, Dorothy R. and Gladys Sollew, *Textbook of Pediatric Nursing,* 3d ed., W. B. Saunders Co., Philadelphia, 1969.

Nelson, Waldo E., *Textbook of Pediatrics,* 9th ed., W. B. Saunders Co., Philadelphia, 1969.

PRETEST ANSWERS
1. 30 and 40 per minute   2. Irregular   3. Deficient   4. Immaturity of the enzyme system   5. Placing an object in the palm of the hand or sole of the foot of the newborn   6. Moro or startle reflex   7. Held upright with the foot on a flat surface   8. Proteins; carbohydrates   9. Greenish yellow   10. Breast   11. Normal   12. Equally

POST-TEST ANSWERS
1. F   2. F   3. F   4. F   5. F   6. F   7. F   8. T
9. T   10. T   11. F   12. T   13. T   14. F

CHAPTER THREE

BEGINNING INTERACTIONS WITH THE NEWBORN

OBJECTIVES *Identify two major influences on the psychological development of the neonate.*

Identify how the "parental feeling" develops.

Identify the major aspects of the feeding process.

Identify the typical changes in the newborn's weight.

Identify special information relevant to the bathing of the newborn.

Identify the pattern of interactions between the parents and the newborn.

Identify specific guidance given by the nurse to the parents in the areas of: taking the newborn outdoors, traveling, and medical care.

PRETEST   In the spaces provided, fill in the word or words that best complete(s) the statements. Then turn to page 314 and check your answers.

1. The newborn's psychological development is dependent upon interactions with the _____ and _____ .

2. The parental feeling develops _____ _____ .

3. Normal phenomena of the infant should be _____ _____ .

4. Feeding time is significant for the _____ and the_____ .

5. At the first several feeds, the newborn will take a _____ .

6. The newborn normally has a weight loss of_____ _____ of his body weight.

7. Tub baths are given_____ .

8. Uric acid crystals are often confused with _____ _____ by the parents.

9. Swelling of the infant's breast is due to the_____ _____ .

10. Rooming-in is helpful to the parents since it _____ _____ _____ .

11. The infant will have passive immunity if the_____ _____ _____ .

Now that you are cognizant of the physiological adaptations of the neonate, we will focus on the psychological adaptations that are taking place concurrently. These *psychological changes,* which at first may seem subtle to the observer, occur as the *newborn interacts* with *the environment* and with the *significant persons* who are providing for his care.

The beginning interactions of the newborn with his parents often set a pattern of expected behavior among the members of this evolving family. For example, if the baby is alert and responsive to the mother's stimulation and voice, then the mother in turn feels more comfortable and relaxed and can better handle the baby. This sets the tone for positive interactions to occur in the future. If the baby should exhibit the opposite type of behavior, crying, fussing, and not feeding well, the mother often becomes nervous and anxious about her ability to provide satisfactory care for her infant. When this occurs, the next time the mother begins to care for the baby, she is likely to be nervous, and the baby senses this and in turn responds by crying. The pattern then becomes cyclic.

The newborn's psychological adaptations are dependent upon the

_____ and _____ .   environment; significant persons

The early interactions of the infant and the parents often establish

_____ .   a pattern of expected behavior

As the interactions continue, they become _____ .   cyclic

Nursing interventions at this time can aid in the establishment of positive interactions by reducing the stressors. The *"parental feeling"* that the mother and father expect to feel the moment they first see their infant often is not present immediately, especially with the first child, but develops over a period of time. Knowledge of this fact can reduce much parental anxiety. This identification process usually takes time. It is accomplished through *physical contact* and *exploration* of the infant by the mother and father. The nurse can render assistance by *providing time* for the parents to become familiar with their offspring and introducing them to the *normal phenomena* exhibited by their infant. The nurse is an essential element in providing support to the parents as they assume the parental role and as they establish beginning relationships with the new infant.

The parental feeling develops by _____   physical contact and exploration

_____ .

The nurse can provide support by_____   allowing time together;

_____ and _____   explaining normal phenomena

_____ .

One of the first major caretaking tasks that the parents learn to perform is that of feeding. Much has been written about the significance and the psychological aspects of the act of feeding as well as the long-range effects of this experience. We will focus on the immediate interactions of the feeding process, which form the basis of the future patterns of behavior.

The infant's physiological need is to take in and assimilate nutrients. As an integral part of this, the infant must feel comfortable and secure during the process for the need to be met satisfactorily. The parent, on the other hand, needs to feel that he/she is successful in providing for this need of the infant by *giving* food to the infant. As the infant receives this food, he is thereby *accepting* the parent. Therefore, through the *feeding interaction, the needs of both parties can be met.* Difficulties arise if the parents do not realize the *small amounts of food* which the newborn normally takes during the first few days of life. The newborn is often *sleepy* and not responsive at feeding time, and when the parents are not able to give to and provide for the infant, they may feel angry and rejected. Also, recognition of these feelings may give rise to guilt: How can one be angry at a helpless infant? If the nurse does not intervene and supply information and support, many of these common reactions and feelings of the parents may persist.

During the feeding process, the infant has two needs: _____ _____ and _____ .

> taking nutrients;
> feeling secure

The parent's need at this time is to _____ _____ _____ .

> feel successful in **providing or giving** food

It is important that the parents realize that the infant is often _____ and takes _____ _____ .

> sleepy; small amounts of the food

The nurse can be helpful by_____ and _____ .

> giving information;
> providing support

If the mother is breast-feeding the infant, there is stimulation of _____ as the baby sucks; this aids in releasing the _____ and at the same time causes discomfort due to _____ often called _____ .

> oxytocin;
> milk let-down;
> uterine contractions;
> after-pains

Frequently, if there is much *discomfort* experienced by the mother and she perceives the feeding time as a painful ordeal, she then becomes very *tense,* and this in turn *heightens* the level of discomfort. It is at this time that often the mother gives up and no longer wants to breast-feed; should she do this, frequently she will experience feelings of inadequacy. During the early feedings the nurse can relieve some of this discomfort by administering an *analgesic* within one-half hour before feeding. The quantity of the drug which would be passed to the baby is negligible.

If the mother experiences after-pains while breast-feeding, she then becomes _____.

tense

The nurse can alleviate some of the mother's discomfort by _____ _____.

administering an analgesic

Effective nursing intervention can assist the mother during the feeding by helping to get the baby to grasp the *entire areola* of the breast within his mouth so that the sucking action is more effective and the baby is able to obtain more milk. This position is much more comfortable for the mother than if the baby has only grasped the nipple. Although the baby gets the major portion of the milk during the first five to ten minutes, he often needs a longer *sucking time* before he feels complete satisfaction. When the baby has finished feeding or needs to be burped, the *suction* can be broken effectively by the *insertion of a finger* between the baby's mouth and the breast.

While assisting the mother who is breast-feeding, it is important to get the baby to grasp the _____ within his mouth.

entire areola

After the infant takes in the required milk, he needs _____ _____.

sucking time

When taking the infant from the breast, it is important to _____ by _____ _____ _____.

break the suction; inserting finger
between baby's mouth and breast

Often, each doctor and each institution develops his or its own schedules for breast-feeding. However, all of the schedules have the purpose of *alternating the breast for the beginning* of the feeding and starting with *short periods* at the beginning. This helps to ensure that the breasts get emptied and toughens the nipple, preventing the development of fissures and cracking of the nipples. It is also important to keep the breasts dry so that there is no breakdown of the skin. Exposing the breast to the air after feeding and wearing a good supporting bra is helpful.

The breast on which the mother begins the baby should be
_____ .

At first, feedings should continue for _____

in order to _____ .

> alternated
>
> short periods;
>
> toughen the nipples

When the parents want to bottle-feed their infant, they must be in a comfortable chair or in bed so that they can relax as they hold the baby. The nipple of the bottle should be filled with formula so that the baby will not swallow large amounts of air. The parents should be taught to test the nipple before trying to feed the infant. Often the nipple can become clogged and will need to be changed. The formula is given to the infant either at room temperature or warmed. The parents should be instructed to burp the baby every ½ to 1 ounce so that all of the formula will not come up with the expulsion of one gas bubble. Placing the baby over the shoulder and rubbing the infant's back gently is an effective way of burping the child.

Before the parents start to bottle-feed the infant, they should relax by
_____ .

The baby will not swallow a lot of air if _____

_____ .

It is important to burp the baby _____

_____ so that the baby will

be comfortable and so that _____

_____

_____ .

> sitting or lying comfortably
>
> the nipple is full of formula
>
> every ½ to 1 ounce;
>
> he will not bring up all of the
>
> formula

Often parents assess the well-being of their infant by their ability to provide nourishment, and this is gauged by the amount of weight the baby gains. It is therefore imperative that the parents be aware that a *normal weight loss* of 5 to 10 percent of the birth weight occurs during the first three to four days of life. Within about ten to 14 days, the infant has regained his birth weight, and then he continues to gain.

During the first several days, the infant loses about _____

_____ .

This weight loss is regained in _____

_____ .

> 5 to 10 percent of birth weight
>
> ten to 14 days

Other caretaking tasks the new parents learn are changing diapers and bathing the infant. Many hospitals set up classes in which the new mothers watch a demonstration of a bath given to an infant or doll and then may return to the bath demonstration the following day with their own infants. In this way, techniques of handling the baby securely are easily learned. Also, in the group common problems and feelings are shared.

The baby is given a sponge bath until the cord drops off and the stump is *healed.* The cord drops off at five to ten days of life, and several days later the area is dry and healed over. Early cord care is geared toward keeping the *area dry*; often applying *alcohol* will dry and toughen the skin. Guidance about bathing should include the information that a tub bath may be given in a small plastic tub in a convenient area *away from drafts* or in the sink with the faucet turned so that the hot water cannot be turned on by the baby. The infant should be *constantly held and supported by the parent's arm* while being washed. The diaper area of the newborn should be kept clean and dry; with each change of diapers the area is *washed and thoroughly dried.* Should a diaper rash develop, the buttocks can be left exposed to the air. This promotes healing and at the same time prevents the urine from being a constant irritant.

The baby is given a tub bath _____ | several days after the cord falls off and is healed
_____ .

The care of the cord is to _____ | keep it dry;
and _____ . | use alcohol

When a bath is given at home, the spot chosen should be convenient and _____ . | away from drafts

During the bath the infant must be _____ | constantly held and supported
_____ .

With each change of diapers, the area is _____ | washed and thoroughly dried
_____ .

In the case of a diaper rash, you can _____ | expose the area to air;
_____ because this | promotes healing
_____ .

During the parents' exploration of their newborn, they may show concern about some of the normal phenomena such as *milia,* which are tiny white spots under the skin usually seen over the bridge of the nose; these spots are due to the inactivity of the sebaceous glands and are present for several weeks.

Since the *uric acid* concentration is high in the urine of the newborn, harmless *crystals* with a brick-red color are often formed. Parents tend to confuse these crystals with blood in the urine.

If the *maternal hormones* have been at a *high* level, then in the female infant there is often seen a white, mucoid vaginal discharge and occasionally a slight amount of vaginal bleeding. This is a normal occurrence. Also, in both sexes the breasts may be engorged due to the maternal hormones. This condition subsides and is nothing to worry about.

Milia are seen as _____ tiny white spots;

and are due to _____ inactivity of sebaceous **glands**

_____ .

Uric acid crystals appear as _____ brick-red crystals

_____ .

When the mother's hormonal level has been high, the female infant may

have both a _____ and _____ vaginal discharge; **engorged breasts**

_____ .

You would advise the mother that, should these conditions be present,

_____ they are often **seen** and **subside**

_____ . with no problem

The parents may decide that they want to have the boy *circumcised*. If this procedure is done by the doctor, it usually necessitates a consent form signed by the parents and it is done before the infant goes home. If the parents wish a religious service with a rabbi, special arrangements are made. The circumcision itself is the cutting of the foreskin, after which a surgical dressing, usually gauze covered with petroleum jelly, is applied. It is important to *observe the amount of bleeding* and report any excess. The dressing is left on until it comes off of its own accord, or it can be removed by gentle soaking if desired. No other special care is needed.

If the boy is not to be circumcised, then the mother can be instructed to *gently ease the foreskin back* while giving the daily bath in order to clean around the glans. No force should be applied in attempting to retract the foreskin, since it may be several months before it is easily retractable.

Once the infant is circumcised, it is important to watch

_____ . the amount **of bleeding**

Once the dressing comes off the circumcision area, the care necessary is

_____ . nothing special

If the boy is not to be circumcised, the mother can be shown how to _____ to _____ .

> gently retract the foreskin;
>
> clean around the glans

We have established that there is a *dynamic interaction* among the members of the family, that the behavior of each individual in turn affects the reactions and responses of the other person. This interaction occurs when the baby cries and the parent picks him up to comfort him; then when he stops crying, the parent will usually feel satisfied. If the infant does not stop crying, the parent often will feel distressed. Nursing intervention is based on the knowledge of the pattern of interactions; the assessment and support provided is geared to *promoting the optimum dynamics.*

The parents need to feel that they are *prepared to handle the common reactions* of their infant, so that their stress level will be reduced should the baby start crying and not stop when picked up. What are some of the things the parents can do to relieve the infant's discomfort? First, they should *check the diaper* to be sure that it is dry and clean. Then they can determine when the infant was *last fed*—Is it time for more food or does he have a gas bubble? Often, the infant fusses just before passing a *bowel movement*; if there is squirming at the same time, this is probably what is happening. If there is *no pin* sticking into the skin, the bed seems clear of objects, and no *sudden noises* have occurred, then often a little *cuddling* will quiet the child. A certain amount of crying is normal for the infant, and the parents should not be unduly distressed if, after they have checked the infant, he cries for a short period. A crying child in an apartment house often causes the parents and the neighbors to be upset; thus, the parents are fearful if the infant does not quiet immediately. Sometimes a *warm bath* will soothe and calm the infant, or giving a *supplementary bottle* of water or sugar water as suggested by the doctor will relieve the infant's discomfort. If the infant has any signs of interruptions of his health state, such as fever, diarrhea, or vomiting, the doctor or hospital should be notified immediately.

Family members relate to each other through a _____ _____ .

> dynamic interaction

In order for the nurse to promote optimum family interactions, the parents must feel equipped to _____ _____ .

> handle common reactions

If the infant continues to cry after the parent has picked him up, you would first check _____ .

> the diaper

If the infant is squirming, he may be _____ _____ .

> having a bowel movement

The infant is often calmed by _____ , _____

_____ , or _____ .

If the parents feel equipped to handle the normal occurrences, they will be much more relaxed, and they will communicate this to their infant. The process of adapting to the new member will be much smoother. The parents will know that there is no problem when the baby hiccups. Some hospitals foster early parent-child relationships by providing rooming-in. That is, the newborn stays in the mother's hospital room with the mother and father during the postpartum stay, usually just during the day period. In this way the parents can learn the normal responses and care of the newborn with the assistance of the nursing staff, who can provide support to the parents as they learn and assume the care of their newborn. This is also an excellent opportunity to give guidance and teaching.

Rooming-in means that _____

_____

_____ .

the infant stays in the room

with the parents

This allows the parents to _____

_____ .

learn normal responses and care

Preparation of formulas is often taught in a class in which there is a discussion of the costs and advantages of the various types of formulas. The actual procedures for terminal sterilization of the bottles and the formula are usually demonstrated, and explanations and reasons for both procedures are given.

Often one of the first questions the parents ask as they prepare to go home is, "When can I take the baby outside?" This often depends on the *climate* and the philosophy of the pediatrician. Usually in warm weather there is no problem as long as the infant is *protected from the direct heat of the sun.* In the winter, if it is very *windy* or very *humid,* it may be wise not to take the baby out for *several weeks.* Usually, when the mother feels like going out, it is fine for the baby to go out.

If the parents are traveling with the baby in the car for long periods, it is important that they *do not put the baby on the floor of the car,* where exhaust fumes tend to collect. Usually the back seat of the car can be set up for the baby.

Some physicians feel that the baby should not *fly* for the first several weeks because the middle ear has not developed to the point at which it can adapt to the changes in pressure. When the infant flies, it is important that at the time of *takeoff* and *landing,* the baby is *sucking* on a bottle or nipple to assist in his adjustment to the change in pressure.

You would advise the parents to take the baby out when _____ _____ and when _____ _____ .

the mother feels like going out;

not windy or very humid

When traveling with the baby in a car, it is important _____ _____ because _____ _____ .

not to put the baby on the floor;

this is where fumes collect

When the parents are flying with the infant, you would advise them to _____ _____ .

have the baby suck on takeoff
and landing

The parents should have information about the medical care needed by their baby. Medical care of the baby can be provided either by a private physician or through a hospital clinic or well-baby clinic. The care is free in the clinics, where the baby is *assessed for normal growth and development patterns* and is given a series of recommended *immunizations*. Previous to this, the infant will have *immunological protection* for the various diseases— mumps, diphtheria, and measles—against which the mother was immunized. This passive immunization lasts for a period of several weeks to several months. The time that regular immunization is started is when the infant's immunological system is able to produce antibodies, about two to three months of life.

Medical care for the infant provides _____ _____ and _____ .

assessment of growth and
development;
immunization

Passive immunity in the infant lasts for a period of_____ _____ .

several weeks to several months

Now let us see how your knowledge of the beginning interactions of the family with the newborn is applied to some actual family situations.

You are with Bill and Jean and their new baby, Jennifer, during evening visiting hours on the first postpartal day. Bill asks you how Jean is doing and then, turning to her, tells Jean how excited the grandparents are about the new baby.

Shortly thereafter, Jean suggests that Bill might want to hold and feed Jennifer. Nervous and apparently unsure, he tells Jean, "Well . . . ah . . . I don't think I better do that now. I have a feeling I am catching a cold."

Later that evening, after all her visitors have left, Jean, appearing perplexed, asks you: "I wonder why Bill didn't want to hold the baby? I know that he is not getting a cold! Why is he making excuses?"

Which of the following choices is the most helpful response to Jean at this time?

A. "How can you say that! I am sure that he really does want to hold the baby but is afraid that he might contaminate her with his cold."

Go to page 311.

B. "You seem upset about Bill's response, but this occurs quite frequently since most men have had little exposure in handling infants."

Go to page 310.

C. "If I were you, I wouldn't worry about that. Next time just put the baby in Bill's arms without asking him to hold her."

Go to page 312.

Excellent! Your selection of *B*, "You seem upset . . . ," demonstrates your ability to recognize the need for Jean to express her feelings, while at the same time you provided information that in itself will reassure her that Bill's behavior is normal.

Advance to page 313 and take the post-test.

Your selection of *A*, "How can you say that! . . . ," indicates that your assessment of the situation was limited; you did not observe Bill's hesitation and you did not listen to Jean. Your response would effectively close the matter so that Jean could not express any other feelings.

Return to page 308. Review the material and choose another response.

By selecting statement *C*, "If I were you . . . ," you have indicated that your understanding of therapeutic intervention is limited. You are denying Jean's feelings and suggesting a confrontation with Bill the next time he visits.

Return to page 308. Review the material and choose another response.

POST-TEST   Indicate whether each statement is true or false by circling the appropriate letter. Then turn to page 314 and check how well you have done.

1. The environment does not affect the psychological development of the newborn. T F

2. The interactions of the newborn and parents evolve from previous interactions. T F

3. The parental feeling always occurs when the parents first see their child. T F

4. Feeding is important for both physical and psychological development. T F

5. The newborn is often sleepy during the first feeding times. T F

6. The mother is often tense and uncomfortable while breast-feeding because of after-pains. T F

7. It is important that the baby have sucking time. T F

8. The mother should cover her breasts immediately after feeding to keep them clean. T F

9. When bottle-feeding, one should ascertain that the formula fills the nipple. T F

10. The baby begins to gain weight by the second day. T F

11. Alcohol should be used on the skin around the cord to aid in drying. T F

12. No care is required at the time of diaper change. T F

13. Uric acid crystals are harmless. T F

14. Rooming-in provides parents time to become acquainted with the newborn. T F

15. The infant receives passive immunity from the mother for some of the contagious diseases. T F

In the specific areas with which you had difficulty, return to the material and review.

BIBLIOGRAPHY   Clark, Ann, "The Adaptation Problems and Patterns of an Expanding Family: The Neonate Period," *Nursing Forum,* Vol. 5, No. 1, pp. 92-105, 1966.

Clark, Ann, "The Beginning Family," *American Journal of Nursing,* Vol. 66, pp. 802-805, April 1966.

Dyal, Lorraine and Kahil Dyal, "When Mothers Breast-Feed," *American Journal of Nursing,* Vol. 67, p. 2555, Dec. 1967.

Jeffcoate, T. N. A., "Emotional and Physical Stress After Baby Comes," *Briefs,* pp. 38-39, March 1966.

Keaveny, Mary E., "Breastfeeding," *Nursing '72,* pp. 31-34, Nov. 1972.

La Leche League: *The Womanly Art of Breast Feeding,* 2nd ed., Franklin Park, Ill., 1963.

O'Grady, Roberta, "Feeding Behavior in Infants," *American Journal of Nursing,* Vol. 71, pp. 736-739, April 1971.

Rubin, Reva, "Basic Maternal Behavior," *Nursing Outlook,* Vol. 9, pp. 683-686, Nov. 1961.

———, "Maternal Touch," *Nursing Outlook,* Vol. 11, pp. 828-831, Nov. 1963.

Sullivan, Harry Stack, *The Interpersonal Theory of Psychiatry,* Norton and Co., New York, 1953.

PRETEST ANSWERS   1. Environment; significant persons   2. Gradually with exposure to the infant   3. Explained to the parents   4. Infant; parent   5. Small amount   6. 5 to 10 percent   7. After the cord heals   8. Blood in the urine   9. High level of maternal hormones   10. Allows them to become acquainted with their newborn   11. Mother had been immunized against certain diseases

POST-TEST ANSWERS   1. F   2. T   3. F   4. T   5. T   6. T   7. T   8. F
9. T   10. F   11. T   12. F   13. T   14. T   15. T

CHAPTER FOUR

THE NEW FAMILY: GOING HOME

OBJECTIVES *Identify seven stressors affecting the new family system.*

Identify five tasks the parents and/or siblings must accomplish.

Identify the nursing responsibilities in assisting the family to adapt successfully.

PRETEST   In the spaces provided, fill in the word or words that best complete(s) the statements. Then turn to page 326 and check your answers.

1. When the new baby comes home, the interaction between the members is

   _____ .

2. While the parents are adapting, the grandparents are also going through _____

   _____ .

3. The family often finds that with the new infant their mobility is limited, resulting in

   a changed _____ .

4. Economics change because of the requirements of _____ ,

   _____ ,

   _____

   _____ , and

   _____ .

5. Maintenance of personal autonomy is a task that is accomplished by _____

   _____ ,

   _____ , and

   _____ .

6. Siblings often verbalize their feelings of _____ .

As the family expands, the whole system goes through an upheaval, and the various members must reestablish or reassert themselves in former roles and adapt to new and *changing roles*. Often the lines of responsibility and support are altered because of these changed roles.

When the family returns home with the first baby, the *interaction* between the family members is *altered*. A triangle has been formed and, as one-to-one relationships occur, there often is an exclusion of the other family member. Should the exclusion of one member exist over a period of time, feelings of anger and jealousy frequently arise; thus, it is important for the parents to take turns in the care of the infant and include the other parent in the interaction with the baby.

The parents must *reestablish* their own *relationship,* which has undergone many alterations during pregnancy and now evolves into a new and often more expanded relationship as they assume more responsibility.

There may be outside influences—friends and extended family members who now attempt to or do participate within the family dynamics. There may be a certain vying for care and attention of the infant as the extended family enters into the family structure. It is important to recognize that the *grandparents* are in the process of working through their own *role changes* and the implications of being grandparents.

The alterations of membership within the family cause the lines of communication to be altered between the members. Also, routines and schedules change to meet the new needs.

In the new family, it is important not to exclude a member; this can be effectively handled by _____

_____ .

    including the other members in the interaction

At the same time, the grandparents are working through _____

_____ .

    their own role changes

The communication between the various members is often

_____ .

    altered

The living space within the apartment or house is changed, and often a certain amount of sharing or giving up space is necessary to accommodate the new member. It is important that the older sibling be moved out of the crib and use the new bed much before the arrival of the baby so that feelings of displacement do not arise.

As the parents plan for the *scheduling of routines* for the care of the infant and household duties, it is important that they allow *special times* for the older siblings. At this early age, the infant sleeps most of the time when he is not eating, and it is the older siblings who need the attention and special projects.

The mother often finds that her activities are more limited and that she has *less mobility* now with her new baby at home. Her *social activities* and those of the father often undergo change. Now they frequently move in circles with other couples who have children, sharing their experiences and common interests.

The *budget* must be altered to cover medical expenses and to provide for the needs of the infant: special formulas and clothing. If the parents go out, the expense of the babysitter must now be added into the cost of entertainment.

The *family's goal* is often changed from one of social-centeredness or education to one that is more family-centered.

There often are alterations in the living space. If there is a young sibling, one should change his or her _____

_____

_____.

sleeping arrangements before

the arrival of the baby

As the schedule of routines is planned, it is important when there are other siblings to _____

_____ .

The family's social activities often are changed because _____

_____

_____.

provide special time and

activities for them

there is less mobility and more

expense

With all these stressors acting as the family adapts to the new member, there are certain tasks to be accomplished. The tasks that are to be accomplished by the parents and/or the siblings for successful adaptation are as follows:

1. The identification of the baby as a person

2. The maintenance of personal autonomy

3. The development of skill in caring for the child

4. The reestablishment of mutually satisfying roles

5. The adjustment of the siblings to the new member

6. The establishment of priorities that are effective for the family system

The first task is the *identification of the baby as a person*. This involves a separation of the parent from the offspring so that the infant is not thought of as an extension of self and so that the parent is not assuming the child's personality or needs. Often, during the first three months, the parents experience difficulty in relating to the infant as a person because the response of the infant is directed towards them not as people but rather as stimuli. When the infant becomes more social, the parents are better able to relate to the child as a person. The father often has more difficulty than the mother in relating to the small infant.

The second task that is important at this time is for the parents to identify their own needs and establish their own personal *identities*. This means that they do not lose their own senses of themselves as distinct autonomous beings separate from other family members. Each parent should set aside a certain specific time during which to pursue his own interests.

As the parents separate themselves emotionally from the infant, they are accomplishing the task of _____

_____ .

> identification of the baby as an individual

The baby does not respond as a social being during the very early months, and often the parents find it difficult to _____

_____ .

> relate to the baby as a person

Through identifying their own needs and setting aside time for their own interests, the parents are _____

_____ .

> maintaining their own identity and autonomy

Usually, both parents have begun to learn the *skills* necessary to *care for the baby* while they were in the hospital. The parents' confidence and skills increase as they continue the care, but they need reassurance from each other that they are performing these skills effectively. Encouragement from the professional staff is also very important.

As the parents come home having assumed *new roles* for which they have been preparing during the months of pregnancy, their relationship with each other must undergo alteration. They must reestablish a mutually satisfying relationship and adjust their functional roles—supportive, companionship, power, and status—within the new, expanded family.

The parents need reassurance about their capacity to perform

_____ .

> skills of child care

As the family adjusts to the new or altered roles, they must reestablish a _____ .

> mutually satisfying relationship

Often the *siblings* are the members of the family who most easily verbalize the difficulty of *adjustment* to this new member; they often say, "Take him back." Frequently, during the time that the mother is in the hospital, the young child at home feels deserted, angry, and guilty that he did something bad and caused his mother to go away. Thus, the young sibling needs much support to cope with these feelings, and this is difficult since all the members of the family are working through their own fears and doubts. The parents should be counseled that jealousy on the part of the siblings is a normal response to this new member. Jealousy is often seen as the sibling kisses the new baby while pinching or squeezing him at the same time. It is important not to leave young siblings alone with the new baby since they frequently act out their feelings. It is very difficult for the young sibling to adjust to the new baby if he has been promised that the new baby would be for him, if he has been told, "We are going to bring you a new brother," and then he is not allowed to do what he wants with the baby when the infant is brought home. It takes time for the siblings to work through their feelings, and if they are given support and reassured by the fact that they are still considered special and that their parents care for them, the adjustment is easier and much more positive.

The family must establish a *set of priorities* placing outside responsibilities, friends, and household duties in perspective according to the family's needs so that the various members of the family have time for themselves and each other.

As the young brother verbalizes, "I don't want him," he is

_____

_____ .   indicating his difficulty in
                                                  adjusting

The sibling's adjustment to the new baby is easier if _____

_____   parents reassure him that he is

_____   special and that they care about

_____ .   him

Often the schedule and responsibilities can become overwhelming for
the family if they do not _____   establish effective priorities

_____ .

Let us examine the following situation as an example of a family preparing to bring home their newborn infant:

Sandra Cummings is preparing to go home with her four-day-old son. You are discussing her plans after discharge. Her mother is coming to help with the household care for a week, but Sandra is worried about her young son's reaction to his new brother.

As you help her explore the possibilities, you keep in mind:

A. The older sibling always feels love and admiration for the baby. Sandra's concerns are unfounded.

Go to page 322.

B. Since the older sibling will be jealous of the baby, he should not be allowed to participate in the infant's care or be present while the infant is being cared for.

Go to page 323.

C. The older sibling will normally experience jealousy as part of his response to the baby, and he can be helped to deal with this if he is made to feel secure in his position within the family.

Go to page 324.

Your choice of statement *A* indicates that you did not recognize that the older sibling will experience other feelings. This information is incorrect and would be of no help to Sandra.

Return to page 320. Review the material and choose another response from page 321.

Your choice of *B* shows that you recognize that jealousy is a sibling reaction; however, your selection does not follow through with a therapeutic suggestion for dealing with the sibling's feelings.

Return to page 320. Review the material and choose another response from page 321.

In your choice of *C*, you have demonstrated an excellent ability to recognize the need for guidance about normal sibling reactions and about how to provide positive support in handling the situation.

Advance to page 325 and take the post-test.

POST-TEST   Indicate whether each statement is true or false by circling the appropriate **letter. Then** turn to page 326 and check how well you have done.

1. The interaction between the family members remains constant after **the** baby comes home.   **T   F**

2. The grandparents often wish to participate in the family's activities **after** the infant is home.   **T   F**

3. The parents often find that their activities are limited because of **the** newborn.   **T   F**

4. It is important that the baby be thought of as a person.   **T   F**

5. The functional roles of the members of the family remain the same.   **T   F**

6. The siblings normally are often jealous of the new baby.   **T   F**

In the specific areas with which you had difficulty, return to the material and review.

BIBLIOGRAPHY   Bell, Norman and Ezra Vogel: *A Modern Introduction to the Family,* Free Press, New York, 1968.

Caplan, Gerald: *Concepts of Mental Health and Consultation: Their Application in Public Health Social Work,* U.S. Children's Bureau, Washington, D.C., 1959.

Goode, William: *The Family,* Prentice-Hall, Englewood Cliffs, N.J., 1964.

Marlow, Dorothy R.: *Textbook of Pediatric Nursing,* 3d ed., W. B. Saunders Co., Philadelphia, 1969.

Senn, Milton, J. E. and Clare Hartford (eds.): *The First Born: Experiences of Eight American Families,* Harvard University Press, Cambridge, 1968.

Sullivan, Harry Stack: *The Interpersonal Theory of Psychiatry,* Norton and Co., New York, 1953.

PRETEST ANSWERS   1. Altered or changed   2. Role changes of their own   3. Social life   4. Medical costs; special formula and supplies; a babysitter when the parents want to go out for entertainment; new housing   5. Preserving one's own distinct identity; fulfilling one's own needs; pursuing one's own interests   6. Jealousy

POST-TEST ANSWERS   1. F   2. T   3. T   4. T   5. F   6. T

UNIT V
EXAMINATION The following multiple-choice examination will test your comprehension of the material covered in the fifth unit of this program. Do not guess at the answers; if you need to do this then you have not learned the content. Return to the program and review areas that give you difficulty, before going on with the examination.

Circle the letter of the best response to each question. After completing the unit examination, check your answers on page 332 and review those areas of difficulty before proceeding to the next unit.

1. The puerperium is the period in which:
   a. Maternal body systems are stable and no psychological alterations occur
   b. Balance of the maternal and infant psychological systems occurs within 24 hours
   c. Both physiological and psychological systems of the mother go through vast changes
   d. A nonhealth state is present as the mother's systems adapt

2. If the mother experiences exhaustion on the day of delivery, you would recognize that this is:
   a. A normal occurrence
   b. A sign of rejection of the baby
   c. An indication of a severe psychological problem
   d. A lack of sufficient vitamins

3. During the "taking-in" phase, you would expect to find the mother:
   a. Relaxed, outgoing, and happy
   b. Passive, dependent, and somewhat tense
   c. Active, independent, and calm
   d. Abounding with energy and excitement and very sociable

4. The first several days after delivery, the father usually has many conflicting feelings and experiences fatigue as he assumes greater responsibility. The primary nursing intervention at this time should be aimed at:
   a. Explaining the reasons why he should do as his mother-in-law wishes
   b. Recognizing his feelings and concerns
   c. Determining why he was not constantly in attendance during labor and delivery
   d. Assuring him that he should have no problems in adjusting to his new responsibilities

5. During the "taking-hold" phase, the nurse can be most helpful to the mother by:
   a. Allowing her to rest and doing the care of the infant for her
   b. Explaining that she should practice holding the baby more often since she is awkward
   c. Allowing her independence and encouraging her in the care of her infant
   d. Explaining that many mothers do not adapt well for several months

6. The term "postpartum blues" refers to:
   a. A period of mild depression in which the woman cries often and becomes irritable
   b. A period that is characterized by severe depression
   c. A period in which the mother rejects the baby
   d. A period of hormonal imbalance causing psychosis

7. The process of involution occurs by:
   a. Autolysis and atrophy
   b. Autogenesis and antibody formation
   c. Anabolism
   d. Regeneration

8. Lochia is the vaginal discharge indicating the progression of involution. Lochia changes from:
   a. Rubra to alba to serosa
   b. Serosa to rubra to alba
   c. Alba to serosa to rubra
   d. Rubra to serosa to alba

9. It is important during the puerperium to assess the mother's intake and output since:
   a. The oral intake is greater than the output during the first several days
   b. The bladder has decreased sensitivity and diuresis occurs
   c. The oral intake should equal the output
   d. The hormonal changes cause fluid retention

10. Lactation is initiated by the release of the lactogenic hormone, and on the second to third day engorgement occurs. This is:
    a. Painful but not accompanied by any rise in temperature
    b. An abnormal process that needs treatment
    c. A normal process for the non-breast-feeding mother after receiving Deladumone
    d. A highly dangerous situation, and the milk should be expressed immediately

11. The mother often does not have her menses while she breast-feeds the infant. It is important to:
    a. Inform her that as long as she breast-feeds, she cannot get pregnant
    b. Inform her that she still can become pregnant since she is ovulating
    c. Remind her that if she uses oral contraceptives, she will produce more milk for the baby
    d. Instruct her that no method of contraception will be effective at this time

12. When assessing the functioning of the neonate's respiratory system, you would normally find:
    a. Regular rhythmic respirations
    b. Thoracic and diaphragmatic respirations
    c. Respirations that are irregular in rate and rhythm
    d. Oral breathing

13. You are caring for a newborn with acrocyanosis. This means that:
    a. The infant's breathing is abnormally slow
    b. The circulatory system is functioning poorly at the extremities
    c. The infant needs to be fed
    d. The infant is too warm

14. Physiological jaundice may be found in the newborn. It is normally found:
    a. When the total bilirubin is at or above 15 milligrams per 100 milliliters
    b. During the first 24 hours of life
    c. Between 48 and 72 hours of life
    d. In infants with mongolian spots

15. Vitamin K_1 is often administered to the newborn to:
    a. Prevent clotting
    b. Increase the prothrombin time
    c. Increase erythropoiesis
    d. Prevent jaundice

16. The Moro reflex is seen when the infant:
    a. Turns his head to one side, extending the arm and leg on that side
    b. Turns his head to the side where the cheek was touched
    c. Makes swimming or crawling movements
    d. Makes a sudden outward movement of the arms while drawing the knees upward

17. The newborn's body temperature during the first several days is:
    a. Dependent upon the environment
    b. Stable
    c. Dependent upon the sweating mechanism
    d. Immune to environmental changes

18. The stools of the newborn who is bottle-fed in comparison with those of the breast-fed infant will be:
    a. Firm, frequent, and sour-smelling
    b. Firm, less frequent, and brownish yellow
    c. Soft, frequent, and golden yellow
    d. Soft, less frequent, and sour-smelling

19. The newborn's interactions with significant persons will:
    a. Have no effect on further development
    b. Form a basis for subsequent interactions
    c. Have no relationship to the newborn's response
    d. Not be dependent upon the reactions of the significant person

20. When the first child is born in the family, the "parental feeling" is a phenomenon that:
    a. Occurs immediately at the time of delivery
    b. Is present before the time of delivery
    c. Is learned through the gradual processes of identification
    d. Is not present until there is a second child

21. During feeding time, you as the nurse would:
    a. Make sure that the mother has enough diversion so that she will not be bored
    b. Comfort her by taking over the feeding if the mother seems hesitant
    c. Ascertain that the mother is relaxed and comfortable before she begins feeding
    d. Arrange that the father feeds the infant every time he is present during the feedings

22. The first several days, at feeding time the newborn is often:
    a. Alert and aggressive
    b. Responsive and social
    c. Very hungry and angry
    d. Sleepy and unresponsive

23. The normal weight loss during the newborn period is:
    a. 20 percent of body weight by the sixth day of life
    b. 1 percent of body weight over two days
    c. 5 to 10 percent of body weight during the first four days
    d. 15 percent of body weight during the first 10 days

24. Guidance to the parents about giving the infant a tub bath should include the information that:
    a. Tub baths can be given as soon as the baby goes home
    b. Tub baths should be given in a room where there is fresh air
    c. Tub baths can be given after the cord area is healed
    d. Tub baths should not be given before two months because of the danger of chilling

25. In the nursery you are caring for a three-day-old infant and observe uric acid crystals in the diaper. These are:
    a. Signs of kidney malfunctioning and an indication of a problem
    b. Crystalized uric acid and harmless
    c. Greenish in color and important to report
    d. Bluish in color and indicative of a nonfunctioning kidney

26. A high level of maternal hormones may cause certain phenomena in the newborn. These can be observed as:
    a. A slight, mucoid vaginal discharge in females and a swelling of the breast in the female or male
    b. An increased state of activity in the female
    c. An inactivity of the sebaceous glands in the male
    d. An increased size of the liver in the female

27. The new family going home undergoes many changes. Guidance to the parents should include:
    a. Suggestion that the father should get a second job because of higher expenses
    b. Suggestion that the grandparents are most helpful if they take charge of the newborn

    c. Information that it is important for the time being to lose oneself in the family needs

    d. Information that this is a difficult time and that as they reestablish relationships they should establish priorities

28. The parents going home with a new baby help the young siblings to adjust by:
    a. Sending the sibling to nursery school
    b. Ensuring that the older sibling does not have any jealousy
    c. Explaining to the older sibling why the mother and father have no time to play with him
    d. Providing special time for the older sibling and allowing for expression of feelings

**ANSWERS
TO UNIT
EXAMINATIONS**

Unit I:	1. d	2. b	3. b	4. b	5. c	6. d	7. a
	8. b	9. d	10. a	11. d	12. b	13. b	14. d	15. a
	16. d	17. d	18. d

Unit I: 1. d   2. b   3. b   4. b   5. c   6. d   7. a
8. b   9. d   10. a   11. d   12. b   13. b   14. d   15. a
16. d   17. d   18. d

Unit II: 1. d   2. a   3. c   4. c   5. b   6. c   7. d
8. a   9. b   10. a   11. c   12. c   13. d   14. d   15. c
16. a   17. b   18. d   19. d   20. c

Unit III: 1. d   2. b   3. d   4. c   5. a   6. c   7. d
8. c   9. a   10. b   11. d   12. b   13. a   14. c   15. c
16. b   17. d   18. b   19. a   20. c   21. c   22. a
23. b   24. d

Unit IV: 1. b   2. b   3. a   4. b   5. c   6. b   7. b
8. c   9. c   10. c   11. d   12. b   13. d   14. c   15. c
16. a   17. c   18. a   19. d

Unit V: 1. c   2. a   3. b   4. b   5. c   6. a   7. a
8. d   9. b   10. a   11. b   12. c   13. b   14. c   15. b
16. d   17. a   18. b   19. b   20. c   21. c   22. d
23. c   24. c   25. b   26. a   27. d   28. d

INDEX

A

Adaptation, defined, 10
Afterbirth (*see* Labor, Stage IV)
Amenorrhea, 129, 140, 141
Amniotic fluid, 111-112
Anatomy
  bony pelvis, 83
    axis, 85
    classifications, 94, 95
    demarcations, 83, 84
    diameters, 84-85, 91-93
  uterus, 100
    ligaments, 101
    muscles, 221
Antepartum period (*see* Pregnancy)
Apgar score, 258-259
Atrophy, 269, 278
Autolysis, 269, 278

B

Ballotment, 131
Birth control (*see* Conception
    control, family planning)
Bony pelvis, anatomy 83
  axis, 85
  classifications, 94, 95
  demarcations, 83, 84
  diameters, 84-85, 91-93
Braxton-Hicks contractions, 131,
    175, 197, 199, 218, 220
Breast care (*see* Pregnancy, Puer-
    perium)

C

Cervix
  dilatation, 220, 229, 233
  effacement, 220, 229
  mucus plug of, 142
Chadwick's sign, 130
Childbirth education, 183-189
  Lamaze method, 186
  Read method, 186

Chorionic gonadotrophic
    hormone, 141
Chromosome
  diploid number, 105, 108
  haploid number, 105
Coitus
  defined, 50
  during pregnancy, 147, 175
Colostrum, 125, 142
Conception, defined, 50
Conception control
  criteria for, 53
  folk methods, 54
  modern methods, 55
  traditional methods, 54
Conditioning, 185
Condom
  defined, 50
  use, 54, 58-59
Continuum, defined, 3
Contraception, 50-70 (*see also*
    Family planning)
Contraceptive, defined, 50
Contractions (*see* Braxton-Hicks
    contractions, Labor, Uterine
    contractions)
Corpus luteum, 137, 141
Crowning, 244

D

Decidua
  basalis, 106, 110, 112
  capsularis, 106, 110-111
  defined, 106
  vera, 106, 110-111
Delivery
  baby (*see* Labor, Stage II)
  placenta (*see* Labor, Stage III)
Diaphragm
  defined, 50
  use, 55, 59
Dilatation
  cervical, 220, 223, 229
  phase, 229

336

Index — 336

New family
  role changes, 317
  changes of routine, 317
  task, 318-320
Nidation, defined, 51
Norms, 20
Nulliparous, defined, 51
Nursing assessment
  defined, 42
  steps in, 43-44
Nursing diagnosis
  defined, 41
  development, 43
Nursing intervention
  defined, 41
  establishing and initiating, 43
  during labor and delivery, 210, 229-238
  with the neonate, 294, 300, 302
  during postpartum, 247, 275-280
  during pregnancy, 146-149
Nursing process
  defined, 41
  steps in, 43-44

O

Oral contraceptives, 55-56, 61
  in breast-feeding mothers, 56
  use of, 61

P

Pain, 185-186
Parental feeling, 300
Pelvic diameters
  anterior-posterior diameter, 91-93
  bi-ischial diameter, 89, 91-93
  conjugata vera, 89, 91-93
  diagonal conjugate, 89, 91-93
  interspinous diameter, 89-94
  transverse diameter, 89, 91-93
Pelvimetry, 91-93
  internal measurements
    inlet, 91, 92
    outlet, 91, 93
Pelvis
  articulations, 82
  bones, 81

Pelvis (cont.)
  boundaries, 83-84
  diameters, 84-86
  types, 89, 94, 95
Phases, defined, 51
Pituitary gonadotrophins, defined, 51
Placenta, 106, 112-114, 141, 160
Positive signs (see Pregnancy)
Potential, 3
Pregnancy
  antepartum care, 144, 145
  basal metabolic rate, 143
  blood volume, 143, 173-174
  body image changes, 159
  breast care, 147, 160
  breast changes, 129
  cardinal danger signs, 145-146
  clothing, 146
  constipation, 162
  employment during, 146
  flatulence, 162
  frequency, 130, 142
  glycosuria, 162
  heartburn, 162
  hemorrhoids, 174
  hypotensive syndrome, 173
  insomnia, 173-174
  mood swings, 147
  nausea and vomiting, 130, 140
  nutritional requirements, 143, 161, 163
  palpitations, 143
  positive signs, 125, 132
  presumptive signs, 125, 129-131
  probable signs, 125, 129
  psychosocial changes, 147, 148, 158, 159, 172
  role changes, 147-148, 158-159, 172-173
  skin changes, 125, 130, 160
  tasks of, 140, 148, 172
  travel during, 146
  varicosities, 174
  weight gain, 140, 141, 159, 173
  weight loss, 199
Pregnancy tests
  biological, 125, 132, 134
  immunological, 125, 131
Presumptive signs (see Pregnancy)
Preventive medicine, defined, 42

U

Uterus
  cervix, 98, 100-103
  changes during pregnancy, 162, 174
  contractions, 222, 223
  corpus, 98, 100-103
  fundus, 98, 100-103
  involution of, 278
  ligaments, 98, 100-103
  muscle layers, 221

V

Variable, 3
Vasectomy, defined, 51
Voluntary sterilization, 61-62

W

Weight changes during pregnancy
      (*see* Pregnancy)